D1569407

SPORTSPOWER

SPORTSPOWER

A Comprehensive Program to Put Power, Speed, and Endurance into *Your* Game

by Ralph and Valerie Carnes

St. Martin's Press | New York

Library of Congress Cataloging in Publication Data
Carnes, Ralph L.
    Sportspower.
    Includes index.
    1. Physical education and training.   2. Physical
fitness.   I. Carnes, Valerie.   II. Title.
III. Title: Sports power.
GV711.5.C37   1983   613.7′1   82-16886
ISBN 0-312-75344-6

First Edition

10 9 8 7 6 5 4 3 2 1

This book is dedicated to Robert Fusaro,
5th Dan, All America Karate Federation

Honored Sensei
Honored friend

Contents

Acknowledgments

We wish to thank the following people for their help, inspiration, and advice: Myron Nidetz, for his illuminating exhortations to moderation in training; Al Phillips, President, Chicago Health and Racquetball Club; Michael McGovern, Asst. V.P., Chicago Health and Racquetball Club; Dr. Miles Pohunek, President, Sports Fitness Institute; Hidetaka Nishiyama, 7th Dan, All America Karate Federation; Takiyuki Mikami, 5th Dan, Japan Karate Association; Jon Thor, athlete/model, Chicago Art Institute; Robert Julian, athlete/model, U.S. Army, Ordnance; Rex Lord, U.S. Army Infantry; Carina and Paul Ellis, U.S. Navy, athletes/models; Robert McNeill, Director of Public Administration, Roosevelt University; Andy Dumpis, athlete/model; Phil Zerillo, athlete/model.

Preface

Sportspower will show you how to develop strength, speed, power, stamina, and endurance in a way that is specifically applicable to the sport of your choice. It is a comprehensive system of training, based on proven biomechanical and physiological principles, that will improve your performance whatever your chosen sport may be.

The sportspower method of training, summarized and codified in the final chapter, is a unique new approach to performance improvement, in which sequences of exercises form "movement clusters" that approximate the specific movements of particular sports. Specific programs have been worked out for a wide variety of sports, from running to football, from baseball to karate, from skiing to judo.

Each sportspower training program makes direct links between the physical demands of particular sports and the exercises needed to meet those demands. Further, the pretraining and basic training chapters will enable you to lay a solid foundation for progress, whether you are a novice or a seasoned athlete. And for those who want to live on the edge, there is an appendix on injury treatment and prevention.

If you want to improve your performance, *sportspower* will give you practical, step-by-step instruction on how to do it, from pretraining right on up to specific sports programs.

Good luck and good training!

Ralph and Valerie Carnes

Chicago, 1982

Introduction:

Why You Need Sportspower Training and What It Can Do for You

During the last decade, Americans have become more physically active than ever before. The health and fitness industry has opened the doors to physical activity for millions of people who never dreamed that they could become—and remain—agile, strong, and fit.

As these people have become more aware of their physical potential, they have also become more and more interested in trying out their new-found strength and endurance by participating in a variety of recreational sports. In the old days, they played a few rounds of golf, a few sets of tennis, or a game of sandlot baseball with the kids on Sunday afternoons. Now people of all ages play racquetball, squash, or handball. They also jog, run, hike, swim, ski, cycle, skate, weightlift, bodybuild, and perform the martial arts.

To stay in shape, people in the old days took their "morning constitutional" walk around the block the way that President Harry Truman did. Now they join health clubs, family fitness centers, or sports fitness institutes. They follow workout programs developed by exercise physiologists, with exercise movements that have been analyzed and formalized by the application of the principles of biomechanics. They work out with barbells, and with isotonic and isokinetic resistance machines.

Whereas in the old days, people played a sport to "keep in shape," most people are now sophisticated enough to know that there is a vast difference between participating in a recreational sport and conditioning the body through a scientifically based exercise program. Sports are games to be played that require specific skills and conditioning. Exercise, on the other hand, is a method by which conditioning can be attained and skills can be enhanced.

Each sport uses the body to achieve a particular set of goals. Depending on the nature of those goals, different muscles and different neuromotor responses are required. Insofar as any single sport is different from any other in the total collection of the bodily movements, speed, timing, strength, and endurance it requires, the exercises used to enhance performance in that specific sport will differ from those used to enhance performance in others.

Consequently, heavy bench presses will not help you run marathons. All the jogging and running in the world will not help you add poundage to your bench press. The exercises used to enhance performance in a specific sport must to a certain degree simulate the movements and the strength and endurance requirements of that sport. Some trainers strive for precise simulation; others simply work the muscles that are used in the sport.

That's what this book is about. It tells you how to develop your own general conditioning routine, and how to do the exercises that will enhance your performance in the sport of your choice. It does it through a simple, easy-to-follow program that you can apply to any sports activity:

• Pretraining, to overcome muscular and structural deficiencies such as weak legs, arms, or injured joints
• Basic training of the muscles in major groups and in isolation, using strength, speed, and endurance-building exercises
• Cluster training of specific muscle groups, for strength, speed, and endurance
• Specific sports simulation exercises that coordinate movement clusters into the space-time matrix that the particular sport requires

In addition to general information about fitness evaluations, injury treatment, training methods, and a wealth of sports skills lore, there are specific programs for each sport, offered in detail so that you'll know exactly what to do and how to do it. No matter what your sport is, you'll find what you need to develop a program tailored to your specific needs.

A Note on How to Use This Book

Sportspower is a step-by-step manual that will help you to improve your performance in the sport of your choice. It begins with a section on physical profiles: ways to evaluate your potential for particular sports, and tests that you can take to measure your performance potential in terms of strength, power, endurance, stamina, and cardiovascular fitness.

The chapter on pretraining covers the fundamental movements at the joints of all the limbs. A complete program of pretraining exercises is included that will build strength and flexibility in the joints, increase range of motion, and help prevent injuries. The pretraining program is the foundation for the basic training program that follows.

The basic training chapter offers general conditioning programs designed to build strength, power, stamina, and endurance as a foundation for specific sports movement training. This section will tell you what you need to know to get your body in shape, no matter what your chosen sport may be.

The sportspower training chapter brings pretraining and basic training together into a comprehensive set of programs designed to improve performance in particular sports by providing a way to achieve maximal-intensity overloading of neuromuscular systems while performing actual sports movements. Each specific sports performance improvement program is divided into sequences of exercises which constitute "movement clusters" that approximate the movements of the sports themselves. These movement cluster sequences will enable you to make gains in strength, power, stamina, and endurance while retaining the timing and neuromotor coordination that your particular sport requires.

Thus, the fundamental movements described in the pretraining program and the foundational exercises described in the basic training program are linked to specific movements that the body makes in particular sports, and to the demands that those movements make on the body. The linkage is made by movement cluster training and by overloading body systems *during* actual sports movements instead of merely during the exercise sequences.

This means that the neuromotor conditioning necessary for genuine sports performance improvement occurs within the context of the sport itself and not merely during simulations or exercise bouts. In turn, this means that you will be able to gain in strength, power, stamina, and endurance while retaining the form and timing called for by your sport.

In short, sportspower training is a way to make a direct connection between what you do in the exercise room and what you want to do on the playing field. It'll give you what you want fast, effectively, and consistently.

And if you become overzealous, there's a section on the care and prevention of injuries in the appendix.

Now, get to work!

Chapter 1

PHYSICAL PROFILES

Who You Are and What You Can Expect to Do

The next time you're down at the gym, take a good look around you. Nobody is the same. Some people are tall and skinny, while others are short and fat. Some are heavily muscled, while others are lean and bony. Some seem to have incredible strength, while others can hardly make it around the track or through a set of machines. Some run three laps; some run a hundred. Some lift 400 pounds in the bench press, while others struggle to get up 145.

In the locker room, the differences are even more apparent. Some people are asymmetrical: they are more heavily muscled on one side of their body than on the other. Some have spinal abnormalities: scoliosis, a condition in which the spine forms an "S" instead of coming down from the head in a straight line; or lordosis, where there is a deep curve at the small of the back. Some people have long legs, some have short arms; some seem to have little fat at all, while others are larded from head to toe.

While most men collect fat around the belly and above the hips to the sides, and most women collect fat in the lower buttocks and at the sides of their thighs, the combinations and permutations of these normal weight distributions seem to be endless.

So no two people are exactly alike. But people who share certain physical traits perform well in certain physical activities. Take another look around the gym.

1

Who's doing well at the bench press? The guys with short upper arms and deep chests, that's who.

Who's lifting the heaviest squat poundages? The guys with short upper legs, wide pelvic girdles, straight backs, and solid midsections.

Who's gliding effortlessly around the running track, making all the gladiators and munchkins alike angry? Why, it's the guys and girls with long, lean legs, narrow hips and shoulders, and light musculature in the chest and arms.

Who's dominating the swimming pool, turning in lap after fast lap, leaving all the others behind? It's the girls or guys with the strong shoulder girdles, powerful hip muscles, and enough adipose tissue to make them buoyant.

Finally, who's getting disgusted with his or her lack of progress? Well, it's the long-armed person trying to set a record on the bench press; the long-legged person who's trying to squat with 480; the short, stocky, heavily muscled person trying to keep up with the long, lean gazelle on the running track; and the lean, bony, fatless gazelle who is wearing himself out trying to learn how to float in the pool when his specific gravity is less than that of the water around him.

The first set of people are doing what their bodies—their lever systems, neuromotor responses, musculature, and weight distribution—do best. The latter group are fighting the tide: they're doing things that their bodies can do, but cannot do as well as they could if they were built for it.

It all has to do with body types, and we don't mean merely the old somatotypes that all the popular magazines keep referring to. Those body types—ectomorph, mesomorph, and endomorph—are useful rules of thumb, but they don't tell the whole story. Let's review them, so we'll be able to see where they fail to tell us what we need to know about physical profiles.

Ectomorphs are characterized by light bone structure, lean muscles, low fat, and light weight. All other things being equal, the ectomorph has a better chance at, say, track and field events than an endomorph.

Mesomorphs are medium in height, weight, and musculature. They grow muscle (if they are men) more easily than the ectomorphs, and they tend to be more agile, stronger, and better than the ectomorphs at sports such as gymnastics.

Endomorphs are fleshy, large-boned, and heavy. They can grow muscle tissue, but they are inclined toward fat, too. They tend to be soft, and usually do not follow physically active lives.

Nobody can change his or her body type. But anybody—barring

structural or organic abnormalities—can push his or her body type to its potential limit through exercise, training, diet, and lots of determination. An ectomorph can fill out a narrow frame so that he's lean instead of skinny. A mesomorph can go all the way and grow immense muscles, or he or she can train for a hard, trim physique. An endomorph can diet and exercise down to normal weight ranges instead of giving up and sitting around eating chocolates. You won't change your body type, but you'll look, feel, and perform better than you would if you did not train.

What the somatotypes do not tell us is the importance of individual variations within the types. Let's talk about the bench press by way of example. "Benching" is one of the most popular lifts in any gym that has barbells as well as exercise machines. The serious bodybuilders and weightlifters always gather around the bench press. To do this lift, lie on your back, reach up and grasp the barbell that rests on the rack, lift it off the rack, lower it to your chest, then push it up toward the ceiling with your arms until your elbows are straight.

Sounds simple, doesn't it? If it's so simple, why is it that Ralph, at a bodyweight of 175, can bench press only 275, while Chang, at a bodyweight of 142, can do repetitions with 300? The answer lies in the difference between Ralph's and Chang's lever system. Ralph is five feet ten inches tall, but his outstretched arms are six feet one inch from fingertip to fingertip. Chang is five feet four, but his arms measure only four feet eight. While Ralph's humerus (upper arm bone) reaches down past the top of his pelvic bone, Chang's elbows are at least three inches above the hips.

Although Chang is lighter than Ralph in total bodyweight, the amount of muscle mass in their upper arms is about the same. But when Ralph does the bench press, the bar travels a full one foot, six and one-half inches from his chest to the end of the lift. Chang does the same movement with only one foot, one-half inch of travel. Consequently, Ralph doesn't have the leverage that Chang has. If Ralph had Chang's lever system, he could do 300 pounds. If Chang had Ralph's lever system, he would not have the distinction of being the only 142-pound person in the gym who can bench press 300 pounds.

Another example: Keith is a tall, beautifully proportioned ectomorph. He has practically no bodyfat, and his muscles are developed in almost perfect symmetry. When Keith gets on the running track, everybody else gets out of the way. He's built for running, and he does it with such effortless grace, people sometimes stop and stare.

Keith, however, does not have the lever system for heavy squats, in which the barbell is held across the shoulders and the person drops down into a deep knee bend, then up to a standing position. He has little leverage for such a lift, and could never be a record holder in squatting if he decided to become a powerlifter.

But there are ectomorphs with short upper arms, short upper legs, and heavy trapezius muscles who do well in powerlifting. And there are mesomorphs (such as Jesse Owens) who are world-class runners. And there are mesomorphs (like Ralph) with long arms. And endomorphs with small bones. In short, there is no such thing as a perfect somatotype, someone who fits into one of the three classifications perfectly. Even if there were such a person, there might very well be anomalies in the musculature or the lever system that would make it possible for him or her to do things physically that are not ordinarily associated with the body type given to them by their parents' genes.

So when you make a decision about the kind of sport you want to play, don't put all your money on the old somatotype classification. The important things are the lever system, the musculature, the neuromotor system, and sheer grit.

Other factors are equally important in determining what you can do well and what you can do with only moderate success. Among them are cardiovascular fitness, muscle tone, weight distribution, bodyfat percentage, sex, and traumas to and diseases of the joints, organs, muscles, bones, and nervous system.

You can be strong, but lacking in cardiovascular fitness. You can be fit as far as your heart, lungs, and circulatory system are concerned, but unable to perform basic feats of strength. You can be strong and fit, but not coordinated, either through lack of kinaesthetic sense or because of the aftermath of a childhood disease. You can be fast, but weak; strong, but slow; fast, strong, but clumsy. There are many variables, and there are many ways to overcome physical problems.

Muscles are made up principally of two kinds of cells or fibers: red, slow-twitch, aerobic fibers, and white, fast-twitch, anaerobic fibers. The reds use a lot of oxygen and come into play in any kind of endurance sport or exercise such as running or jogging. The whites are the strength-giving fibers, use less oxygen, and come into play in sports such as weightlifting. These two types of cells are trained differently.

● *Aerobic training.* "Aerobic training" is "oxygen-utilization" training. When you train aerobically, you are for the most part exercising the red muscle fibers, which use oxygen during their contraction as well as during recovery. Aerobic training, because of the high oxygen demands, is the prime way to condition the cardiovascular system.

• *Anaerobic training.* Also known as "strength training," anaerobic training involves chiefly the white, fast-twitch muscle fibers, which do not utilize oxygen in their contraction phase. While aerobic training involves repetitions of a movement over a long period of time, the anaerobic energy system depletes itself in about 20 seconds. That's why it is possible to have a superbly muscled individual who has no endurance at all. He's been working the white cells to the exclusion of the reds. Recent research indicates, however, that the aerobic energy system helps replace the depleted anaerobic energy system, so athletes training for strength do get some aerobic conditioning indirectly. The best training program for someone in sports includes both strength and endurance training, both anaerobic and aerobic conditioning.

Although recent research indicates that it is possible to make red cells behave like whites (and vice versa) with a tremendous amount of specialized training, people born with more reds than white fibers will not excel in strength sports (such as weightlifting), and people born with more white than red fibers will not excel in endurance sports (running, jogging, and so forth). This is true regardless of their somatotype or lever system.

What does all this say about what you can do with what you have? Let's make a few helpful distinctions to clear the air.

First, distinguish between sports and exercise programs. Sports include a variety of physical activities, all of which involve some amount of exercise, but which may or may not provide the kind of conditioning a systematic exercise program would give you.

Exercise programs, on the other hand, are systematic, progressive physical activities that do not necessarily involve winning or even keeping score.

The goal of any participant in a sport is to win or to help the team win. The goal of a participant in an exercise program is to achieve strength, endurance, and health. If it's the right kind of program, it will also enhance his or her performance in the chosen sport. Sports involve games that people play. Exercise involves movements whose primary function is to condition and train, strengthen and coordinate.

Thus, *weight training* is a form of exercise that can be used to enhance performance in any sport that calls for strength or short-term speed. Weightlifting, whether Olympic lifting or powerlifting, is a sport for which weight *training* provides the conditioning.

You may tire your legs playing football, but it takes a progressive training program in addition to the game to build real strength in your legs. You may feel bushed after a night playing softball with the company team, but you won't condition yourself aerobically unless you embark on a systematic cardiovascular conditioning program. In short, your sport may give you some exercise, but it will be neither systematic nor necessarily progressive. It will consist merely of the movements and demands of the specific sport.

So separate exercise programs from sports. Realize that no sport will give you overall conditioning, either for the cardiovascular system or for individual muscle tone. The very movements that make one sport different from another preclude general conditioning as a result of playing that sport.

Exercise programs can give you the kinds of conditioning that you need to perform well in sports, all other things being equal. But there are many elements that go into success in sports. Don't let your body type discourage you from participating in the recreational sport that you want to play. If you are a high-school athlete, and plan to compete in national or world class events, you should take a good long look at yourself in the mirror and ask yourself if you resemble the people who are the world champions in the sport in which you're interested in competing. If you don't fit the mold of the champions, and if the difference between you and the champs lies in body type, lever system, and musculature instead of simply the difference between being in shape and being out of shape, you should probably think twice about choosing that particular sport. Otherwise, you'll spend your life trying to become something that is beyond your reach. There are always notable exceptions to the rules, but statistics are against you.

On the other hand, if you are not a state, national, or world-class athlete, but are an ordinary man or woman who wants to enjoy participation in recreational sports, then choose the sport that interests you. Choose the one you can have fun with without endangering yourself.

You're short and stocky, but you want to run marathons? Go to it! The fun is in running itself.

You're long and lean and you love swimming but hate basketball? Dive in! The fun is in being in the water.

You're a well-muscled mesomorph whose arms are too long, but you want to bench press? Go for it! There's nothing more satisfying than setting a record that's new *for you.* The enjoyment is in playing the game.

When the fun is in playing the game, then you always win. The problems start when the competition bug bites and you begin to think of your recreational sport as some kind of contest whose outcome will decide once and for all whether or not you're really a valuable human being. This is when the joggers become runners, and begin to have the kinds of physical problems and injuries that competitive runners have. Or "weekend athletes" develop the kinds of problems that powerlifters, pro ball players, pro skiers, Olympic swimmers, and all the other athletes have.

While you mentally separate sports from exercise programs, you should also mentally separate amateur sports from competitive ones. The former is recreational. The latter is a way of life.

Age is also a factor in choosing a sport. You can avoid injuries if you admit to yourself that a twenty-year layoff from physical activities calls for some careful pretraining before you start to hit the old ball around again. You can save yourself considerable pain and expense if, when you first join the local health club, you take it slow and easy instead of trying to show all the young guys what a great former athlete you are. The worst offenders in this category are the ones who really *were* athletes twenty years ago, but who've done nothing but swill beer and smoke cigars since that last scrimmage in college.

Older people's muscles "jell" faster than those of younger people. That's why if you're fifty-five, your muscles feel stiff after prolonged sitting, while your grandchild can bound out of bed after a night of immobility. This means that the older person should do a more extensive warmup, in order not to strain or tear the muscles.

Further, if you've been inactive for a long time, you should never start a vigorous sport or training program without first consulting your physician. A lot can happen between checkups, especially if they come five or six years apart. If you've experienced shortness of breath, tightness in the chest, low back pain, discomfort in the joints, racing or irregular pulse, unexplained sweating or "flushed" feelings, dizziness, chronic constipation, rectal or genito-urinary tract bleeding or discomfort, chronic indigestion or chronic heartburn, blurred vision, or any of a host of other complaints, you should consult with your physician not only about your general health, but about the suitability of both specific recreational sports and general conditioning exercise routines.

All too many people, especially men, become frightened on their thirty-fifth, fortieth, or fiftieth birthday, join a health club, buy jogging shoes, join the company touch football team, and launch themselves with full commitment into what they think will be health-producing activities. These are the people who keep the orthopedists, the podiatrists, the cardiologists, and the morticians working overtime.

Age should be no barrier to reasonable exercise and well-chosen recreational sports. Ralph is fifty at the time of this writing, and he works out with weights three times a week, using barbells, dumbbells, and a variety of Hydra-Fitness, Nautilus, Dynacam, Universal, and Paramount machines. But he didn't get into it overnight. He started back on his fortieth birthday. It was a long climb (complicated by the effects of childhood rheumatic fever and rheumatoid arthritis), but at fifty he is stronger and has more endurance than he had at twenty.

Don't let your age deter you from starting on an exercise program or from participating in a recreational sport for the fun of it. But while you're exercising, also exercise the wisdom that your years imply.

What are the criteria for choosing a recreational sport? Easy. Choose what you'll enjoy doing. Do it for the sheer fun of doing it. Do it because it makes you feel good. Do it because it makes you happy. Do it because it's good for you. Even the pros once played touch football in the corner lot just because it was fun. There is no reason for you to become a hardcore somadynamic who'll do anything to win. If you're playing for the fun of it, playing itself is a kind of winning.

All too often, sports-oriented health clubs become absolutely deadly in their pursuit of performance improvement. We've seen gyms where nobody smiled, although most of the adult membership was composed of ordinary men and women who just wanted to get in shape, trim down, and look and feel good. In these places, training is always serious business, and exercise is a form of penance paid for tomorrow's expected performance. We've even seen gyms where "ordinary" people were discouraged from joining on the grounds that they did not have the "competitive spirit" or the "killer instinct" required to excel in physical activities.

This, of course, is nonsense. It's no sin to enjoy what you're doing, especially if it's healthful and invigorating and gives you a feeling of accomplishment. So don't let overzealous would-be sports trainers infect you with the idea that you've got to train like a demon six days a week just to play softball on the company team. Avoid them. If they were really that good, they would be trainers for pro ball clubs.

Choose the sport that suits your needs as well as your body type. And make playing the game something you do *for* yourself, not *to* yourself.

Common Structural and Muscular Problems

Nobody is perfect. While we all know this, we have a tendency to forget it when we exercise or play sports for which we have no training.

The popular myth that sports themselves will give you all the training and conditioning you need is partially responsible for our temporary loss of memory.

When jogging became popular in the United States several years ago, people who had never given a thought to jogging or running suddenly went out and bought a $50 pair of running shoes, an $80 warmup suit, some terrycloth headbands and wristbands, and commenced to rack up the miles on sidewalks, streets, park trails, roads, and bridle paths. According to a podiatrist friend of ours (who has built a lucrative practice around jogging injuries), around 82 percent of them sustained injuries within the first thirty days of jogging.

Since almost all joggers began jogging because they thought it would make them healthier, you can imagine their frustration when they discovered that it was breaking down their ankle and knee joints, and bringing them closer and closer to the orthopedist's surgical table. What happened?

What happened is that many of them began jogging because they were primarily concerned with avoiding heart attacks. With all the ballyhoo about the beneficial effects of jogging on the cardiovascular system, many writers neglected to tell aspiring joggers that most of them probably needed some kind of pretraining before they took to the trails. While you can gradually increase your jogging distances from practically nothing to several miles, your joints and muscles, ligaments and bones, tendons and cartilage get a pounding from the very beginning.

If you're young and resilient, you probably won't have any difficulties. If you're older (many joggers are middle-aged and beyond), you will run into trouble. Your joints aren't used to the compacting force that jogging brings to bear upon them, and your muscles aren't used to the stress that they're getting.

It's not all a matter of being out of shape. Sometimes there are structural problems that increase the probability of injury.

PRONATED OR SUPINATED FEET

Stand in front of a mirror with your feet together. Look at your ankles and feet. Does the ankle joint appear to turn inward and downward? Do you have a high arch or are your "arches" really flat on the bottom? If you answer yes to these questions, you probably have pronated feet, which means that your feet rotate along the axis of the foot (from heel to toe) and that your ankle, instead of being a stable structure, skews inward. This condition is the result of one or more of the following:

- Injury to the ankle or foot
- Weak muscles in the foot and calf
- Misaligned bones in the foot or calf
- Poor posture habits that have become chronic
- The aftermath of a childhood disease (such as juvenile rheumatoid arthritis)
- A secondary effect of a long illness that necessitated an extended period in bed

If your feet are pronated, your knee joint will tend to shift toward the body's centerline, thus making the knee even less stable than it is to begin with. If the knee shifts inward, the hip joint will have to take up some of the slack, with the resultant hip problems that sometimes follow.

If you have these problems with your feet, ankles, knees, and hips, every time your feet hit the ground as you jog the problems will be accentuated. The outcome: torn or strained ligaments, tendons, and muscles in the feet, ankles, knees, and hips. And if you have problems in these areas, the lower back is right up the line, and you can look for pain there, too.

Supinated feet offer similar problems, except that the foot rides on the outside ridge, the ankle shifts to the outside, as does the knee, and the hip receives stress from another angle. The damage and pain is similar, except that it's on the other side.

What should you do? Easy. See a competent orthopedist or podiatrist and get yourself fitted with an orthosis, which is a device that slips into your shoe. The orthotic device will be especially designed for your feet, and it will help correct the problem. Orthotic devices can be used for both pronation and supination of the foot.

WEAK ANKLES, KNEES, OR HIPS

One of the causes of weak ankles, knees, or hips is malformation of the foot, as described above. Other causes include all the things that cause pronated or supinated feet. In short, the body is an organism, an organic system, and when something goes wrong with one part of it, something usually goes wrong with another.

The problems don't always arise from the feet, however. Sometimes they come from other parts of the body. For example, Ralph's mother underwent three surgical procedures for a hip problem that developed when she was in her fifties. The problem started when she was eleven years old. Unfortunately, nobody noticed.

She developed osteomyelitis in the left tibia (shin bone) when she was eleven. The condition appeared to clear up when she was twelve. No one noticed that her left leg was slightly behind her right leg in growth.

By the time she was fully grown, her right leg was about a quarter of an inch longer than her left. But still, nobody noticed, and besides, she had compensated for the difference in length in the way that she walked.

By the time she was fifty-two, the longer right leg had pounded the acetabulum (hip joint) nearly to pieces. She had three ball-and-socket joints installed before the surgery finally came out right. By that time, her health was ruined for good.

An evaluation by an orthopedist or a podiatrist, and a forty-dollar orthotic device could have saved both her hip and her health.

Sometimes weak ankles, knees, and hips are the result of long illnesses in which a person is required to stay off his feet for a prolonged period of time. When Ralph had rheumatic fever, he was confined to bed for six months when he was seven, another six months when he was eight, and an entire year when he was nine. By the time he got back on his feet at ten years of age, his ankles simply shifted to the inside and his feet pronated. Of course, at that time, nobody talked about "pronated" feet. Consequently, Ralph still has problems with his feet and ankles.

Often the problem is not the result of any of the above, but is merely the result of malformed joints. There's many a slip between conception and birth, and early malformations are often not caught in time to do anything about them. We have a friend whose son was born with feet that were both supinated and inverted (he was both flat-footed and "pigeon-toed"). The pediatrician caught the problem immediately and prescribed corrective shoes, and the problem was a thing of the past by the time the child was four.

BACK PROBLEMS

Problems with the feet, ankles, knees, and hips share one thing in common with back problems: they are the result of the force of gravity acting in combination with the various factors cited above. There is a great deal of lore about the spinal column, some of it true and some of it fanciful. However, it is no joke to the person with chronic lower back pain.

At the beginning of this chapter, we talked about scoliosis and lordosis (a spine with an "S" curve and a spine with a deep inward curve at the small of the back, respectively). If you have either of these problems, you can expect some discomfort from sports that involve jogging, running, leaping, diving, or lifting heavy weights.

Some people have had scoliotic spines corrected by surgery. It's a painful procedure, but worth it to those whose condition precludes normal activities. Lordotic curves are easier to treat, and can sometimes be corrected (or at least improved) by developing the muscles of the "core": the abdominals, external and internal obliques, *erector spinae*, and *iliopsoas* muscles.

Our friend George has a lordotic curve, but through consistent weight training has overcome the condition almost completely. He does repetition squats with 450 pounds, and he has a column of muscles in his back and midsection that would make Hercules jealous.

A strong back is absolutely necessary if you want to be a powerlifter or an Olympic lifter. Dead weight lifts call for strong *erector spinae* muscles, as well as solid abdominals and side muscles. Heavy squats call for the same kind of strength. Bench presses demand strong shoulders, elbows, wrists, and arms, but it is the strength of the rest of the body that gives you stability on the bench.

Back problems are not confined to abnormal curves of the lower and middle back. Many people suffer from a curving upper back that can be caused by anything from polio to being dragged forward and down by a fat belly. Another friend of ours, who went into the paratroopers with a high chest and a straight back, came out of the Army 10,000 beers later with an enormous belly, sloping shoulders, and an upper back curvature. Two months of diet and exercise brought him down from 225 to 205, and straightened his back to where it had been five years before.

Ironically, although the medical profession has villified chiropractors for decades, modern orthopedists are beginning to develop a new field that some call manual orthopedics. This is a form of spinal manipulation, and has many elements in common with chiropractic adjustments. The purpose is to provide short-term relief from pain caused by pinched nerves, abraded tissue, and misaligned vertebrae.

WEAK OR INJURED NECK

Neck injuries are common to wrestlers and football players. Weak neck muscles set you up for such injuries. Since the neck muscles develop relatively quickly, if you plan to wrestle or play one of the hard contact sports, you should spend some time developing neck strength before you start to play.

Some exercises that involve odd postures for the neck are not recommended. The Yoga "plow" position is notorious for the number of injuries it has caused. To do the "plow," you must lie on your back, then curl the torso upwards until your entire weight rests on your radically flexed cervical vertebrae and your shoulders. Depending on the formation of the first few cervical vertebrae, the nerves that run through little holes in these vertebrae could be pinched or severed. You won't know whether you're one of the unlucky ones until things begin to go black. Better to use one of the modern neck exercise machines made by Hydra-Fitness or Nautilus, or simply use an old-fashioned neck harness with a couple of barbell plates. They'll give your neck all the workout you need.

You may also find that you have problems with your neck that are the result of compensations for other kinds of injuries. The first time Ralph tried to walk an oscillating balance beam, he was told to look straight ahead into a mirror, and to keep his body perfectly straight at all times. He kept falling off the balance beam to the right. Since he rides a motorcycle, does karate, and performs other activities that require balance, it seemed mysterious that he should not be able to stand erect on a balance beam.

The mystery was solved the next day when he tried to walk the balance beam without the help of an overzealous instructor. Here's the answer: over the years since he lost his left eye, Ralph has turned his head slightly to the left, to compensate for the narrowing of the cone of vision. When the instructor put him on the balance beam, he lined Ralph's head up so that he looked directly to the front. This, of course, threw him off balance, with a fall to the right. When he turned his head to the position that he has been using since 1948, he had no trouble walking the balance beam. Problem solved.

Not quite. The compensation for the narrowed visual field set him up for injuries that come as a result of not having the bones of the neck aligned. It explained some of the problems that he has experienced with balancing heavy weights on his shoulders in the squat, and it also explained the intermittent neck pain that he suffered for several years after losing the eye. A competent orthopedist or physical therapist could have cleared up the mystery in a moment.

WEAK HANDS, WRISTS, ELBOWS, AND SHOULDERS

Weakness in these areas is not compounded by the force of gravity, as are weaknesses in the legs or back. The fault here lies in underdevelopment of the forearms, *triceps brachii, biceps brachii, brachialis* (the muscle that runs along the outer edge of the biceps), and the muscles of the shoulders and upper back (*deltoideus, infraspinatus, supraspinatus, rhomboideus, teres major* and *minor*, and *trapezius*).

Weak hands can be strengthened by finger and forearm exercises. Weak wrists respond to wrist flexes and extensions. Weak elbows benefit from wrist flexes and extensions, as well as from rotational movements of the forearm. They also respond well to biceps, triceps, and *brachialis* exercises such as curls, presses, and reverse curls, respectively (see page 106 for a description of these movements).

Inability to pull things toward you and to push them away from you calls for both curls and presses. If you are weak in movements of the arm in which the elbow is stationary but the shoulder joint is brought into play, you should work the deltoids and the other muscles that stabilize and strengthen the shoulder.

Unless you are afflicted with a degenerative muscle or nerve disease such as muscular dystrophy or myasthenia gravis, your muscles should respond to systematic exercise. This is true all the way into your fifties and sixties. Ralph recently added 75 pounds to his bench press during the last few months of his forty-ninth year. Stimulate them and they'll grow and grow stronger. As the old saying goes, "Tweak 'em and you'll keep 'em. Don't use 'em and you'll lose 'em."

If you are weak in any of the areas mentioned in this section, you should begin a pretraining program before you embark on any general exercise program. You certainly should train before you go into a sport, no matter how mild the activity may seem to you. If you have obvious structural problems such as deformities or malformations of joints or bones, see your physician before you start any exercise program. You can save yourself time, money, and a lot of anguish.

But don't be discouraged if you have a problem. Even the pros have physical problems, some of them far worse than anything we ordinary people have. And yet, with proper training, determination, and systematic progressive exercise, they're back on the field week after week in the wide world of sports.

You've got problems? The next section will give you some tips on pretraining routines that will help you solve them.

Body Composition, Muscle Strength and Endurance, and Cardiovascular Fitness Tests

Our seventies-induced exercise consciousness and fitness mania have had quite a big impact on our lives. The good effects first: the fitness boom has made us, individually and collectively, start moving more and eating less, take vitamin supplements, watch our salt and sugar intake, and, sometimes, stop smoking.

But there's a negative side to the fitness mania too. Part of it stems from the tremendous media impact of all the sports consciousness. Your favorite magazine or newspaper in the last six months probably has run an article on the joys of (choose one): tennis/running or jogging/training with weights/swimming, water-skiing, or surfing/playing one of the ball sports. Or you've looked out your window and seen the hosts of brightly clad runners or cyclists or sandlot softball players. It looks so effortless and so much fun! And over there on your couch, beside the half-smoked cigarette and umpteenth cup of coffee, is that article that ends "all you need is a good pair of shoes. . . ."

So you're hooked. You dash out to the local shopping mall and buy a sweatsuit and what looks like a reasonably good pair of shoes. You run back home to pump up the old bike's tires. Presto! You're a weekend athlete! Come Sunday, you go for a half-mile run and a cycle ride. By Sunday night you need two aspirin every three hours just to get to sleep. By Monday morning, you drag your aching bod out of bed and wonder how all those Saturday-morning athletes managed to look so bright-eyed and alert. You feel more dead than alive after your first brush with the Fitness Genie.

So much for the negative side of the fitness boom. We Americans are a democratic folk, and love to think that *everybody* can do *every* sport. The less complicated the activity and the less expensive the gear, the more we believe that it's truly "the people's exercise." After all, everybody *can* run/swim/cycle/play tennis/throw a ball, can't he?

The answer, surprisingly, is no. And it's no for a variety of reasons, some of which we've touched on in earlier sections. Everyone can find *a* physical activity or sport, but not everyone can play competitively or well at every game, and there may even be some sports that you can't play at all. Your lever system may not be right. You may have sustained an injury in the past that prohibits your participating in a certain sport. You may have an undiagnosed illness or chronic condition that will limit your participation. That's why all responsible exercise coaches or experts will include with their presentation or program a warning, "Do not participate in this or any other exercise program without first seeking your physician's advice."

That's right: go see your doctor *first*, before you even put down the bucks for that first pair of running shoes or that new bicycle pump. He or she can tell you, with relatively little trouble or expense, whether or not you'll have any serious trouble with your new sport. The testing is simple and may involve as little as a resting EKG or stress test, and some standard diagnostic work. On the other hand, if you have sustained serious injuries in your lifetime, you should mention these to your physician—you may need X-rays before you begin a program.

Remember, though, that your MD isn't a mind reader. It's helpful to supply him or her with as much information as possible. Be specific about your goals. Saying "I'd like to start running" isn't very useful except as a starting point. Why do you want to run? For relaxation? Weight loss? Companionship of the other singles on the jogging path through the park? Something to do on Saturday morning? Winning the Boston Marathon? Running in local races? The more precisely you can define your goals, the better off you and your doctor will be. If you've a munchkin's frame and accept it, you and your doctor can plan comfortably for a program that will let you shed fifteen pounds, attain conditioning, and spend many a happy morning bounding through the park in your new sweatsuit. But if you're bent on becoming a marathoner, despite your build, say so. It just may be that your doctor can help you work through those problems that your pronated feet, weak ankles, and short legs are going to present.

The answer is obvious: get the testing *first*. There's always the possibility that you have some undiagnosed ailment—diabetes, a heart or respiratory problem, arthritis—that hasn't shown up yet in your sedentary life. But it may well surface now, as you become more active. Don't assume that just because you can sit behind a desk and move papers you can become an athlete—even an amateur one—without medical consultation.

On the other hand, if your doctor isn't savvy about exercise or is prejudiced toward some particular form of training, it may be difficult to convince him or her that you know what you're doing. Many doctors today are devotees of walking, running, or jogging to the exclusion of other exercises. If your goal is to become a racquetball player or train with weights, you may get nowhere. In that case, get the necessary testing, have the results evaluated, and go your merry way. But if you become serious about your sport, you may need to find another doctor whose specialty is sportsmedicine or injury rehabilitation. These people can be located through associations connected with your sport (such as the Road Runners of America), through reference works such as Dr. Gabe Mirkin's *The Sportsmedicine Book*, or through a call to some local teams. If there's a gym in the area that has a reputation for training top athletes, find out which doctors train there or consult with the trainers.

At worst, you can call up your local high school or college to see who the team doctor is. These men and women are usually more sympathetic to, and knowledgeable about, sports-related problems than your average gynecologist, allergist, or dermatologist. Continue to see your specialist for his/her specialty, but for sports-related questions, seek out your local sportsmedicine authority.

So let's assume for the purposes of this chapter that you're not a pro athlete, but just an ordinary man or woman who wants to trim off a little excess fat, relax, play a new sport or return to an old one, and generally get in better condition. You go to see your doctor for an "all clear" sign before you start working out. What can you expect?

It pays to be honest with your friendly MD. Start with a short medical history, making sure you include all the following points if they apply:

- Diabetes, diagnosed or "borderline" symptoms
- Cardiac difficulties or irregularities
- A history of shortness of breath
- Serious allergies or asthma
- A recent weight loss or sudden gain of over 10 pounds
- Serious sprains or any fractures
- Menstrual irregularities; a past history of miscarriages or other abnormalities (for women)
- Chronic back, knee, ankle, elbow, or shoulder problems that interfere with your activities
- Arthritis
- Hypoglycemia, diagnosed or suspected

If any of these show up in your medical history, your doctor can advise you about further tests or X-rays. Many of these conditions can be treated or controlled so that you can exercise despite having had them, so don't automatically assume you've a good excuse not to exercise! Unless you're in the middle of a cardiac arrest or are about to go into diabetic shock, your chances of being put in a therapeutic exercise program are fairly high. Most doctors today encourage even patients with serious or chronic conditions to exercise as soon as possible. Gone are the days when complete bed rest was the order of the day for every small ache and pain.

But assuming that you've none of these problems that require special testing, a complete routine physical may be quite sufficient. Here is a brief list of the tests you can expect if you've elected to go the full annual physical route:

- Review of medical history, including family history
- Examination of the skin, head and neck, chest, heart and lungs, abdomen and genitalia
- Spirometry test (for breathing capacity)
- Eye examination for glaucoma
- Electrocardiogram (resting or in motion)
- Breast and pelvic examination (for women), including Pap smear
- Hemoglobin count (for diagnosing anemia)
- White blood cell count (for infections or blood disorders)
- Blood chemistry tests: cholesterol, sugar, urea nitrogen, uric acid, triglycerides (tests for diabetes, fat metabolism, gout and kidney function)
- Serological test for syphilis
- Urinalysis (tests of kidney, liver, and urinary tract functions)
- Proctoscopic examination of rectum and colon (for over-thirty-fives)

Who should be tested? The simplest answer, of course, is "everyone beginning an exercise program, regardless of age or health." But even within that category, there are a number of variables. Age, previous exercise history, and general physical condition have quite a lot to do with how extensive the testing should be and how recent the checkup before you begin your workouts. Aerobic expert Dr. Kenneth Cooper's guidelines, as set forth in *The Journal of the American Medical Association,* provide this list of age-adjusted and fitness-adjusted variables. According to Dr. Cooper:

- If you're under 30: you can start exercising without immediate medical supervision, providing you've had a medical checkup within the last year and received a clean bill of health.
- If you're between 30 and 39: have a checkup within at least three months of the time you plan to start exercising. The exam should include an EKG at rest.
- Between 40 and 59: same as for the 30–39 group, with one important addition: have your doctor do an EKG in motion (while you are exercising).
- Over 59: same requirements as for the 40–59 group, except that exam should be performed immediately before you start the exercise program (the "last three months" rule no longer holds).

All right: you've completed all the tests. But you're not done yet. While these tests in the standard annual physical checkup battery may be all a sedentary person needs, if you plan to begin a more strenuous exercise program, you'll need some more specific tests for cardiovascular fitness. The three most common of these tests are the treadmill, the ergometer, and the step test.

Of the three, the "step test" is the simplest and easiest to administer. According to Dr. Cooper, it dates back to the early 1940s when soldiers were first weighed, then given backpacks of 40 to 75 pounds, and asked to step up and down on a 16-inch stool 30 times per minute for 5 minutes. Recovery heart rate was then measured at three 30-second intervals. After the war, civilian versions of the test were developed—among the most famous, the so-called "Harvard step test," which eliminated the backpack and changed the stool height from 16 to 20 inches. A two-step test designed by Dr. Masters at Harvard University was intended specifically to identify patients with serious cardiac problems. Other physicians eliminated the steps entirely and simply had patients jump or run in place to get the pulse rate up.

Over a period of time, it was found that the step tests were too inaccurate, so treadmills and ergometers became the chief ways of measuring cardiovascular fitness. Both of these are less subject than the step test to variables such as emotional state or motivation to perform.

It's useful to know something about the procedure as outlined by Dr. Cooper if you are going to take an ergometer or treadmill test. Usually you'll be told to get a good night's sleep and eat lightly at least three hours prior to the test. At the lab or testing center you put on gym clothes or sweatsuit and running shoes. You are weighed and a medical history is taken. You'll be asked something about your recent exercise history so that the treadmill can be set accordingly—a person in good condition can tolerate a higher work load setting.

Then electrodes for the EKG are attached to your chest so that testers can monitor your pulse rate during the test. (A careful tester will stop the run the minute any abnormality develops.) Next you are connected to a system that enables the tester to collect your expired air during the run. This air is used for measuring both oxygen and carbon dioxide in order to see just how much oxygen your body utilizes during a run.

The test itself will probably consist of at least three 3-minute runs, which become progressively more difficult. If you are in average to good condition, with no special problems, a "typical" first run would be 5 mph and a 5 percent uphill grade—"level" running is too easy to test accurately for cardiovascular conditioning.

After each 3-minute run, the treadmill is stopped and the tester takes your recovery heart rate for 15 seconds at 1-minute intervals. Then the other runs are completed in the same way. When you reach your maximum performance level, your heart rate will peak out at about 180 beats per minute, or higher.

Total oxygen consumption is measured in milliliters (ml) per kilogram of body weight per minute. This measurement basically tells the tester how much oxygen your body is consuming. Dr. Cooper points out that a person in poor condition might exhale 18 percent oxygen, with his body consuming only 3 percent of the oxygen inhaled. A person in good condition, by contrast, will exhale only about 16 percent oxygen, meaning that his body can consume 5 percent of the oxygen inhaled.

Although treadmill tests remain the standard fitness measurement for most American doctors, ergometers are also gaining in popularity. (An ergometer is a measuring device usually built into a stationary bicycle on which the subject works or pumps against a work load that's fed into the machine.) While it's an excellent way to test cardiovascular conditioning, all but the most sophisticated models depend on individual motivation much more than the treadmill. Since the subject himself/herself has to furnish the leg power to pump against the work load imposed by the machine, motivation alone determines whether he or she will push hard enough to reach maximum effort. By contrast, on the treadmill, the machine supplies the power and the subject has to keep up with it or stop the test altogether.

As for the cost and general availability of these special cardiovascular tests, both will vary widely, depending on your location and the resources available to you. In large cities, the tests are often offered at locations other than a hospital, clinic, or laboratory. Many universities, health clubs, gyms, family fitness centers, and YMCAs provide the tests at a reasonable fee. If you've no serious medical problems and don't suspect any, consider getting the tests run through a school or public health facility. If you're a diagnosed cardiac or respiratory-disease patient, you may not have to foot the bill yourself—your insurance may cover the tests if they're prescribed by your physician. Average "healthy" people may not get off so lightly, however, so shop around for a less costly testing site before you commit yourself.

A couple of *caveats* about the tests: first, while they are designed to detect and help diagnose cardiovascular and respiratory ailments, they may actually do damage to a person in the advanced stages of undetected cardiac or respiratory disease. If you feel your pulse rate developing a severe arrhythmia (irregular pattern), be sure to tell the tester. The irregularity will doubtless have already shown up on the equipment. Insist that the test be discontinued at once if the tester wants you to go on. Be sure you wear running shoes on the treadmill or ergometer.

Ralph permanently injured his right foot and ankle while taking a treadmill test barefoot the morning after surgery in a Chicago hospital. If you don't have running shoes with you, make sure the lab or hospital provides a pair.

Popular as it is, stress testing is not universally accepted among all doctors, exercise physiologists, and exercise experts. Indeed, there are many MDs who are highly critical of stress testing. Among them is Dr. George Sheehan, the noted physician and authority on running. He quotes other colleagues—among them, Dr. Gordon Cumming, the Canadian cardiologist—as saying that the test is highly restrictive, expensive, and probably an unnecessary precaution. Dr. Stephen Epstein of the National Heart Institute also confirms Sheehan's suspicion that the tests are of no great value in the diagnosis of serious coronary disease. Dr. Albert Kattus of UCLA found that even tests given without a preliminary warmup to otherwise healthy people yielded 70 percent "abnormal" results. Sheehan reminds us: "Don't forget that laboratory tests are just that: performed at 70° temperature and 40 percent humidity with no wind. Changing meteorological conditions, proximity to meals, presence of tension or excitement all change the demands on our cardiopulmonary and muscular systems" (from *Dr. Sheehan on Running,* World Publications, 1975, p. 127).

On the positive side, however, there's much to be said for the tests. The screening of patients for serious heart or respiratory conditions is the most obvious reason for including such testing in your pre-exercise workup. If the test is properly supervised and monitored, it will be stopped at the first hint that the heart is overtaxed by the exercise or that the work is too strenuous for you to perform. In a real sense, the most useful function of the tests is to indicate levels of performance in healthy people. If no serious problems show up on the monitors, you, your physician and trainer or coach can use the material to gauge your ability to exercise, determine which exercise or sport is best for you, and then decide at what level you should start.

As important as stress testing "in motion" may be, it is not automatically a part of every battery of tests run by every doctor or clinic for every patient. Even as strong an advocate of stress testing as Dr. Cooper admits that "stress testing everyone is not practical. There are not enough treadmills or physicians to provide all the tests. Furthermore, not all the people are going to have enough money to take the test" (Dr. Kenneth Cooper, "Views from the Aerobics Center," in B. Anderson, ed., *Sportsource,* World Publications, 1975).

What are the alternatives, then? If time or money is severely limited, there are some fairly valid, safe ways to test cardiac and respiratory fitness. Here is a test that you can try for yourself, provided you've first checked with your physician to make sure the test is safe for you.

The test is called the Kasch Pulse Recovery Test and was developed by Dr. Fred Kasch of San Diego State University. It requires only three things: a twelve-inch bench or step, a watch with a sweep second hand, and a friend to help count.

Dr. Kasch advises that you not smoke or engage in any physical activity for at least two hours before the test. Here's the procedure from an unpublished paper by Dr. Kasch's Exercise Physiology Laboratory, San Diego State University, as quoted in Charles Kunzelman's *Rating the Exercises:*

> To begin, step up onto the bench or step, stand fully erect, then step back down from the bench. Do this for three minutes, at the rate of 24 steps per minute (that's a full step-up-step-down every 2.5 seconds). Both feet must step onto the bench and return to the floor each time. The action should be even and relaxed.
>
> . . . When you've done that (performed the test) for three minutes, sit down and relax—without talking—for five seconds. Then take your pulse rate for 60 seconds.
>
> To get an accurate pulse rate, place the middle three fingers of one hand on the underside of the opposite wrist. If you have difficulty locating your pulse there, try placing the same three fingers on either side of your throat just below the joint of the jaw. Count each "push" or "throb" you feel against your fingertips. . . .

For this test, fitness level is determined by age-adjusted charts. The three age ranges are 6–12, 18–26, and 33–57.

At 18–26 years, the ranges for men are as follows: *excellent,* 69–75; *good,* 76–83; *average,* 84–92; *fair,* 93–99; and *poor,* 100–106. For women, *excellent* is 76–84; *good,* 85–94; *average,* 95–105; *fair,* 106–116; and *poor,* 117–127.

In the 33–57 age range, men range from 63–76, *excellent;* 77–90, *good;* 91–106, *average;* 107–120, *fair;* and 121–134, *poor.* Women in the same age cluster score 73–86 for *excellent;* 87–100, *good;* 101–117, for *average;* 118–130, *fair;* and 131–144, *poor.*

One point should be made about this test: this is *not* a substitute for a stress test done in a clinic, hospital, or aerobics testing center. But it does give you a rough-and-ready idea of where you fall on a general fitness continuum that's age-adjusted for various groups. Obviously, if you fall in the "fair" to "poor" range—or fail to complete the test altogether—you should proceed with caution. Be on the safe side: go visit your physician and have some further testing done. If you're in the "average" to "excellent" range, then start exercising cautiously and then retest yourself at the end of four to six weeks after you've begun your program.

As to the subject of target pulse rates to be obtained, both during the tests and during your program itself, this is a particularly controversial subject among fitness experts. Most doctors, trainers, exercise physiologists, coaches, and athletes agree that cardiovascular fitness (which *Sportsmedicine* author Dr. Gabe Mirkin defines as simply "the ability of the heart to do work") involves pushing the heart rate to a certain point and maintaining it at that level for a certain period. The controversy centers around what that target pulse rate must be and how long the period of time for maintaining it is. Mirkin, for example, says that in order to achieve cardiovascular fitness, "you must push your heartbeat to more than 60 percent of its maximum for at least 30 minutes three times a week."

Other authorities differ. Dr. Paul DeVore, in an article, "Cardiovascular Benefits of Strength Training Exercises" (*Iron Man*, July 1979), maintains that a trainee's heart rate must be maintained between 70 and 85 percent of maximum heart rate, as figured according to age-adjusted maximal heart-rate charts for at least 12 consecutive minutes. He finds 10–12 minutes "sufficient" for conditioning, but he adds that 20-minute segments are better.

Dr. Kenneth Cooper's view, as stated in *Aerobics*, is that "if the exercise is vigorous enough to produce a sustained heart rate of 150 beats per minute or more, the training benefits begin about five minutes after this exercise starts and continue as long as the exercise is performed." Thus we're left with the following summary: the exercise we do (whatever it may be) must be aerobic, or oxygen-burning; must be sustained between 12 and 30 minutes; must be repeated at least several times each week, and must push the heart rate to 150 beats per minute or more—somewhere between 60 and 85 percent of maximum heart rate for the individual who is doing the exercising.

All right. Let's say you've been to your family doctor or internist and have received a clean bill of health. You've been pronounced ready to exercise. Are you really set to go invest in the long-awaited workout gear?

Not quite. In addition to all the tests that have been run, there are at least two more areas that need checking before you start your exercise program. The advantage of these tests is that they can be self-administered, so they won't cost you anything. If you want help with the testing or results, find a workout partner or get some advice from your coach or trainer, if you've already picked one. These are really tests for your locomotor apparatus and for minimum strength and flexibility in sports. They won't determine whether or not you're "pro" material, but at least they can indicate if you'll be able to play your sport on a competent amateur level.

There are seven of these tests in all, as recommended by Dr. Hans Kraus in *Sports Injuries*. Here is a list for your home testing program:

Test 1. Lie on your back with hands clasped behind your neck. Flex your knees. Put your ankles under a heavy piece of furniture, or have someone hold your feet down to make sure you're not "cheating." Now roll up slowly into a sitting position, and back down, as a test of the strength of your abdominal muscles.

Test 2. Stand up straight with your legs together. Slowly bend over and reach down as far as possible. A flexible person can touch the floor with his/her fingertips. Don't force the movement or bounce up and down; this might cause severe back strain.

Test 3. Get on your knees and settle back until you're sitting on your heels.

Test 4. Do three deep knee bends, going down until your thighs are parallel with the floor.

Test 5. (two versions): For men: do three chins while hanging from a bar by your arms. For women: do a modified chin by placing a broomstick between two chairs. Then lie flat on the floor and pull yourself up three times.

Test 6. (two versions): For men: do three full pushups. For women: do three modified pushups, keeping your knees on the floor, but raising the upper body.

Test 7. Lie on your back on the floor. Extend your arms so that your elbows are straight and the backs of your arms touch the floor.

Obviously, this isn't a series of tests that you can "pass" or "fail" in any absolute sense. However, if one or two of the movements give you difficulty, you should start on an intensive pretraining routine before you get into your sport. Don't rely on the sport itself to give you the flexibility and strength you need; you may want to do some pretraining first before you begin to play seriously.

Muscular strength is a more complex area to measure. One relatively accurate way to measure it is with a grip-strength test, since it's been found by researchers that the results of this test correlate very closely with overall body strength. The test is administered with a hand-grip dynamometer. The instrument is held in the hands and is squeezed as tightly as possible. The dynamometer records in pounds or kilograms the strength of the subject's grip. Some machine manufacturers have designed equipment that will test muscles throughout the body for strength (Cybex, for example), but the machinery is fairly costly and highly specialized.

If you are looking for a home test of strength, however, you can use multiple repetitions of the Kraus tests for flexibility as tests of *minimum* strength. Inability to perform any one of the movements indicates, according to Dr. Kraus, a weakness in the muscle area worked—for example, the inability to perform one or more simple situps suggests weakness in the abdominal and *psoas* muscles.

There's one final area we need to discuss—the all-important question of your weight. How do you know when you're overweight, underweight, or "just right"? The answer isn't always as simple as it sounds. You may know that you're 10 pounds heavier than when you graduated from college, or when you were married, or 15 pounds lighter than last Christmas. But what do all these figures really mean?

Keith looks gazelle-like at 165, while Robert is developing a spare tire and a decided paunch at that same figure. Joyce at 5′9″ is overweight at 175, but considers herself "thin" at 140. But Kathy, small-boned and lightly muscled, is 5′4″ and feels "grossly" fat at 102. How do we judge which person is really overweight and which is at ideal weight or below?

Let's clear the air with some important distinctions right away. The scales tell only a very small part of the total story on ideal weight. A man who is muscular and well-conditioned may look and feel trim and terrific at 160, while another man who's desperately out of shape may be 15-plus pounds overweight at the same reading on the scales. Measurements of critical areas—hips, thighs, waist, midriff, upper arms—reveal quite a bit but still can be misleading. Much depends on the place where the measurement is taken, as well as how tight or loose the tape measure is.

The critical factor in determining overweight/underweight/ideal weight is the proportion of bodyfat to muscle—fat weight vs. lean weight. The problem with the scales is that it records total pounds, not what percentage is muscle and lean body tissue, and what is excess fat. A man in good condition is 11–12 percent bodyfat, while a woman in good condition is about 15–16 percent bodyfat. Dieting alone can produce a decrease in bodyfat with a corresponding decrease in muscle mass and lean body tissue, anywhere from 25 to 80 percent, depending on the length and severity of the diet.

How, then, can we determine what percentage of our total weight is fat and lean? There's only one totally accurate method, of course, and that's hydrostatic weighing done in an immersion tank. The subject is literally placed in a tank and immersed in water. The amount of water displaced is recorded and other measurements, such as residual lung volume and bodyweight both in and out of water, are also made. The proportion of bodyfat to lean tissue can be calculated from these measurements.

Unfortunately, this test, accurate though it may be, is expensive, time-consuming, and often not readily available. Even in large metropolitan areas, there may be only a handful of places that provide hydrostatic weighing. You may find yourself called on to travel miles and shell out big bucks for the privilege of learning what percentage of your weight is fat and what is lean.

Fortunately, there are do-it-yourself methods that provide some accuracy. In most people under the age of 50, at least 50 percent of the bodyfat is stored directly beneath the skin (subcutaneous fat). If we measure the thickness of the fold produced when the skin and the tissue just under it are firmly grasped in the fingers, we can get a good measure of the presence of bodyfat. The common spots for measuring are the back of the upper arm, subscapular region (middle of the back at the shoulder blades), waistline, biceps (front of upper arm), and iliac crest (waistline right above the hip bone). Bear in mind, however, that the average triceps fat measurement increases slightly with age—for males, from .433 mm to .55 mm from 18–24 to the 24–44 age group. Women increase from .708 mm as teenagers to .984 mm in their mid-thirties and beyond.

Looking for a quick, homespun method to get an idea of the shape you're in? Do the old pinch test, which will give you a rough idea of how you'd come off with the more sophisticated calipers test. Just pinch the skin at the triceps of one upper arm (back of the arm) midway between the shoulder and elbow. If the skin fold is more than ½ inch to 1 inch, you're probably sliding into the range of overweight.

The skin-fold thickness test, incidentally, is probably the best compromise today between the expensive, time-consuming if accurate hydrostatic weighing and the old look-in-the-mirror method. The National Center of Health Statistics in Washington points out that "skin folds permit a closer estimate of bodyfat than do the tables of relative weight. . . . Skin folds are becoming established as the easiest and most direct measure of body fat in the doctor's office, the clinic, or in a large-scale population survey."

The most accurate way to perform the skin-fold test is to do the measurement with calipers of various names (such as the Fat-o-meter, Slimguide, and Physique Meter; Harpenden makes the most accurate but also the most expensive metal calipers). These are small devices that allow you to pinch small skin folds. They come with clear instructions, usually in manual form, about how the measurements are to be taken and interpreted. Some manuals such as Fat-o-meter's recommend using four measurements for men—triceps, biceps, upper back, and above the iliac crest (the top edge of the hip bones at the sides)—but only the triceps and iliac crest for women. Others recommend all readings for both sexes. Along with your calipers you'll usually receive a chart on how to read and compute the percentages. If the reading is done by your doctor or trainer, he or she will help you determine the percent of bodyfat and the amount you need to lose to be in good shape.

Your doctor, like as not, isn't inordinately concerned about the five extra pounds you picked up over vacation. What he or she is looking for is serious obesity (20 percent or more above normal for your height, bone structure, body type, and age). Thank goodness, we all are growing more sophisticated about what "ideal weight" is. No one pays much attention to the height-weight tables anymore—least of all the MDs, who are now discovering that these norms are, if anything, a little low for the average American adult. Your doctor is looking for patterns of severe overweight or underweight, metabolic or eating disorders, and circulatory or digestive problems that might interfere with your exercising safely.

If you're seriously overweight and need to lose, have your doctor or trainer show you how to do the bodyfat tests with a set of calipers, and keep weekly and monthly records for the duration of your program. Rely on these measurements as well as the scales to monitor your progress.

And don't be tempted by the latest new fad diet. The danger of these for the new athlete is especially grave. If you eat a diet that's so unbalanced that you don't have the energy to exercise, you can end up seriously fatigued, lose muscle tissue and lean body tissue, and finally abandon the sport altogether. Result: you're now back to your old sedentary ways minus a pound or two. Furthermore, you're now so discouraged that you give up on exercise completely. The unwanted pounds creep back on and the cycle starts all over again. Stay on a weight-loss program that's safe and balanced, for maximum bodyfat loss and the best in sports performance. That's the only real way to build your sportspower and keep it up to par!

Nutrition for Sports Performance Training

While many people participate in recreational sports for the sheer joy and experience of playing the game—not to mention the thrill of competition and the even greater thrill of winning—a growing number of us weekend/weekday-evenings athletes participate in sports to shape up, lose bodyfat, and reduce our weight. So if you are among this growing number of men and women participating in sports and also dieting at the same time, you'll find the first part of this section directed at you. If you're among the lucky ones who have already reached ideal weight—or never had a weight problem in the first place—you'll be most interested in our nutritional information and suggestions for eating for top athletic performance. Either way, you can use this section to help you plan your eating regimen for maximum performance and also for good looks, strength, and health.

If you're a perpetual dieter, you're probably tired of all the well-meant "diet advice" that descends on us every day, and bored by all the miracle diets, reducing drugs, pills, and miracle cures that promise "ten pounds off in three days." Your goals, after all, are more complex than those of the person who just wants to lose a quick ten pounds for a special vacation or party. *You* want a diet that will give you the energy you need to play your sport or participate in exercise while maintaining good health and an energy level that keeps your athletic performance at peak condition. Of course, you also want to shed excess bodyfat and, more importantly, learn to keep it off. But if you want to improve your sports performance, it's a must that you maintain high energy levels while you train.

A pretty tall order, but certainly far from impossible. But before we recommend some diet plans we need to review briefly exactly how the body utilizes the food it takes in and stores.

You need energy for your body to do work. Energy is measured in units called *calories.* If you don't eat enough calories in the form of carbohydrates, fats, and proteins, your body will begin to *catabolize* (burn up) stored energy. Carbohydrates are stored in the form of fat, and are also present in the form of glucose in the bloodstream and as glycogen stored in the liver and in the muscle cells themselves. Fats are stored in adipose tissue. Proteins are stored as fats when excessive amounts are eaten, and also are *anabolized* to form lean tissue.

The body has a preference about which fuel sources it taps first. This is called the principle of "preferred energy fuel." All other things being equal, the body will first catabolize its carbohydrates, then its stored fat, then its lean tissue protein.

As long as there is enough glucose in the bloodstream, carbohydrate catabolism begins when glucose enters the cells and is broken down into pyruvic acid by a process called *glycolysis.* If there is not sufficient glucose in the bloodstream, glycogen stored in the liver and in the muscle cells will be converted into glucose by the process of *glycogenolysis* and will then enter the cells to be broken down into pyruvic acid. The pyruvic acid then enters what is called the *citric acid cycle,* through which ATP (adenosine triphosphate) is produced. ATP is further broken down by the *mitochondria* (tiny cellular organs) into ADP (adenosine diphosphate), phosphate, and energy. It is this energy that the body uses to do work.

When fats are catabolized, the first part of the process is different from the catabolization of glucose, but the final stage is the same. If you don't take in sufficient calories and there is not enough glucose in your bloodstream or glycogen in your liver and muscle cells, fat will be mobilized and will leave the adipose tissue where it is stored and will travel through the circulatory system to the liver. There it will be broken down into acetoacetic acid. The acetoacetic acid will then go to the muscle cells, become acetyl-coenzyme A, and then enter the citric acid cycle to produce ATP, then ADP, and usable energy.

If your diet is really poor or unbalanced, and if you have neither sufficient glucose, glycogen, or stored fats, your body will begin to catabolize lean tissue or protein. Protein catabolism begins with a process called *deamination,* in which an amino group (NH_2) is separated from an amino acid molecule to form one molecule of ammonia and one molecule of keto acid. The greater portion of the ammonia is converted into urea, to be excreted by the kidneys. The keto acid is either converted into glucose (to enter the cells and go through the citric acid cycle to produce ATP, then ADP, and energy), or fat (to go to the liver to be broken down into acetoacetic acid, which then enters the cells, becomes acetyl-coenzyme A, and enters the citric acid cycle to produce ATP, then ADP, and energy), or the keto acid enters into the citric acid cycle directly without first being converted into glucose or fat.

The body needs a balance of carbohydrates, fats, and proteins. For the normal person, books such as the *Mayo Clinic Diet Manual* (by the staff of the Mayo Clinic, Rochester Methodist Hospital, and St. Mary's hospital of Rochester, Minnesota; Philadelphia, London, Toronto, and Sydney: W. B. Saunders Company, 1981) recommend 60 percent carbohydrates, 20 percent fats, and 20 percent protein.

It has long been a common practice of competitive athletes to "load" or "pack" carbohydrates before a game. To do this, carbohydrates are eliminated from the diet until hours before a game, then added in large quantities. The theory is that the body will react to the period of carbohydrate starvation by overcompensating in its carbohydrate storage when fed massive amounts of carbohydrates at the end of the deprivation period. This, it is thought, will yield a greater store of energy than if the carbohydrates had not been eliminated from the diet.

This practice has recently come under fire. It places stress on the kidneys as well as the heart. If you have potential problems in either of these areas, you may be in for disastrous results. Alternate carbohydrate deprivation and loading can cause an irregular heartbeat. The catabolism of stored fat and protein during the deprivation period places a heavy load on the kidneys. Further, the actual benefits of carbohydrate loading have yet to be conclusively demonstrated in consistently higher scores and athletic achievements.

Far better to eat a balanced diet, with sufficient carbohydrates, fats, and proteins to sustain normal bodily processes. You won't need massive amounts of protein, either. This is another popular myth among athletes. Excess protein will simply be stored in the form of fat, as will excessive amounts of carbohydrates.

The key to having more energy is in training the muscle cells themselves to store more glycogen and to manufacture and store more ATP (adenosine triphosphate). This is best done by a vigorous training program in combination with a sane, balanced diet of sufficient calories to sustain the energy demands of your sport and the exercise program that you use to supplement and improve your sports performance.

Let's turn now to some familiar diets, and find out why they are not always wise regimens for someone who is trying to reduce total bodyfat percentages while improving his or her game.

ZERO-CALORIE OR MINI-CALORIE DIETS

These regimens are all the 500-calories-a-day-or-less variety. Advocates claim that such a diet cleanses the system and helps detoxify the body. But the disadvantages are far more serious: overly rapid weight loss, especially water loss; loss of potassium, sodium, and other necessary minerals and a resulting upset to the body's electrolyte system; possible tissue loss and cardiac irregularities.

HIGH-PROTEIN, LOW-CARBOHYDRATE PLANS

Let's make an important distinction among these diets at the beginning. Zero-carbohydrate diets can be quite dangerous and disruptive to the system. *Low* carbohydrate diets, with proper medical monitoring, usually are not. That means a cautious green light to levels 2 and 3 of the Atkins diet, the Scarsdale diet, the Woman Doctor's Diet for Women, the Adrien Arpel "sacred cow" diet, and generally for all other diets that stress protein but permit 30–60 grams of carbohydrate daily and also are low-fat, low-salt, and low-cholesterol. The forbidden diets are level 1 of the Atkins diet (the zero-carb phase), the Stillman diet, the quick-weight-loss diet, and the liquid-protein diets that came and went in the late seventies. The dangers of these regimens, as with fasting, include ketosis, potassium loss, fatigue caused by carbohydrate depletion, a disturbance in the body's electrolyte system, and an excess of fat, protein, cholesterol, and sodium caused by the high-fat staples such as butter, mayonnaise, unskinned fowl, untrimmed beef, and sour cream.

High-protein programs should never be undertaken by people with undiagnosed kidney ailments, diabetes, or a history of cardiac problems. If your blood cholesterol level is high, you'll find that the diet adds to your difficulties unless you conscientiously monitor the amount of cholesterol you ingest each day. You'll also have to take plenty of vitamin and mineral supplements and add fiber in the form of fiber tablets or a few tablespoons of unprocessed bran each day.

Also beware of the myth that protein is "the food of athletes" and that you can't eat too much protein. An average-sized man or woman, even one in a tough athletic training program, needs only one gram of protein for each two pounds of body weight at most. Any excess is excreted or stored as fat. You *can* gain weight on a very high-protein regimen, as many unhappy ex-Atkins dieters can testify.

HIGH-CARBOHYDRATE, PROTEIN-POOR DIETS

If the high-protein diets are dangerous, these are equally so, since many are drastically lacking in necessary proteins and fats. Regimens like the rice diet, macrobiotic and vegetarian diets, the "inches-off" diet, salads-only regimens, and even extreme versions of the highly respected Pritikin program are examples of such plans. The advocates claim that if only we'd drop animal protein and fat from our dinner tables, the pounds would melt away.

It's certainly true that we Americans eat far too much untrimmed beef, unskinned fowl, and fats such as butter, sour cream, and salad dressings; that generally whole grains, fruits, and vegetables are healthy fare. It's also true that, as the U.S. Government Report called *Dietary Goals for the United States* reminds us, we need to increase our complex carbohydrate intake and reduce refined sugar, salt, and cholesterol.

Remember that vegetable protein is incomplete protein, and at least a small amount (12–20 percent of daily total food intake) of animal protein is needed to digest your salads and bean curd. Even if your major source of protein is vegetarian, plan to average at least 20 to 30 grams a day of animal products (eggs and dairy products are acceptable if you've sworn off meat) to make sure you get the essential amino acids necessary for digestion and other bodily processes. Also be aware that combining vegetarian protein is essential—for example, corn and beans, eaten separately, are incomplete proteins but together are complete. It takes more than just a trip to the local farmer's market to be a healthy practicing vegetarian—a sophisticated knowledge of nutrition is also required.

One more word of warning: many of the more extreme vegetarian regimens—for example, the Kempner rice diet, consisting of juice, 3 ounces of fruit and ⅓ pound of cooked rice per meal—were designed for use with medically obese patients and were never intended for the general public to use. Persons on the Duke University rice diet are monitored daily for abnormalities and signs of trouble. It's not a diet that a working person leading a normal working, exercising existence could live on for a long-term period. Don't try to use any of these diets in ways for which they weren't intended!

In the same low-protein category is the newest diet fad, the Beverly Hills diet. It's a regimen built almost exclusively on fruits for the first two weeks. The diet, like all reducing programs, has a few good points. The sheer regimentation and boredom of the mono-meals will finally force most dieters into eating less. It's certainly low enough in refined sugars, salt, and fat and rich in fiber, minerals, and vitamins.

But the diet has the general flaw that plagues all one-food diets: it's woefully unbalanced. The digestive enzymes are all there in the fruit, but as author Richard Smith points out in a July 1981 *New York Times* review, the ptyalin and hydrochloric acid in the stomach have no protein to work on for the diet's first three weeks. Result: massive diarrhea, excretion of water, ketosis, possible acidosis, and electrolyte imbalance. Most of the fruit is fiber that simply goes undigested—hence the quick weight drop. Even a low-protein diet, such as the Pritikin program, recommends at least 15–20 grams of protein per day—more than the Beverly Hills diet offers even in its third and fourth weeks.

SINGLE-FOOD DIETS

These are almost too numerous to mention, and chances are you're familiar with many of them: the drinking man's diet, the bananas diet, the junk-food diet, the fast-food diet, the pizza-only diet, the yogurt diet, the grapefruit diet. Their effectiveness stems largely from boredom. If you're really limited to a single food or food group, how much of it can you eat? Besides the boredom, one-food diets are also nutritionally unbalanced. Most are heavy on one or two nutrients or vitamins and low on everything else. The grapefruit diet, for example, is an excellent source of potassium, unrefined carbohydrate, and fiber, not to mention vitamin C, but is low on protein, fat, and many essential minerals and vitamins. You can't live forever on such a regimen. The very lack of balance means that you don't reeducate yourself about eating nor do you reform your eating habits. So when you go off you *really* go off and regain all your lost poundage.

Finally, many of the foods are claimed to have magic, fat-burning properties. While there are some lipotropic (fat-burning) vitamins and minerals, these "magic" foods are not. More misinformation, less real help for the overweight.

"HEAD" DIETS

These are all the diets where you're encouraged to "think yourself thin" or are told that it's your head, not your body, that's making you overweight. The head tricks are numerous, ranging from hypnosis and acupuncture to tricks such as always eating in the same place or from the same dish, eating only at certain times of the day, never ingesting more than 100 calories at a time. While all the tricks may be perfectly fine for teaching a form of behavior modification—which is what most of the elaborate trickery boils down to—they don't help you decrease your total caloric intake, ingest fewer fats, fewer simple sugars, or less cholesterol or salt. Nor do they help you burn calories through exercise, which is perhaps the most helpful behavior modification "trick" that can be taught a heavy person.

DIET GROUPS AND CLUBS

For many people, these are the only real solution, since they seem to provide just the right amount of support, punishment and ego-gratification (plus the social occasions of the meetings) to make the whole thing work. Into these categories fall Weight Watchers, the Diet Workshop, TOPS, and Overeaters Anonymous, as well as many smaller groups. The "fat farms" and spas, in a more limited sense, provide the same thing: support, a controlled environment, and a regimented plan that must be followed to the letter. The success of these depends heavily on the individual dieter and his or her preferences.

The "fat farms" and spas, widely criticized for years, are now coming into their own. Many spas offer medically tested, moderate exercise programs and imaginative, nutritionally sound meals for the money. The drawback: you put down your money, spend the week or two weeks, lose the obligatory ten pounds, and leave, looking and feeling like a million dollars. Trouble is, you *live* in a city, small town, or suburb, not in that sequestered paradise where the chef makes special enticing low-calorie meals and the svelte exercise instructor *makes* you get out of bed for that 6 A.M. walk. Once back home, your incentive fades before the daily realities of going to work, eating fast-food lunches at the desk, making dinner for the kids, and dealing with social and business engagements. Unless you take the knowledge that you gained on your retreat and incorporate it into your daily life—reeducate yourself about diet and eating, in other words—nothing will change in your life and you'll regain those pounds with interest.

With all the bad stuff around, then, what's a "good" diet? More to the point, what's a safe, nutritionally balanced program that an active person can follow and still maintain good health and high energy levels?

WHAT IS A GOOD DIET?

It's hard to find such diets amidst all the hustles and scams, but they're there. The diets recommended by Weight Watchers, the Diet Workshop, and Overeaters Anonymous, for example, are all sound and nutritionally balanced, low-calorie diets. Even if you don't have time for the meetings, you can certainly go on the diets safely and effectively. Carbohydrate-sensitives, beware, however: some of the prepared dishes are very high in carbs and may slow down weight loss because of all the vegetables, grains, and pastas. The diets recommended by some of the top spas—for example, the Golden Door—are excellent, very imaginative, and a real plus for the gourmet cook, since he or she can still show off kitchen talents while losing. For the same reasons, check out Craig Claiborne's new low-salt diet cookery and some of the *nouvelle cuisine* cookbooks.

Three excellent regimens to try are: Dr. Rechtschaffen's diet (Random House, 1980, based on the Claiborne low-salt diet), low in salt and fat, high in fiber, and moderately high in protein and unrefined carbohydrates. It's sane, nutritionally balanced, tasty, and could be followed indefinitely. Also sample Dr. Norman Jolliffe's "Prudent Man's Diet," originally designed for members of his Anti-Coronary Club. It's also balanced, low-calorie, low in fats, cholesterol, and salt. While you're at it, check out *The American Heart Association Cookbook* (David McKay, 1973) and *What You Need to Know about Food and Cooking for Health* (Viking, 1973).

Finally, try the *New York City Health Department Diet*, published as a pamphlet by the Bureau of Nutrition, Department of Health, City of New York. It's a basic 1,200-calorie-a-day diet that's frequently reprinted and is available in pamphlet form directly from New York City's Bureau of Nutrition. A good diet, particularly since there's a 1,200-calorie version for smaller-frame people and an expanded 1,800-calorie one for the larger-frame or more active person. You couldn't go wrong with this one.

There are other diets that are also acceptable with slight modifications—for example, the Pritikin program, which provides for only 13 percent protein. That's rather low for the very active person who wants to train vigorously. But if the amount of lean meat, low-fat cottage cheese or farmer's cheese, egg whites, fish or skinned fowl were increased, the diet is an excellent choice for a sports-minded person. Another way to up the amount of protein without adding a significant number of calories: try a soy-based or milk-egg-based protein powder as a supplement to mix with low-fat skim milk, yogurt, or cottage cheese—an easy, calorie-conscious way to enrich this basically sensible diet.

For the carbohydrate-sensitive, Dr. Barbara Edelstein's "Woman Doctor's Diet for Women" is a prudent version of a low-carb diet. You can live with it on a long-term basis, provided you slowly increase the carbohydrate grams by adding more salad greens, some low-carbohydrate fruits such as melon or berries, and perhaps some high-protein, low-carbohydrate bread or crackers. Once you've found a maintenance level that's right for you, you can play with the diet until you've adjusted the carbohydrate/protein/fat ratio to suit your own needs.

THE ATHLETE'S DIET

But suppose the athletic bug bites? You decide, after all, to go into competition. Or the sport or activity you took up to shed a few extra pounds has taken on a new importance. You find yourself spending more and more time in the gym, on the running track, cycling through the park on weekends. Or you try cross-country skiing, the martial arts, tennis, racquetball, golf and steadily improve your skills. Don't you need to eat differently from the average person?

The answer is both *yes* and *no*. *Yes*, in the sense that certain foods act on the body in certain specific ways and, depending on the requirements of your sport, you need more of certain nutrients and less of others. But the answer is *no* in the sense that much of the mythology surrounding athletic diets is just that. We're always seeing or reading endorsements by athletes for one or another product, or hearing tall tales of fantastic pregame meals. The fact that much of this is advertising or media hype escapes the overzealous beginner. Dr. Gabe Mirkin sums it up very well in *Sportsmedicine*. After relating various menus for pregame meals—ranging from tomato juice mixed with the blood squeezed from two pounds of raw hamburger, a meal of lentils, seeds, and nuts, or a snack of two bunches of bananas—he summarizes: "These stories prove a point. Whether you're a meat eater, a vegetarian, a faster or a gorger, you can be a standout in competitive sports."

Obviously, then, there's no royal dietary road to good athletic performance. However, the basics are the same. Athletes, like everyone else, need a variety of foods balanced among the four basic groups: fruits and vegetables, cereals and grains, high-protein foods (eggs, meat), and milk and other dairy products. Four servings from each of the first two groups and two from the last two should provide everyone, athlete or not, with all the nutrients, minerals, and vitamins he or she needs. And to that extent, the athlete's diet should be only a better-planned, better-orchestrated version of everyone else's.

First, a little basic nutrition. The most important substance for any person, athlete or not, is water. Whether or not you exercise, your body requires 6–8 glasses of fluid per day. Some of this fluid requirement is met by the food we eat—particularly foods high in water content, such as fruits or vegetables, or foods such as other complex carbohydrates (grains, breads, cereals), which aid the body in retaining water. If you're training vigorously or playing competitively, particularly in hot weather, your body may lose 2–3 pounds of fluids through excretion and perspiration. Replace this lost fluid by drinking water and also potassium-rich juices such as grapefruit and orange juice, or by drinking commercially prepared electrolyte drinks such as Gatorade. (Electrolytes are those mineral salts—sodium, potassium, and so forth—that control the electrical potential of nerve cells and regulate fluid levels.)

Next in importance is protein, an organic substance that forms the primary structural material of cells and tissues. It contains 23 essential different amino acids, only 14 of which the body can manufacture. The other 9, often called the essential amino acids, must be obtained from food.

There's a lot of mythology surrounding protein for athletes, and much of it is false. For example, protein is not a source of immediate energy. And contrary to belief and media hype, protein requirements do not increase significantly with exercise (with the sole exception of bodybuilding). The myth that an athlete needs immense quantities of protein in the form of huge pregame steak meals is false. Excess protein can add body fat, just as can excess carbs or fat. Any excess amount of protein, beyond the body's normal requirements, is either excreted or stored as fat. So much for the theory that you can't get fat on protein!

Before protein is absorbed into the bloodstream, it's broken down into amino acids. Hence the body can't recognize whether its sources of protein are animal, vegetable, nut, or seed. Its only concern is with getting those essential amino acids.

We classify food sources of protein as either complete (containing all nine essential amino acids) or incomplete (lacking one or more of the essential amino acids, as is true of most vegetable proteins). Meat contains all the essential amino acids and is the surest, simplest way to obtain them all. But vegetarians can fulfill their dietary requirements by combining carefully—for example, eating corn (seven essential acids) with beans (which contain the two missing ones). Together they make up a complete protein.

Carbohydrates are components of foods that are composed of carbon, oxygen, and hydrogen. They provide the primary source of energy for daily activity, especially for vigorous exercise. If you're low on carbs, you'll feel listless, depleted of energy and weak during your workout.

Although carbohydrates were for years considered dietary villains and dieters were warned to avoid all desserts, breads, pastas, cereals, rices, and potatoes, we're now coming to realize that some of this was bad advice. Carbs, it seems, are the dieter's and the athlete's friends, not enemies. While simple refined sugars, such as "junk foods" and desserts, table sugars, cola drinks, refined bread, sweetened cereal, and many sugared processed foods are anathema to the dieter and athlete alike, complex carbohydrates (fruits, vegetables, unrefined and whole grains, potatoes, whole-wheat breads, rices, and pastas) are both excellent sources of quick energy and good bargains calorically. They provide plenty of fiber, water, and essential minerals and vitamins in addition to the quick energy boost. In fact, *Dietary Goals for the U.S.* recommends that we increase our intake of complex carbs from 28 percent to about 48 percent of our diets. (Refined and processed sugars, by contrast, should drop from 45 percent to 10 percent.)

Fats are easy to recognize, since they're greasy to the touch and are not water-soluble. While they aren't immediate energy sources like carbohydrates, they do provide energy late in endurance events after muscles have been depleted of glycogen. (Glycogen is the form in which glucose or sugar is stored in the liver and in muscle cells.) Visible fats include margarine, butter, salad and cooking oils, bacon, fat, cream, and the fat on meat. Invisible fats are found in egg yolk, meats, olives, whole milk and milk products, avocados, and nuts. Fat gives us 4,082 calories per pound, or more than twice as much as a pound of carbohydrates.

While competition bodybuilders and persons trying to lose weight often go on severely fat-restricted diets, people who participate in endurance sports such as long-distance running, race walking, or cycling need the long-term energy benefits of some fats in the diet. Restricting fats too severely may cost you dearly in terms of endurance in your sport or exercise.

What about vitamins and minerals? We've heard them widely touted as prime ingredients for athletic success so that each time we hear about some new product or discovery, we're off in pursuit of yet another tiny expensive bottle that's hyped as the latest Fountain of Energy.

First, it's useful to know that a vitamin is simply a component of an enzyme that regulates the rate at which chemical reactions proceed in the body. Vitamins, contrary to popular myth, aren't direct sources of energy. And our vitamin requirements, unlike mineral requirements, do *not* increase significantly because of exercise.

Also remember that since vitamins alone are not nutrients, taking massive amounts of a certain vitamin can't make up for a total deficiency in the diet. Thus, using vitamins in place of meals rather than as supplements to them makes no sense at all.

The essential vitamins and their recommended daily allowances are as follows: A—5,000 units; B_1—2 mgm; B_2—2 mgm; niacinamide—20 mgm; B_6 (pyridoxine)—3 mgm; biotin—.3 mgm; panthothenic acid—15 mgm; folic acid—.4 mgm; B_{12}—6 mgm; C—60 mgm; D—400 units; E—30 units; and K—2 mgm. All the minimum daily requirements cited above (as drawn from Mirkin's *The Sportsmedicine Book*) are typically supplied by a balanced diet and at worst are obtainable from a good extra-strength multi-vitamin tablet. The drugstore or supermarket variety is often quite as good (that is, as high in content of specific vitamins) as the more expensive specialty or health-food-store kind; just be sure you read the label.

The big "fad" vitamins for athletes are currently C, E, and B_{12}. These are all vitamins that have a reputation for increasing athletic prowess. But do they really live up to their PR copy? Let's look at each in turn and see what it actually does.

Vitamin C is one of the easiest of the vitamins to obtain in natural form. Even if you're exercising strenuously, you shouldn't really need C supplementation. If you're eating your share of fruits and vegetables, especially citrus fruits and such green vegetables as peppers and cabbage, you'll have all the vitamin C you need. If you overdose on C, the excess is excreted anyway, so taking megadoses is literally a waste of money. Incidentally, as *The Sportsmedicine Book* tells us, Americans spent $80 million for vitamin C supplements in 1976 alone.

Despite the popularity of C as a supplement, there are some very real dangers attached to overdoses. Over 2,000 milligrams daily can prove to be toxic. In lesser doses, bad side effects include diarrhea, kidney stones, spontaneous abortion in pregnant women, liver damage, bone fractures, destruction of B_{12}, and iron poisoning. Some people even claim that steady doses cause a mild addiction. The only instances where a C supplement might be indicated are cases where fruits and vegetables are highly restricted. If, for example, you're on a low-carb diet at your physician's advice and are eating few citrus fruits or green vegetables, a C supplement might be indicated. Fortunately, the best C sources are also low-calorie, so even dedicated dieters seldom run the risk of a serious C deficiency.

Vitamin E is another of the most-hyped vitamins. The vitamin E fad actually started in the 1920s when two researchers found that doses of E would help white rats become fertile. In the sixties and seventies, E was credited with practically magic powers—everything from being a youth vitamin to increasing sex drive and aiding memory. As a result, by the late 1970s Americans were spending $100 million a year on E capsules.

Like C, E occurs naturally in so many foods that true deficiencies are very rare. Cereals, wheat germ, margarine, soybeans, corn and other oils, muscle meats, fish, and green leafy vegetables provide ample sources of vitamin E. Dr. Mirkin wittily sums up the current E research: "To date, the only solid scientific fact that has been established is that vitamin E has value if you are a rat who wants to become pregnant."

The third vitamin invested with mythic powers, B_{12}, is another fad supplement. People with pernicious anemia benefit from B_{12} injections since their stomachs do not have the necessary chemical balance to absorb B_{12} from the foods they eat. Normal people, on the other hand, take in B_{12} from all animal products, eggs, milk—in short, most non-vegetable products. Only total strict vegetarians need worry about a B_{12} deficiency, and it is easily corrected by a mild supplement. No need for expensive B_{12} injections, which are costly—if painful—placebos.

So what's the safe and sane approach to vitamin supplements? As we've already said, unless you are on a highly restricted and thus unbalanced diet, you can probably get by without any supplement at all, or with only a mild multiple-vitamin tablet. Ask your doctor's advice. He or she will probably prescribe a supplement, if one is indicated, at the same time your diet is recommended. A good diet, remember, will not cut out all of any food, be it breads, cereals, fruits, or fats; it will simply restrict them, so a general supplement should be all you need.

Minerals, as distinguished from vitamins, are basic elements found in the soil. They are picked up from the soil by plants and ingested by both animals and man. There are many different minerals, but the four that our bodies require in large amounts are sodium, potassium, magnesium, and calcium. In trace amounts, 14 others are necessary in very small dosages: aluminum, boron, chromium, cobalt, copper, iodine, iron, zinc, manganese, nickel, molybdenum, selenium, tin, and vanadium. The trace minerals are available from most normal diets or, at worst, from a multi-mineral tablet.

The four major minerals have very specific functions. Calcium is the material that makes bones and teeth hard. Sodium regulates how and where water is distributed in the body. Potassium regulates muscle heat and nerve impulse conduction. Magnesium regulates muscle contractions and also controls carbohydrates being converted to energy. Recommended daily dosages for each of these minerals are calcium—25 mgm; magnesium—200 mgm; potassium—mgm not established, but the requirements *do* increase with exercise; and sodium—2 gm.

Of these four, the most important is sodium. It's the most abundant mineral in the blood and in its absence, we become dehydrated and weak, and develop muscle cramps. Too much salt also dehydrates, increases potassium loss, and may even cause blood clotting. It can also cause or aggravate hypertension.

It's almost impossible for people in twentieth-century America to develop salt deficiencies. Salt is contained in all milk products, such as yogurts and cheeses, unless they're specifically labelled low-salt. It's also found in all margarines, butters, meats, fish, chicken, rye, wheat, and corn products, and most canned and processed foods. Same for natural sources of sodium, such as bran, spinach, celery, and many nuts and grains. The more difficult task is to avoid salt. Now that low-salt diets are so plentiful for people with high blood pressure, edema, cardiac problems, and other medical conditions, we're beginning to look more critically at the amount of salt in the average American diet and to be rather appalled at it. The average American takes in from 6 to 18 grams of salt per day, or about 60 times his or her MDR (minimum daily requirement). The recently published *Dietary Goals for the U.S.* recommends we cut salt consumption to about 5 grams a day—a modest goal in view of the fact that we can survive nicely with 2 grams daily.

If you're an athlete, you've probably heard of the practice of feeding salt tablets to players in hot weather to replace salt lost in sweat. Forget it! Taking salt supplements is dangerous and may even cause stroke or heart attack in hot weather. Better to take an electrolyte drink or some fruit juice with a potassium tablet to help regulate the sodium-potassium balance in the body. And forget the myth that excess salt helps athletic performance. Often athletes on salt-restricted diets outperform players on traditional diets in hot weather. One word of warning: start your salt restriction in cooler weather when you perspire less so that the body can adjust a bit. Then, come summer workouts, you'll have no trouble and can probably play your sport better as a result.

Two minerals in which athletes often are deficient are potassium and magnesium. Weakness, tiredness, irritability, and a tendency to low endurance and early fatigue are signals that you may lack these two minerals. Fruit juices are rich in potassium; so are many vegetables, molasses, bananas, pecans, rye flour, soybeans, walnuts, and wheat germ. Magnesium is found in almonds, beans, beer, Brazil and cashew nuts, corn, dairy products, peas, pecans, meat, oatmeal, peanuts, rice, soybeans, green vegetables, wheat, and walnuts.

Potassium is one of the few substances in the body that is depleted with exercise. In order to keep from overheating, the muscle being exercised releases potassium into the bloodstream which in turn widens the blood vessels, increases blood flow, and carries heat away from the muscles. Potassium is constantly excreted from the body through sweat and urine, and the more active you are, the more potassium you lose. Keep replenishing it through potassium-rich fluids and solid foods (bananas, oranges, grapefruit, and other citrus fruits), and you'll improve your game or workout.

Magnesium is one of the most important minerals to the active person, since it helps control muscle contraction and also regulates the conversion of carbohydrates to energy. Low magnesium levels can cause chronic fatigue and muscle cramps. Distance runners and other people who engage in endurance sports lose substantial amounts of magnesium in the sweat and always need to replenish their supply—part of the reason that beer is so popular with athletes!

Calcium, the last of the four important minerals, is the main structural material in bones and teeth. It's also the most abundant mineral in the body. It helps control muscle contractions and regulates many of the body's chemical reactions. Calcium requirements, fortunately, stay fairly constant throughout life except when women are pregnant or nursing. Eating a minimum of calcium-rich foods like asparagus, beans, cabbage, cauliflower, cheese and other dairy products, egg yolks, figs, lentils, nuts, sardines, and turnip greens will give you all the calcium you need.

For a mineral-rich diet sufficient to sustain you through the most intense workout, then, you need plenty of fruits and vegetables for potassium; nuts and whole grains for magnesium and trace elements; small amounts of sodium as they occur naturally in such foods as spinach, celery, nuts, grains, and bran; and low-fat or skim milk and other products for calcium. And remember that you can fight tiredness and lack of energy and endurance in your sport by significantly increasing your potassium and magnesium intake.

As far as a "perfect" diet for athletes goes, then, there's really no such animal. Let's look at our three categories of athletic activities: 1) endurance or aerobic sports that call for long, sustained stretches of activity—running, jogging, racewalking, long-distance cycling, cross-country skiing; 2) "power" sports that call for shorter, more intense bursts of power or strength, such as Olympic lifting or powerlifting, plus sports requiring short bursts of speed (sprinting); and 3) sports requiring a combination of the two, such as the racquet sports, the "ball" sports, and the martial arts. In a category by itself is bodybuilding, a sport where the body itself (especially its musculature and definition) is its own "product" and where certain kinds of highly restricted diets must be followed for long periods before a contest in order to achieve the currently fashionable "cut up," well-defined look.

Let's talk about the aerobic activities first. If you're a runner, cyclist, jogger, or a participant in any of the sports that require long periods of sustained activities, you need plenty of long-chain complex carbohydrates, plenty of liquid, easily digestible foods, and a diet low in sugars, fat, salt, and fatty proteins. But don't forget to include a few fats for better endurance when glycogen stores in the muscles have long since been exhausted.

A new "aerobic diet," developed recently by Dr. Don Mannerberg of the Cooper Clinic for Aerobic Exercise, stresses limiting fat intake to 20 percent of the diet and proteins to 12 percent. Complex carbs comprise the bulk of the diet at 63 percent. Simple sugars and salt should be limited as much as possible. Dr. Mannerberg suggests using only skim-milk, low-fat products, eating unsalted and water-packed canned produce, using lean, trimmed, or skinned pieces of meat, fish, and fowl, and using only brown rice, whole-grain breads, and unsweetened cereals. As a result, the diet he recommends is high in grains, breads, fruits, and vegetables, and also stresses lean cuts of beef, and plenty of fowl and fish. Desserts are limited to fresh or water-packed fruits and an occasional slice of plain low-sugar cake.

A diet for powerlifters, Olympic lifters, sprinters, and other persons whose sports require short bursts of energy or speed should stress unrefined complex carbohydrates. Pregame meals of pancakes or waffles without syrup and only a light drizzle of butter or margarine are recommended for high performance. So are meals of pastas, whole-grain cereals, and breads. High fat and protein levels tend to make a meal indigestible and also are not good sources of immediate energy, although they're needed for endurance activities. On the other hand, avoid the intensive carbohydrate-packing so common among athletes in the past several years. Don't practice such packing unless you have expert advice. (The theory behind carbohydrate-packing, by the way, is to eat only protein and fat for about 3–6 days before an event, after working to exhaustion the muscles to be trained in the event; then for the 3 days just prior to the event, eating many small meals rich in carbs. This forces the muscles to bind large amounts of carbohydrates as muscle fuel in the stress of the event.) But we repeat: the process is full of dangers and should be practiced only under careful supervision. The severe depletion of carbohydrates in the first phase can lead to ketosis, with its accompanying accumulation of toxic substances in the blood, kidney damage, irritability, muscle fatigue, and increased excretion of water. The packing itself can also place a great strain on the heart and in severe cases can cause cardiac problems. Unless the sport requires genuine endurance activity—over 30 minutes of peak sustained performance—it's best simply to eat a carbohydrate-rich diet for the few days before the event but to avoid the strict depletion phase altogether.

The special category, of course, is that odd sport, bodybuilding. It's odd for dietary purposes simply because here the end product is achieving a certain bodily appearance. The prescribed appearance varies from decade to decade; just now, it's maximum definition, plenty of "cuts," vascularity, and an absolute minimum of bodyfat coupled with symmetrical, aesthetically pleasing muscular development. Unfortunately, the only way to achieve the cuts (highly visible separation between muscles) and the vascularity that pro competitions demand is through severely restricting carbohydrates and fats. In the six weeks or so just before a contest, most bodybuilders now go on either zero- or extremely low-carbohydrate diets with very low fat content. While these measures are probably necessary to achieve the kind of body that wins contests today, we repeat: don't do it without supervision. Try not to eliminate carbs completely, watch your mineral intake, especially potassium and magnesium, and be sure to include multi-vitamin and multi-mineral tablets daily during the final restricted phases of the diet. Some good advice for the bodybuilder, from amateur to pro levels, is offered by such magazines as *Iron Man, Strength and Health,* and *Muscle and Fitness.* Check out the copies with special features on diet if you're interested in competition.

Finally, a word of general advice to all categories: follow very restricted programs only at a doctor's advice. Drink 6–8 glasses of fluid daily, keep a close check on mineral and vitamin intake, and periodically re-evaluate your dietary program. That's the best way to develop your own sportspower.

Chapter 2

PRETRAINING FOR STRENGTH AND FLEXIBILITY

A Few Valuable Tips from the Locker Room

The purpose of recreational sports is fun and healthy physical activity. Nobody wants to get hurt, but sports are sometimes rigorous as well as vigorous. Any kind of physical activity carries with it a certain amount of risk. That's part of the fun. It's no fun, however, if you get hurt, especially if the injury makes it impossible to play your game anymore.

Proper pretraining and basic training can help you to avoid many kinds of injuries. This part of the book is devoted to exactly that kind of training. It should help you not only become stronger in your sport, but also avoid the common injuries that are associated with that sport. You'll play with more confidence as well as with more strength, stamina, power, and endurance.

If you already have an injury, and you are trying to get back in shape to play your sport again, you should follow your physician's advice about how much to play, what exercises to perform, and what you may expect of yourself in the way of improvement. For general information about injuries and injury treatment, we urge you to consult Appendix I on injuries at the end of this book. The last thing *you* want to do is get hurt again. The last thing that *we* want is for you to start a program to improve your game before you're really ready for it.

If you're in good health and raring to go, the next section will tell you what you need for your pretraining program.

Pretraining Equipment

In this section, we will describe the various pieces of equipment, some ordinary and some exotic, that can be used to help you overcome deficiencies in strength, flexibility, joint stability, and endurance. The next section will describe a number of exercises to be used for specific deficiencies. Before we get to the exercises, however, here are the pieces of equipment that you can use to do them. Many of these devices are used at the Sports Fitness Institute in Chicago for training by pro ball players and other competitive athletes.

BALANCE BEAMS

Let's start at the bottom and work our way up. The "oscillating balance beam" has become popular throughout the United States as a training device that improves your sense of balance, coordination, and concentration, while at the same time improving strength and endurance in a variety of collateral stabilizing muscles throughout the entire body. The beams are approximately four inches in diameter, and rounded along the longitudinal edges so that they will oscillate and thus be unstable.

They are traditionally about ten feet long, and can be bought at athletic equipment houses. You can also have them made to order at your neighborhood lumberyard. Be sure that you pick out the four-by-four yourself, so that you don't get stuck with a bowed beam.

The beam should be placed on a carpet. The thicker the pile, the better, because the thickness of the pile will make the beam even more unsteady. The trick here is to walk the balance beam, forward, backward, and laterally, until you learn to walk it without a tremble or a misstep. This will strengthen the muscles around the ankles and feet, as well as the knees and the hips. It's a lot harder than it looks, and many a pro athlete has had to hide his head in shame after trying to walk the beam.

TENSION BANDS

Tension Bands are manufactured by the Unique Athletic Equipment Company in Glendale Heights, Illinois. They come in at least two widths, broad and narrow. They are made of natural rubber, and vary in length. The bands are widely distributed to health clubs and rehabilitation centers.

The Tension Bands provide a resilient tension for specific muscle movements. While they can be used for major muscle groups, they are without parallel in exercising smaller, collateral stabilizing muscles. The amount of effort involved varies with the extent to which you stretch the band, so you can accommodate your exercises with the band to your own limitations in strength and endurance.

Because they are light and portable, and can be looped around feet, ankles, forearms, hands, legs, and arms, all with equal facility, they make a fine traveling gym for people who spend a lot of time on the road.

FREE WEIGHTS

Free weights—barbells, dumbbells, kettlebells, swingbells, and other pieces of equipment that are not part of a machine—can be used to good effect in rehabilitating injured muscles, joints, etc. The reason that free weights are so effective in this regard lies precisely in the area for which machine manufacturers criticize them.

When you perform an exercise with a barbell or a dumbbell, you are, in a sense, on your own. Your hands lift the barbell and you perform the exercise for the requisite number of repetitions. When you are through, you set the barbell back down on the floor or rack from which you got it. There are no machines to help you lift it, no preordained "groove" through which the barbell moves, no sturdy rack or mechanical lever system to keep you balanced.

In short, you must find your own lifting configuration, find your own sense of balance, find your own way to stabilize yourself while you're lifting. This means that you must use not only the large "lifting" muscles, but the smaller collateral stabilizers as well.

Free weights have another advantage, also: it is difficult to isolate individual muscles when you are working with free weights. That's one of the reasons why there are so many different exercises. Because of the shifts in balance and the movements of the entire body that are made when lifting a barbell, you learn to exert strength by coordinating the movements of many muscles, not just a few or a single group. This, of course, is what happens in sports movements. Nobody throws a ball with his forearm muscles alone.

You can enhance the utility of free weights with arrangements of pulleys and cables. They narrow the range of muscle groups being worked, but are not as restrictive in use as a machine would be. All the top bodybuilders and weightlifters swear by free weights. Look around the gym and you'll find that the serious athletes are all clustered around the squat racks, the bench press rack, and the weightlifting platform. They may use the machines for specialization work, but they rely on free weights for both strength and muscle size.

EXERCISE MACHINES

For a complete description and evaluation of modern exercise machines, with cross-referenced chapters on exercises, machines, and muscular anatomy, get a copy of our book *Bodypower: The Complete Guide to Health Club Exercise Machines and Home Gym Equipment* (St. Martin's Press, 1981). Exercise machines are the most popular means of weight training for health club members, whether they are training for endurance or strength, or just want to trim off a few pounds. Notwithstanding the serious bodybuilders' penchant for free weights, exercise machines if properly used are valuable tools for improving sports performance.

The machines work muscles either in isolation or in partial isolation. Some machines, such as the Nautilus leg press, work the hips and the thighs, but unlike (for example) the squat (which also works the hips and the thighs) do not give a good workout to the *erector spinae* muscles or to the core muscles (abdominals, external and internal obliques, and *iliopsoas*), or the shoulders and upper back.

Specialization is one of the prime selling pitches for the machines. The machines allow you to concentrate all your effort on one or a few muscles at a time. Further, since the machines are designed so that the weights will not fall on you if you exceed your strength in an attempted lift, you don't need a "spotter" (someone to catch the weight if you can't complete the lift) as you do with free weights.

Machines can also be used with great facility in what are called "circuits" or "circuit training." While it would be a terrific hassle to load and unload barbell plates in order to do a series of different exercises one after another, with the machines you can simply hop from one specialized machine to another, changing the weights by inserting a pin in the appropriate slot.

For those of you who think that you can't get cardiovascular conditioning with machines, try a series of circuits using about 20 percent of your lifting capacity on each machine, with 3 minutes on each machine. If you have a circuit of, say, ten machines, you can maintain your target pulse rate while exercising the entire body for a period of over 30 minutes per workout. If you want to do more, drop the weights to 10 percent of your maximum and spend 4 to 5 minutes on each machine. People who think that you can't get aerobic conditioning with resistance machines are simply ignorant of the ways that the machines can be used.

Some of the new machines, such as the Hydra-Fitness omnikinetic equipment, can be used with equal facility for strength and power training, endurance and cardiovascular conditioning, and simulation of specific sports movements. These machines use hydraulic cylinders for the resistance, so that both the resistance met and the speed with which exercise movements can be performed are determined by adjustable valves and the amount of effort that the individual wants to expend.

The Hydra-Fitness machines are also marvelous for rehabilitation work, since they can be set to accommodate the strength and endurance of the individual in an almost infinite range. The faster you try to move Hydra's lever arms, the harder it is to move them. The slower you try, the easier it is. There are no plates to change, no pins to reset, and no clanking metal. Just a quiet *whish* of the hydraulic cylinder and you're on your way.

Machines such as Mini-Gym are made specifically with sports movement simulation in mind. Mini-Gym has machines to which you can hook up baseballs, baseball bats, tennis and racquetball racquets, basketballs, and a variety of other pieces of familiar sporting equipment. Mini-Gym machines are also isokinetic, using a black box with a friction device.

The following is a brief list of pieces of equipment and the body parts that they exercise. We'll wait until the next section to talk about how free weights are used in the individual exercises. In the case of the machines, they are listed according to the muscle or muscle groups that they are designed to work.

- **Ankles and feet:** Tension Bands; barbells and dumbbells; Nautilus, Dynacam, Paramount calf raise machines; leg press stations on Universal and Paramount multistation machines; Hydra-Fitness Pro Power and Power Squat machines; Mini-Gym Leaper; balance beam
- **Knees:** Tension Bands; balance beams; barbells and dumbbells; Hydra-Fitness Quad Hamstring machine; Nautilus, Paramount, Universal, Dynacam leg extension machines and leg curl machines
- **Hips and lower back:** Tension Bands; balance beams; barbells and dumbbells; Hydra-Fitness Hip Flexion/Extension, Nautilus Dual Hip and Back machine, Dynacam and Nautilus Hip and Back; Nautilus, Dynacam, Paramount, Universal leg press machines; Roman Chair Spi-

nal Hyperextension bench (a bench that enables the user to work the muscles of the lower back)
• **Wrists and forearms:** Tension Bands; barbells and dumbbells; wrist rollers; Dynacam Grip Machine; low pulley work on multistation machines; Hydra-Fitness Forearm Conditioner
• **Elbows and shoulders:** Tension Bands; barbells and dumbbells; Nautilus, Paramount, Dynacam triceps machines; Nautilus Double Shoulder; Dynacam Vertical Shoulder, Lateral Shoulder; pulley stations on multistation machines; Nautilus, Paramount, Dynacam curling machines for biceps; Hydra-Fitness Upright Row/Triceps Equipment
• **Neck:** Tension Bands; barbell plates; Nautilus, Hydra-Fitness, Dynacam Neck Machines

Most of the machines listed above can be found in any up-to-date health club. Many clubs use Nautilus machines exclusively, while others use a variety of machines. Sadly enough, fewer and fewer clubs are featuring free weights, since they are building their memberships around fast, simple, easy-to-do "executive" programs for people who are interested more in general toning up than they are in any real conditioning program.

This is unfortunate in many ways. While some of the machines are superb devices, many clubs stock only a bare minimum. Consequently, you may or may not find the machines that you need to rectify any physical deficiencies that can't be treated with, for instance, Nautilus' basic line.

Fortunately, however, you don't have to be restricted to a health club to train and pretrain for sports. Barbells have become so popular in the United States that they are available almost everywhere from department stores to wholesale houses, from sporting goods shops to drugstores.

Weights are getting cheaper instead of more expensive. Their popularity has resulted in competitive free enterprise as far as small sets for the home are concerned. You can still trot down to Sears or Montgomery Ward's and pick up a 110-pound barbell/dumbbell set for under $35. For a few more dollars, you can also pick up various benches and accessories.

You can outfit a Hydra-Fitness sports circuit in your basement for under $5,000 if you want to go the high road. This would consist of four or five pieces of equipment, and would enable you to do whatever strength, flexibility, endurance, cardiovascular, or power training you want, with low-maintenance, quiet equipment that is attractive and light in weight (so you don't have to worry about cracking the slab).

If your concern is strictly cardiovascular conditioning, and problems with your feet, knees, and hips preclude one of the popular aerobic exercises such as jogging or running, you should look into buying a bicycle or a stationary exercise bike. The former will take you into the fresh air (if there is any where you live) and the latter will allow you to reap the benefits of cycling in the comfort of your home. Machines range from low-cost friction-belt cycles to deluxe ergometric and electronically operated machines such as the new Schwinn (Excelsior) line. Cycling is both fun and healthy, and gives you (if you really go at it) the same rigorous conditioning as jogging without the pounding that jogging gives your ankles, knees, and hips.

You might also keep up with the back pages of *Muscle Builder, Iron Man, Muscular Development,* and *Strength and Health* magazines for advertisements for wrist rollers, neck exercises, and so forth. Except for a few health clubs that have these little-known items, these ads are the only source for many of them; they are still among the best devices known for the rehabilitation of injuries in joints and muscles that are not specifically worked by machines.

In the next section, we'll give you a short compendium of exercises for your problem areas, using the various pieces of equipment we've described in this section. If you work out at home, it will be a handy guide on what to do as you get ready for basic training. If you belong to a health club, chances are that the machines cited are available to you.

The Terminology of Sports Training Movements

Before we describe the pretraining exercises, we should first introduce the terminology that is used by sports trainers to describe the various movements that you will be making as you do the exercises. There aren't many terms, but they are necessary if you are to understand the language of sports training.

The first thing to learn is the names of the fundamental movements that are possible at the joints. We've listed them not in alphabetical order, but in pairs of opposite movements. Refer to the "Body Planes" illustration in the Appendix to orient yourself in terms of bodily movements.

Abduction: Any movement that is in a direction away from the median plane. When you swing the arms out to the sides you are *abducting* the arms.

Adduction: Any movement that is in the direction of the median plane. When you bring your arms back toward the sides you are *adducting* them.

Depression: This term refers to a movement downward. Such movements are therefore *caudal, inferior,* or *distal.* If you stand with your back straight and stretch your arms downward, you are making a movement that is *caudal, inferior,* and *distal: caudal* or *inferior* because the movement is downward and *distal* because the arms are moving in a direction away from their attached ends.

Elevation: This refers to a movement that is *cranial* or *superior.* When you move your shoulders up in a shrug, you are making a *superior* or *cranial* movement. Also, since this particular movement involves moving the arms in a direction toward their attached ends, the movement is *proximal.*

Extension: This term refers to movements that are opposite to *flexion.* In extension, the opposite ends of bones connected by a joint move away from each other. When you extend the leg at the knee, you move the thigh bone and the lower leg bones away from each other. The same is true of extension of the fingers at their knuckles, or extension of the arms at the elbows.

Hyperextension: You *hyperextend* a joint when you make an extension movement on past the point where the limb is straight. Hold your arms out to the sides, with the elbows pointing to the floor. Straighten the arms completely. If your forearm angles down slightly from your upper arm while you hold the elbow so that it is facing the floor, your arms *hyperextend* at the elbow (and you are likely to suffer elbow injuries when doing karate punches if you don't watch out). Lie on the floor on your stomach. Then, arch your back until it is bent in a bow. This is called a spinal *hyperextension.*

Flexion/Flexing: This term refers to movements in which the opposite ends of limbs that are connected by a joint move together. When you bring your arm up with your biceps, bending the elbow in the process, you are *flexing* the elbow joint. The movement is thus a *flexion* movement.

Inversion: To *invert* means to turn inward or toward the median plane. Hold your hand out in front of you with the palm flat as if you were going to do a karate chop. The thumb should be on top and the ridge of the hand on the bottom. Then, rotate your hand so that it *supinates*. When it *supinates,* the ridge used in the karate chop *inverts:* it moves toward the median plane.

Eversion: Eversion is the opposite of *inversion.* If you rotate your karate chop hand so that the hand *pronates,* the ridge with which you make the chop *everts* or moves away from the median plane.

Pronation: When talking about the body as a whole, *pronation* means lying on your stomach. When talking about the hands or feet, it means rotating the hands or feet *medially* so that the palms of the hands and the soles of the feet are turned downward. When the feet *pronate,* they also *evert* and *abduct* in the tarsal and metatarsal joints, so that the medial margin of the foot lowers.

Supination: Supination is the opposite of *pronation.* When your whole body is *supine,* you are lying on your back. When you *supinate* the hands, you rotate them laterally so that the palms of the hands are facing upwards. When you *supinate* the feet, the soles of the feet turn toward the median plane (or, if you have very flexible ankle joints, they face upwards). This also means that the hands and feet are rotated *laterally* and that the tarsal and metarsal joints *invert* and *adduct.*

Rotation: Rotation involves moving along a circular path around an *axis of rotation.* The imaginary line that runs through the earth from the south to the north pole is the axis for the earth's rotation. When you *supinate* your hand, your forearm is making a *lateral rotation* around a line that roughly approximates the position of the bones of the forearm. *Rotation* of limbs can be either *medial* or *lateral,* depending on the direction of the rotation.

As you move your body and limbs through these fundamental motions, you will notice that each joint allows a motion to proceed through a specific range. When you extend your arm at the elbow, the elbow joint stops the arm's motion and keeps it from bending too far. "Tennis elbow" often is the result of repeated snapping motions that cause the bones to be damaged at the elbow joint as they strike each other.

Each joint thus has its own unique "range of motion," or "ROM." Range of motion is figured by kinesiologists in terms of degrees of arc. For example, the elbow has a range of motion of 150°. This measurement assumes zero degrees with the arm straight or extended. It means that it is possible for a normal person to bend his or her arm at the elbow through a range of motion of 150° of arc.

Each person's joints will show a variation from the norm. These variations reflect individual configurations of bones, ligaments, tendons, cartilage, and muscle. It is not necessary for you to know exactly the normal range of motion for your joints in order to do the pretraining program. Measurements of the ranges are difficult, and are better done by an orthopedist.

What *is* necessary is that you try with each movement to increase the range of motion of the joint in question. This is done simply by contracting your muscles so that you move the limbs as far as they will go in the various directions that constitute the fundamental movements of the particular joints.

If you are working the ankle, do the fundamental movements of the ankle to the limits in range of motion that the ankle joint will allow. The same goes for any other joint. Don't try to pull the foot or the arm or the leg past where the muscles of these limbs themselves could pull them. Make the stretch an "active" stretch (caused by the limb's own muscles) instead of a "passive" stretch (caused by pulling the limb with another limb or by forcing the movement on a ballet *barre,* for example).

Active stretches will greatly increase your flexibility, and will strengthen the muscles that stabilize the joints without sacrificing the structural integrity of the joints.

Pretraining Exercises

These pretraining exercises will help you to do the following:

- Increase the strength and flexibility of the joints
- Increase muscular strength, especially in the collateral stabilizing muscles
- Increase endurance
- Achieve a fuller range of motion for the joints
- Improve muscle tone
- Increase circulation to areas where healing is in progress
- Help prevent injuries
- Get you ready for the general conditioning exercises of the basic training program

Before we describe the exercises themselves, we should say a few things about exercise programs in general. This will help you to decide how many repetitions ("reps" for short), how many sets, how much weight or resistance, and the speed at which the exercise is performed. When you are doing the exercises, keep the following in mind:

TRAINING FOR STRENGTH

If you are training for strength, whether it is of the big muscles such as the quadriceps or the small ones such as the flexors for the wrist, remember that strength training involves slow repetitions. Don't try to swing the weight up. Don't try to jerk the Tension Band in an attempt to handle more resistance than you actually have the strength for. If you're training for strength, go slowly and deliberately.

TRAINING FOR POWER

If you are training for power, you are trying to train the muscles to contract rapidly so that you can perform movements with explosive speed. Remember that training is specific, so if you want speed, you'll have to train for it. Make the movements in strict form (no help from other muscles), but do the contraction phase with as much speed as you can muster. Do the eccentric or negative return phase slowly. Remember: fast up, and slowly down, to train for power.

TRAINING FOR STAMINA

Stamina calls for the ability to perform movements with blinding speed for short periods of time. Any stamina-training movement should be performed for about 30 to 40 seconds, at high concentric and eccentric contractions. Don't let the weight simply fall to the starting position, but control it as it comes down. Control it, but move it quickly. A good example of the need for both power and stamina is in performing multiple karate punches. If you can fire off a dozen punches at one or more targets in 14 or 15 seconds, each with power and focus, without exhausting your punching muscles (anterior deltoids, pectorals, and triceps), you have both power and stamina.

TRAINING FOR ENDURANCE

When you train for endurance, you'll want to repeat specific movements for 2 minutes or more—the more the better. When you have performed a movement for longer than 20 seconds, you will have depleted the anaerobic energy supply to the affected muscles. When you continue to perform the movement, you tap onto the aerobic energy supply. If you are doing endurance exercises properly, you will be working with a resistance that is no more than 10 to 20 percent of your maximum. The idea here is not the development of strength, but the development of muscular endurance and cardiovascular conditioning.

During cardiovascular training, you are working at about 60 to 80 percent of your capacity for periods of 30 minutes or more. "Capacity" here refers to the capacity of the heartbeat to sustain itself without complications such as premature atrium or ventricle contractions. These are the infamous "PACs" (premature atrium contractions) and "PVCs" (premature ventricle contractions) that indicate an interruption in normal heart rhythm.

When we talk about working with a resistance that is about 10 to 20 percent of your maximum, we mean that the weight is about 10 to 20 percent of the maximum weight you could lift in the particular movement that you are performing.

One of the amusing things about the advocates of running and jogging is that they do not realize that from a biomechanical point of view, they are simply doing thousands of reps of leg movements, with gravity, wind, and running speed providing the resistance. The legs are carrying most of the weight (literally), and the arms are making balancing movements as they swing back and forth. The torso twists, but the legs do the work. It is primarily a leg exercise: an endurance exercise for the legs, involving one giant set of several thousand reps. The notion that you can get aerobic conditioning *only* from doing giant sets of leg exercises without weight is a little silly. You can also get aerobic conditioning by working all the major muscle groups through circuits of different exercises, with no rest between circuits. Use a small amount of resistance, aim for your target pulse rate, reach it, and keep up the circuits as long as you want to.

The advantage of this kind of aerobic training over running or jogging is that it avoids the kinds of foot, ankle, and knee injuries that commonly come from jogging, and it also works muscles other than the running muscles.

The cardiovascular benefits of circuit weight training are only recently coming to light. If you are a health club member, don't pass up the chance to try circuits. Don't stop at one circuit, however. Do several. Then you'll see what we mean.

BODY AREAS

The following are the body areas covered by the pretraining program: feet and ankles, knees, hips, spinal column, hands, wrists, elbows, shoulders. In the case of each body area, the area itself will first be identified, followed by a list and description of the fundamental movements allowed by the joints in that area. For example, the section on the knee will include extension, flexion, and rotation as exercise movements, and the section on the elbow will include extension, flexion, supination, and pronation.

Each section will explain the movements involved. If you haven't learned the names of these movements, do a quick review of the material on pages 51 through 54. If you're serious about improving your sports performance, you've simply got to learn this basic terminology of sports training.

Ready? Here are the pretraining exercises:

FEET AND ANKLES

Dorsiflexion

In this movement, you should start with the foot at 90° to the lower leg. Pull the foot upwards so the toes approach the front of the lower leg or shin.

Plantar Flexion

In this movement, you will move the foot in the direction opposite that of dorsiflexion. When you rise up on your toes, you are doing plantar flexion. Try to move your foot as far as it will possibly go each time you do the movement.

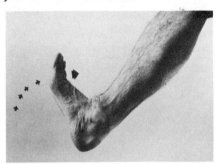

Dorsiflexion of the foot
at the ankle.

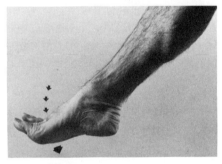

Plantar flexion of the foot
at the ankle.

Inversion

Keep the heel stationary and do not allow the lower leg to rotate at the knee joint. Sit in a chair, and rest the heel against the floor. Inversion is a movement toward the body's centerline, so the right foot will invert toward the left and the left foot will invert toward the right. Move the feet to the end of their range of motion each time.

Eversion

Eversion is the opposite of inversion. Sit in the same position as for inversion, but move the feet away from the body's centerline as far as they will go.

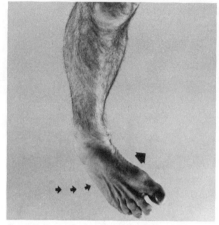 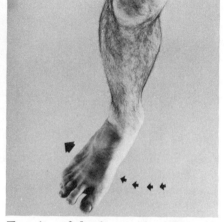

Inversion of the foot at the ankle. **Eversion of the foot at the ankle.**

Supination

Sit in the same position as you would for eversion and inversion. Keep the foot in a line that is perpendicular to the coronal or frontal plane (that imaginary plane that divides the body into front and back portions). Rotate the foot along its own axis until the bottom of the foot is turned upwards. If you are supinating the right foot, it will rotate clockwise. A supinating left foot rotates counterclockwise.

Pronation

Sit in the same position as you would for supination. Pronation is the opposite of supination. Start the movement with the foot supinated and rotate it along its own axis until the bottom of the foot is facing the floor. Again, make the movement to the end of its range of motion.

Now that you know how to do the movements, here is a sequence of exercises that you can do to increase flexibility and strength in the feet and ankles. Try this sequence with no weight or resistance, but with a good solid stretch each time.

1. Dorsiflexion
2. Plantar flexion
3. Inversion
4. Eversion
5. Supination
6. Pronation

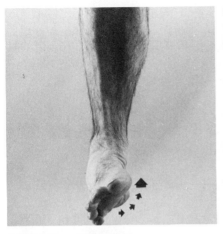
Supination of the foot.

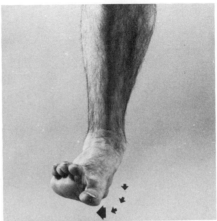
Pronation of the foot.

Be sure to do the exercises in this sequence. Do all six movements; then without a pause, do them again. The third time around, do 2 reps of each one before going on to the next. Now the sequence will go like this:

1. Dorsiflexion (2 reps)
2. Plantar flexion (2 reps)
3. Inversion (2 reps)
4. Eversion (2 reps)
5. Supination (2 reps)
6. Pronation (2 reps)

Even without resistance, if you're out of shape, your calves (especially the front) will be howling for mercy. Before you try the exercises with resistance, work up to 5 reps for each movement, immediately followed by the next movement, until you run through 5 cycles. Remember to stretch as far in each direction as you can. When you do the dorsiflexion movement, you can enhance it by pulling your toes back as far as they will go. When you do the plantar flexion movement, you can do the same by bending the toes down as far as they will go.

Do these exercises three times a day: when you get up in the morning, in the early afternoon, and just before you go to bed. If your ankles are stiff, they should limber up in short order.

When you get to the point where you can do 5 circuits through the movements, try doing them with the resistance provided by a Tension Band. If you don't have access to one of the Unique Athletic Equipment

Tension Bands, get some surgical rubber tubing. Fasten the band (or tubing) around the foot so that each time you do one of the movements, you are pulling against the band. For dorsiflexion, loop it around the tops of the toes and hold the other end with your other foot. For plantar flexion, loop it around the ball of the foot, and hold the other end with your hand. For eversion, inversion, supination, and pronation, simply loop the band so that you will be able to pull against its resistance in the direction of the movement you are doing. If you're interested, Unique Athletic Equipment, Inc., will provide a complete set of courses in Tension Band exercises for a small fee.

Less effective than the Tension Band or surgical tubing is the placement of weighted bands or ankle weights around the toes. If you use ankle weights, make sure that you are actually moving your foot against the pull of gravity. For example, if you are doing eversion movements with your right foot, using ankle weights around the ball of your foot, you will have to lie on your left side in order to work against gravity. Otherwise, you won't get the full benefit of the exercise.

Of course, plantar flexion involves the same movement that you perform when you do heel raises or calf raises with an exercise machine or with a barbell on your shoulders. When you get into the basic training program in the next chapter, this is one of the exercises you will be doing. But for now, we're interested in range of motion and in strengthening and improving the stability of joints. At this stage, let's concentrate on stretching and on high-repetition, endurance movements. You should do the foot/ankle circuit with no resistance at first. Then after a week, add resistance with a Tension Band or with surgical tubing, or with ankle weights around the toes. If you use weights, sit in a chair when you do dorsiflexion, lie on your back with your feet up to do plantar flexion, lie on your right side to do inversion with the right foot (and vice versa for the left foot), lie on your left side to do eversion with the right foot (vice versa for the left foot), sit in a chair for supination and pronation. As you can see, it's a lot simpler with the Tension Band or with surgical tubing.

Now let's move on to the knee.

THE KNEE

The knee allows three basic movements: extension, flexion, and rotation.

When the knee is fully extended, the upper and lower legs form more or less a straight line. When the knee is flexed, it is bent and the foot is drawn up toward the buttocks. Rotation is measured with the knee bent or flexed at a 90° angle.

Range of motion measurements are made with the fully extended knee as the baseline. Extension for the knee is thus figured at 0 degrees. With a fully extended knee as the starting point, the normal range of motion for flexion is 135°. Rotation normally measures 50° of arc from one extreme to the other. Don't be confused by the fact that extension is zero, while everybody down at the gym is doing "leg extensions" on the Nautilus machine. To extend the leg means to straighten it, and the guys are right when they say that they are doing "leg extensions" or "knee extensions." However, for the sake of making kinesiological measurements, you have to have a baseline somewhere. Consequently, it makes sense to start with the knee fully extended, call that point zero degrees, and measure the movement from that point.

The knee is stabilized by a variety of muscles. When you extend the knee, you use the *vastus lateralis,* the *vastus medialis,* the *rectus femoris,* and the *vastus intermedius* muscles. Look at the anatomy chart in the Appendix to see where these muscles are located. The knee is flexed or bent by the *biceps femoris,* the *semimembranosus,* and the *semitendinosus.* The knee is rotated medially by the *popliteus* (it also helps flex the knee), and it is rotated laterally by the action of the *biceps femoris.*

Now, here are a few exercises for the knees. Again, start with a simple performance of the basic movements of which the knee is capable, without using any weight or resistance.

Extension

Begin by sitting in a chair with the knee bent. Straighten the leg until it is fully extended. Now, slowly bring the leg back down until the foot is on the floor. It's better to sit on the side of a table so that your foot does not actually rest on the floor.

Each time you raise the leg, take it as far as it will go. When the leg is fully straight, flex the muscles along the top of your leg until you feel that the joint action has gone absolutely as far as it will go. Do 10 repetitions slowly.

Flexion

Stand on one foot, steadying yourself with your hands (for example, against a doorframe). Bring one of your legs up until your heel approaches your buttocks. Let the leg slowly back down. Work each time for the fullest range of motion possible.

Rotation

Stand so that the knee is bent at a 90° angle. Rotate the lower leg at the knee. Go as far to the right as you can, then go as far to the left as you can.

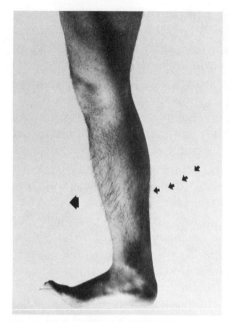

Extension of the leg at the knee.

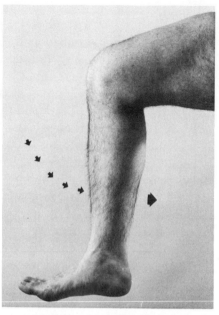

Flexion of the leg at the knee.

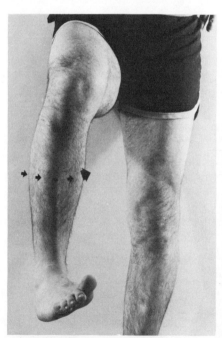

Medial rotation of the leg at the knee.

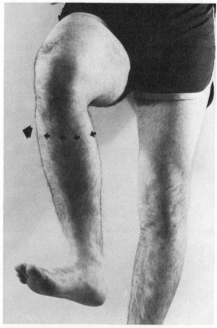

Lateral rotation of the leg at the knee.

Each time you do one of these movements, you will notice that the muscles on the side of the leg opposite the side where the muscles are contracting will be relaxed. It is normal for opposing muscle groups to relax while opposites are contracting. When you contract your quadriceps, for example, the hamstrings (the muscles of the back of the thigh) will naturally relax so that the movement will be possible. The hamstrings will also get a good stretch when the quads extend the knee fully. This kind of stretch is called an "active" stretch, as opposed to the "passive" stretch that would occur if you were forcing the knee to extend, whether the hamstrings were relaxed or not. Active stretches are much less likely to cause tendon pulls than passive stretches, since the leg is moving only as far as its own muscles will let it.

It should be pointed out, however, that many of the guys down at the gym who complain of hamstring injuries probably picked them up because they neglected to work both sides of the leg when doing leg work. The leg extension machine is always more popular than the leg curl machine, which flexes the leg at the knee. Most people neglect their hamstrings, while few who do leg work neglect their quads. The result is often tendon pull injuries to the hamstrings, due to the unequal strength of the two opposing muscle groups. Consequently, while the active stretch is generally safer than the passive stretch, it is quite possible to injure yourself while doing active stretches if the muscles on one side of a limb are disproportionately stronger than the muscles on the other side.

To add strength in the quads, try doing extensions with resistance. You can use iron shoes (strap-on iron "sandals" that are worn over tennis shoes), ankle weights, or a Tension Band or surgical tubing. If you have access to a leg extension machine, use it. But remember, if you are doing pretraining exercises in order to strengthen an injured or deficient joint, make sure that you work with light resistance at the start. Save the heavy poundages for the basic training routine.

The knee flexors or hamstrings can be strengthened by doing leg curls. These can be done with ankle weights, iron shoes, Tension Bands, or rubber tubing. The same cautionary note is appropriate here that was appropriate above. If you have access to a leg curl machine, use a light resistance at first and save the heavy weights for later. You don't want to reinjure your knees.

For rotational movements, use either a Tension Band or a length of surgical tubing. Do the same movement that you did without resistance: rest the heel on the floor, and rotate the lower leg at the knee. You'll have to change sides with the Tension Band as you rotate in opposite directions.

Do a sequence of exercises in this order when you do the movements without weight or resistance:

1. Extension
2. Flexion
3. Rotation
4. Extension
5. Flexion
6. Rotation

If you have knee problems and feel pain in any of these movements, you should check with your physician before embarking on any program that involves adding resistance. These exercises are not meant as a substitute for medical or physical therapy advice. They are meant as a means whereby muscles and joints can be strengthened by the use of progressive resistance exercises.

When you add resistance or weight, you will probably not be able to go from one machine to another without waiting for someone else to get off the machine. The longer you have to wait for a machine, the more rest you will get between exercise bouts, with the result that you lose the "training effect" that comes from intensive exercise. Do 15 reps on each machine, and keep the order as it is given above. Use light resistance at first, and gradually work up to the levels that will be used in the basic training program.

THE HIP

Most people never think about flexibility in the hips until they take up a sport such as karate or ballet, where hip flexibility is a must. In karate, for example, one of the most popular (and beautiful) movements is the side thrust kick. The body is held as erect as possible, and the leg is driven out to the side until the knee is fully extended. The foot is drawn back into dorsiflexion, with the toes turned up to tighten the side of the foot. At the last instant, the leg is rotated medially in the hip joint, to provide for a solid alignment of the bones from the hip to the foot. If you can place the foot at chest or head level, you're in good shape as far as flexibility is concerned.

Unfortunately for most beginning karate students, it is a real effort to get the foot up to waist height. Training will get it higher, and those who are naturally stiff in the hips will have to train harder and longer to get their feet up.

Other karate techniques, such as the front thrust and snap kicks, the roundhouse and the back thrust kicks, also require hip flexibility. Most karatekas, consequently, spend a lot of time doing exercises that are similar to the ones done by ballet dancers. They work at the *barre*, practice the split, and even have their workout partners lift their legs past the point where their own muscles can take them.

In short, they do active and passive stretches of the muscles that connect the femur (upper leg bone) to the hip. Nothing very mysterious here, just hard work and consistency. The hip joint allows for certain movements of the leg. To make the joint more flexible, move the legs in those directions.

The hip joint allows six basic movements, with two "hyper" movements. To visualize these movements in a sequence, imagine that you are *standing perfectly erect* with the legs and the body forming a vertical line. The movements (one leg at a time) are:

1. *Flexion,* in which the knee is brought up toward the chest.
2. *Extension,* in which the leg is moved back down so that it is in line with the body again.
3. *Hyperextension,* in which the leg is moved on backward past the body's vertical line.

Flexion of the leg at the hip.   **Extension of the leg at the hip.**

**Hyperextension of the leg at the
hip (with ankle weight).**

Lateral leg raise (abduction of the leg at the hip).

4. *Abduction,* in which the leg is lifted to the side away from the body's
   centerline.
5. *Adduction,* in which the leg is moved from the side toward the
   body's centerline.
6. *Hyperadduction,* in which the leg is moved past the body's centerline.

Adduction and hyperadduction of the leg at the hip.

7. *Medial rotation,* in which the (right) leg is rotated counterclockwise (the left leg would be rotated clockwise).
8. *Lateral rotation,* in which the (right) leg is rotated clockwise (the left leg would be rotated counterclockwise).

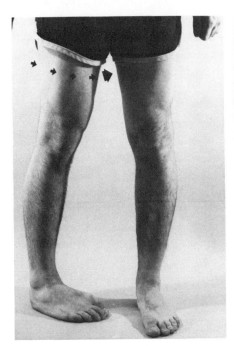

Medial rotation of the leg at the hip.

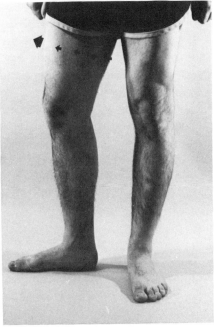

Lateral rotation of the leg at the hip.

As you do each of these movements, don't tilt the hip in order to move the leg farther. The point here is not to see how high you can lift your leg, but how far you can lift your leg without moving the hips. The range of motion for hip movements is relatively small in comparison with other joints, and many people lose the effect of the exercises by forgetting how small the range of motion is.

In all hip movements, the baseline for description is a leg that is in line with the vertical line of the body. When you do rotational movements, don't let your ankle rotate. Keep the rotation in the hip joint.

At first, try to do the motions without any weight or resistance. You can do the flexion movement either standing or lying on your back on the floor. Extension is no movement at all, since it is the baseline for that plane of motion. Hyperextension should be done either standing or lying on your stomach. Abduction and hyperadduction can be done standing or lying on the side, alternating from one side to the other. Medial and lateral rotation can be done either lying on your back or standing.

When you add resistance to the exercises, such as a Tension Band, surgical tubing, or weights, you will have to be careful that you maintain strict form. This means that you should not tilt the pelvis. Again, the purpose here is not to see how high you can lift your leg, but how far you can move the leg *in the hip joint.*

If you use Tension Bands or surgical tubing, always set the band or tubing where you are pulling against its resistance. When you do abduction movements, loop the band around the other leg. If you want a lot of resistance, loop it around the ankles. If you want less resistance, loop it around the knees.

You can also attach the other end of the band or tubing to a hook mounted in the wall or in the frame of a door. Anchor it securely, because you could get a nasty whack if it came loose. You will need an external anchor if you use bands or tubing for hyperextensions and hyperadductions, as well as for rotational movements. In each instance, you can lower the resistance by placing the band or tubing near the joint. You can raise the resistance by placing the band or tubing away from the joint.

If you are training for strength, do the movements slowly. If you are training for endurance, do them for 2 minutes or more. Always work for a complete and full range of motion. When you get to the end point of each movement, try to push a little bit farther. This will increase the flexibility in the joint.

Although the practice is widespread, use caution when you are doing passive stretches, especially if it involves having someone lift your leg up or out past the point where you could lift it alone. If you do engage in this kind of passive stretching, be sure that you are contracting the muscle opposite the one being stretched as hard as it will contract. This will tend to make the opposing muscle relax.

You can use ankle weights to good advantage in these movements. Ankle weights come in various weight ranges, and are usually made of shot-filled leather bands, or lead-filled bands. Iron shoes are also useful, but beware of using too much weight. Form is everything in these movements, since the natural tendency is to tilt the pelvis.

At first, do the movements slowly and deliberately, stretching at the end point of the movement. When you add resistance, you will have a natural tendency to move faster in the contraction phase and even faster in the relaxation phase. Resist the temptation as well as the Tension Band! Go as slowly in the relaxation phase as you did in the contraction phase.

Try the following sequence standing, without weight:

1. Flexion, 2 reps
2. Hyperextension, 2 reps
3. Abduction, 2 reps
4. Hyperadduction, 2 reps
5. Medial rotation, 3 reps
6. Lateral rotation, 3 reps

Now, lie on the floor, add ankle weights, and do the same sequence. Do 5 reps for each movement except the rotations. Do 10 reps for them. Do the exercises every day, and add a rep to each movement each time you work out. Do 1 set the first and second day, 2 sets the third and fourth day, and 3 sets the fifth and sixth day. Take a day off, and start the new week with more weight (add another ankle weight), 1 set, and 5 reps. Work your way up again. Do the program for three weeks, and you should drastically improve your hip flexibility and strength.

SPINAL COLUMN

There is an incredible amount of lore on the spine. It has been taken as symbolic of everything from the order of the universe to the grand step that took the vertebrates out of the muck forever. It is a column of bones (vertebrae) that runs from the pelvis to the skull.

The spinal column is divided into five distinct areas:

1. The *cervical* vertebrae, which are the bones that make up the neck.
2. The *thoracic* vertebrae, which provide the foundation for the thorax or upper torso.
3. The *lumbar* vertebrae, which constitute the lower back.
4. The *sacral* vertebrae, which are fused into a single bone. The *sacrum* is the part of the spinal column that transmits the body weight to the hip joints.
5. The *coccyx*, which is usually two to four fused vertebrae, and is all we have left of what was once a tail.

The spine has natural serpentine curves, and looks like a giant "S" with an additional curve at the base of the skull and at the coccyx. Each vertebra is a complicatedly shaped piece of bone, with a hole in the middle and tabs or *processes* to the sides and to the back. Each vertebra is separated from the next by a *disc*, which is a fibrocartilagenous structure, and which takes its name from its disclike shape.

The spinal cord runs up the center of the spine, through the holes at the centers of the vertebrae and the discs. The spinal cord is part of the central nervous system, which includes the brain, the cerebrum, the brain stem, and the cerebellum. Radiating out from the spine are the components of the peripheral nervous system, consisting of 12 pairs of cranial nerves and 31 pairs of spinal nerves.

Ruptured or slipped discs, fractures of the vertebrae, and other traumas of the spinal cord and the peripheral nervous system are the roots of most of what we label generally "an aching back." Damage to the lumbar discs is common, especially with people who are active in sports. Ralph damaged his fourth lumbar disc in 1952, and could do no weight training for over ten years.

There are as many cures for back pain as there are people who profess to cure it. One thing is certain: when your back hurts, you're miserable and your activities are cut down to nothing. Whether you undergo orthopedic surgery, have an adjustment by a chiropractor, or have heat, cold, vibratory, ultrasonic, or massagic therapy, back pain is no joke, and has ruined many a person's physical activities.

The best way to prevent back injuries, other than not participating in rigorous physical activities, is to make sure that you have a strong set of muscles supporting the spine. This means that you should develop the entire system of spinal muscles, from the pelvis to the cranium. (See the anatomy chart in the Appendix.) This means not only the popular *erector spinae* (usually worked by dead weight lifts in which a barbell is lifted off the floor), but the group of muscles called the *transversospi-*

nalis (which rotates the spinal column), and the *splenius,* which extends and rotates the head.

Further, you should develop the external obliques on either side, the abdominals in front, and the *iliopsoas* muscles that attach to the spine inside the abdominal cavity and to the pelvic bone. These are sometimes called the "core" muscles, and they will give you the solid muscular foundation that the spine needs to do its work and to withstand stresses. If Ralph had developed strength in these muscles, he would not have ruptured his fourth lumbar disc in 1952, and he would not have had to take the ten-year layoff from strenuous physical activities.

The movements of the spine are as follows:

1. *Flexion,* in which you bend forward.
2. *Extension,* which is the baseline for spinal movements.
3. *Hyperextension,* in which you bend backward past the point where you would be standing erect.
4. *Lateral flexion,* in which you lean either to the right or to the left.
5. *Rotation,* in which you rotate the spine either to the right or to the left.

Now you're ready for a few exercises. Let's start with flexion and go down through the list.

Flexion

Lie on your back, with your feet up on a chair. The knees should be bent at a 90° angle, and should be spread apart. Put your hands behind your head. Then, contract your abdominal muscles and flex your body in a bow. Hold it at the top of the movement for a count of 3. Repeat for 10 reps.

Hyperextension

Lie on your stomach with your legs straight and your hands behind your head. Arch your back in a bow and hold it for a count of 3. Do 10 reps.

Lateral Flexion

Stand erect and bend to one side. Make sure that you don't bend forward, but maintain a perfectly vertical plane to the side. Lean as far as you can go, hold for a count of 3, then straighten up. Do 10 reps. Then do it for the other side.

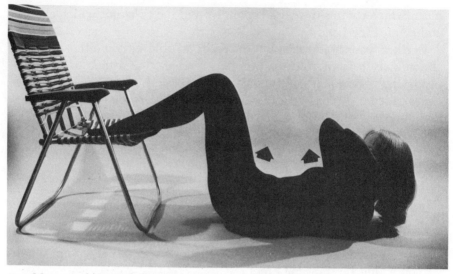

Double crunch (spinal flexion).

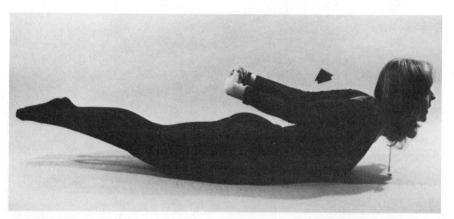

Spinal hyperextension.

Rotation

Sit on the floor to immobilize the pelvis. Place a broomstick across the shoulders behind the neck. Rotate slowly to the left, then slowly to the right. Do 20 reps.

You'll notice that we have not advised you to do the popular "toe-touching" exercise, because it puts a terrific strain on the muscles and nerves of the lower back, especially if your flexibility is low. Touching your toes is a form of passive stretch, in which the weight of the upper

Side lean (lateral flexion of the spine) with a dumbbell.

Seated twist (spinal rotation).

torso is used to bend you down and stretch the lower back muscles. Better to do the abdominal exercises outlined above. They will strengthen the abdominal muscles and at the same time actively stretch the muscles of the lower back.

In order to strengthen the muscles of the lower abdomen, you should do leg raises. Either lie on your back on the floor, or hang in a vertical leg raise rack at the gym. Keep the knees slightly bent, and raise the legs, flexing the hip. If you raise them both at the same time, you will work the lower abdominals. If you raise them one at a time, you will work the *iliopsoas* muscles mentioned above.

You'll need no weight or resistance on the rotational movements at first. Just try for a maximum range of motion. When you do add resistance, do it this way: lie on your back, with your arms outstretched along the floor. Immobilize your upper back against the floor, pull your knees up, and roll your hips from side to side. You can add ankle weights to your ankles for a bit of resistance.

For the hyperextension movements, hold a small barbell plate to your chest. If you have access to a Roman chair (see photograph, page 127), hold a small dumbbell below you as you make the movement. If you do the exercise on a Roman chair, be careful and do not lower your body more than a few inches below the horizontal plane. Put the emphasis on the hyperextension itself. Hold for a count of 3 at the top of the movement. Do 10 reps.

Lateral flexion can be weighted either by holding a barbell across the shoulders, or by holding a dumbbell in either hand. If you do it with a barbell, you may find the movement awkward. If you do it with a dumbbell, use only one at a time. If you use one in each hand, you'll find that the other dumbbell only helps you come back up from the side lean. Do 10 reps for one side and 10 reps for the other.

To work the muscles of the neck, lie on your stomach, on each side, and on your back with your head hanging off the end of a bench. Raise the head against the force of gravity in each movement. If you use a neck exerciser machine, don't use very much weight at first. Neck injuries are common and extremely painful.

Remember that movements of the head are also spinal movements. These movements follow the same pattern as those listed above, but are done with the cervical vertebrae only, while keeping the rest of the spine stationary. If you have a weak neck, or if you haven't worked your neck muscles for a long time, go easy. The muscles in the neck are highly susceptible to injury.

Here are a few stretching and toning exercises for the neck. Later on, you may want to use a neck exercise machine or use a head strap with a weight for more resistance.

Flexion
Stand erect and lean your head forward as if you were trying to touch your chin to your chest. This exercise should be combined with the next one.

Hyperextension
Stand erect and follow the flexion movement with a movement in which you lean the head backward as far as it will go. Do these movements slowly and don't snap your head around.

Lateral Flexion
Stand erect and lean the head from one side to the other as far as it will go.

Rotation
Stand erect and let the head "roll" around in a circle. Rotate first to the right. Your face will be looking sequentially at the wall in front of

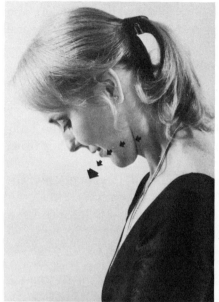

Forward flexion of the cervical spine.

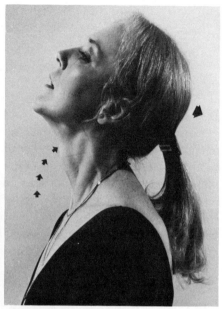

Hyperextension of the cervical spine.

Lateral flexion of the cervical spine.

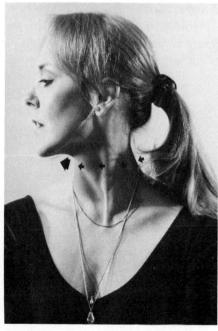

Rotation of the cervical spine.

you, at the wall to your right, at the ceiling, at the wall to your left, and back to the front. Do several rotations in one direction, then do several in the other direction. This is a basic karate stretching exercise.

Let's turn to the wrists and hands now, and make our way up to the shoulders.

HANDS AND FINGERS

Structurally, the hand is one of the most complex of all the body parts. It has muscles of its own, which divide the fingers and then bring them back together. Tendons come down to the hand and fingers from muscles in the forearm to extend and flex the hand, the fingers, and the wrist.

Because of the complexity and delicacy of the hand and fingers, if you have any injuries that have left you with chronically stiff joints but have not seen an orthopedist, let us urge you to see one right away. The loss of the use of a finger is no joke, as many a budding pianist or guitarist will tell you. If you play a musical instrument, count the cost before you go into any of the ball sports. Relatively minor injuries can put you on the musical sidelines for good.

Exercises for the fingers and hand include the following:

Finger Spreads (Finger Abduction)

Hold your hands in front of you, palms down. Spread your fingers apart as far as they will go. Hold for a count of 3, then bring them back together. Do 10 reps.

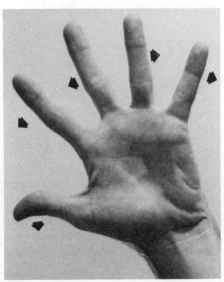

Abduction of the fingers.

Finger Flexion
Hold your hands in front of you again, palms down. Do not bend the fingers at the knuckles, but at the second joint from the tips. It may take a bit of practice, but you can do it. Flex the fingers until the tips touch the area underneath the hand that is under the knuckles. Hold for a count of 3. Do 10 reps.

Finger Extension
Straighten your fingers at the first and second joints and at the knuckle. This is easy to do without resistance, but difficult with even light resistance.

Knuckle (metacarpal) Extension/Hypertension
Hold your hands in front of you, palms down. Extend the fingers at the knuckles as far as they will go. Try to go past the hand's longitudinal line. Hold for a count of 3. Do 10 reps.

Flexion of the fingers at the second joint.

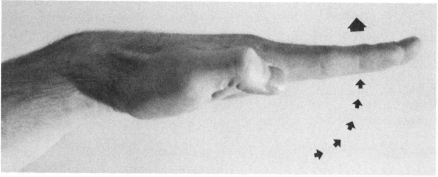

Extension of the fingers at all joints.

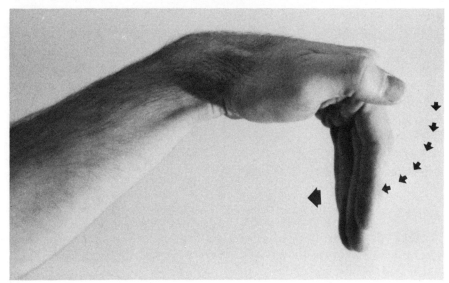

Flexion of the fingers at the knuckles (third joint).

Knuckle (metacarpal) Flexion

Hold your hands in front of you, palms facing each other. Do not bend your fingers at the second joint, but at the knuckle. Keep the fingers themselves straight, otherwise they'll get in the way of full flexion. Hold for a count of 3. Do 10 reps.

If you want to add resistance, the Tension Band or surgical tubing is excellent for these exercises. For finger spreads, wrap the band around the fingers and spread them against it. For finger flexion, hold the band in one hand, loop an end underneath the fingers of the other hand, and flex the fingers against the band's resistance. For knuckle hyperextension, put the loop over the tops of the fingers and pull up. For knuckle flexion, place the loop along the underside of the second finger joints and pull down. If you can't get a Tension Band, get several large rubber bands or a piece of small-diameter surgical tubing.

WRIST

The wrist moves in four directions, and in combinations of those directions.

Extension

Arm and hand in a straight line (this is the base-line from which wrist movements are made).

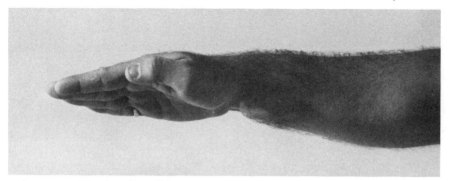

Extension of the hand at the wrist.

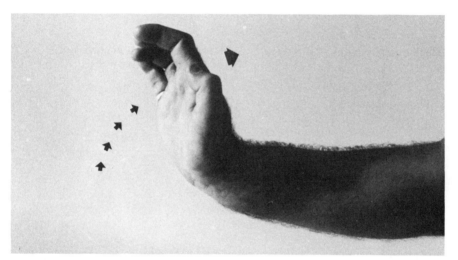

Hyperextension of the hand at the wrist.

Hyperextension
Hyperextension is done by bending the wrist so that the back of the hand moves toward the top of the forearm.

Flexion
Flexion is done in the opposite direction to hyperextension. Bend the wrist so that the palm of the hand moves toward the underside of the forearm.

Ulnar Flexion (also called "ulnar deviation")
Hold your hands in front of you with the palms facing. Keep the bones of the forearm, hand, and fingers in a straight line. Bend the wrist so that the hand moves toward the floor.

Flexion of the hand at the wrist.

Ulnar flexion (ulnar deviation) of the hand at the wrist.

Radial flexion (radial deviation) of the hand at the wrist.

Radial Flexion

Hold the hands in the same position as for ulnar flexion and bend the wrist upward toward the ceiling.

Do each of the movements in succession, bending as far as the wrist will bend, and holding for a count of 3. Do 3 cycles of the sequence in this order:

1. Hyperextension
2. Flexion
3. Ulnar flexion
4. Radial flexion
5. Hyperextension
6. Flexion

To add resistance, use a Tension Band or surgical tubing, looped around the hand at the knuckles. Make a fist and hold the band in place, and hold the other end of the band with the other hand.

These exercises can also be done with weights. Use dumbbells for ulnar and radial flexion, while resting the hand on the end of a table or bench, or along the tops of the thighs. A barbell or dumbbells can be used for hyperextension and flexion of the wrist. Hold the barbell with the forearms resting on the tops of the thighs, palms down for hyperextension and palms up for flexion.

Use light weights at the beginning. Remember, the two main goals in pretraining exercises are flexibility and strength. Make sure that you go through the full range of motion in all the exercises. If you use weights, use an amount that will allow you to do 12 reps for one set. Work up to 20 reps by adding a rep every day. When you get up to 20 reps, drop back down to 12 reps and either add another set or add enough weight to keep you at 12 reps for one set.

ELBOWS

The elbow is one of the most easily injured joints in the body. Tennis elbow and pitcher's elbow both come from the same cause: a quick snap of the wrist at the end of the movement, which places an overload on the tendons of the wrist flexors and extensors that attach at the elbow. You can get injuries in the tendons above the elbow, also, by trying to handle too much weight in movements such as presses and curls that extend and flex the elbow.

These injuries are extremely painful. If you have pain when you move your elbow, you should see an orthopedist. You may have a fatigue or stress fracture, which will not heal until it is diagnosed and a proper therapy prescribed and carried out.

The elbow joint allows two basic movements, extension and flexion. Some people (such as Ralph) hyperextend at the elbows. In Ralph's case, the hyperextension is over 10°, which means that he has to be extra careful about movements that end with the arm straight. If your elbows hyperextend, you should probably wear elastic wraps when you do bench presses.

Supinations and pronations of the hand, more properly called radial-ulnar supination and pronation, also place a strain on the tendons that attach at the elbow. Sudden rotations such as the snap supinations associated with outside and inside mid-blocks in karate can leave you with torn tendons, especially if the movement is done with full focus.

Exercises for the elbow should include not only the familiar curls (flexes) and presses (extensions), but rotational movements as well. Here are a few exercises that will improve strength and flexibility in the elbows.

Flexion: The Zottman Curl

This movement is done with a dumbbell. Stand erect, and hold a dumbbell in each hand. Rotate the forearms so that the palms of both hands are facing the back (that is, they are pronated). Bring the arms up by flexing the elbow joint. The *brachialis* muscle (see anatomy chart in the Appendix) will help on the initial upward movement. As you bring the dumbbell up, rotate the forearm so that the hand supinates by the time it approaches the chest. Don't let the weight fall back toward the chest. You don't want to lose the tension in the biceps and *brachialis*. As you complete the movement, the hand should be fully supinated. This brings the biceps into play fully. Start with no weight at all, then add weight so that you can do 12 reps for one set. Work your way up to 20 reps by adding 1 rep every day. When you've reached 20 reps, drop back down to 12 reps, and either add weight or add a set. Keep it up for two weeks, and you'll be ready to move on to basic training. You can

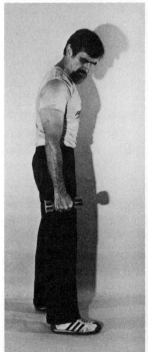  

The Zottman or supinating curl (supination of the hand, flexion of the arm at the elbow), position 1.

The Zottman curl, position 2.

The Zottman curl, position 3.

also do curls either with the palm remaining down, or with the palm remaining up. This gives you three ways to do the curls.

Extension

There are a variety of "presses" that extend the arm to the point where the bones in the forearm and the upper arm are in a straight line. Military presses involve moving the elbow joint while you are extending the arm (as do bench presses). Exercises such as "French curls," kickbacks, and triceps extensions work the triceps while keeping the elbow stationary.

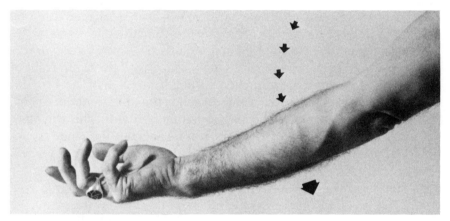

Extension of the arm at the elbow.

Ordinarily, there is less strain on a joint when it is moving. When you immobilize a joint, the joint bears the full stresses that a movement brings to bear upon it. As a consequence, pressing movements are less likely to damage the elbow than are extension movements.

In the beginning, make the movements with no weight at all. Straighten the arms until they reach the point where they will not extend any farther. Alternate between flexion and extension, until you can do the full range of motion without stiffness. Then start with light weight and do bench presses with a barbell. The weight should be lowered to the chest, then raised to a position at arm's length over your chest. Repeat the motion. Use a weight with which you can do 12 reps. Make the same additions of reps that you did with the curls mentioned above. You aren't trying to do record poundages here, nor are you trying radically to strengthen the triceps, pectorals, or anterior deltoids. The goal here is a full range of motion and the development of strength in the joint itself.

When you've done pressing movements for a week, alternate from one day to the next with extension movements. Lie on your back, holding a light barbell in your hands in position over your head. Your arms should be straight. Keep the elbows stationary and slowly lower the weight by bending the elbows. Bring the weight down until it is at the top of your head. Then slowly take it back up in an arc until the arms are straight again. Don't use heavy weights. Follow the same pattern with reps and sets as you did for the curling and pressing movements.

Rotation

Many people simply hold a dumbbell in their hands and alternately supinate and pronate the hand. The only workout that such a movement gives the rotators in the forearm comes from overcoming inertia at the beginning of the movement. You need something to resist the rotation throughout the range of motion. Again, the Tension Band or surgical tubing seems the practical solution. Place the forearm in front of you on a table or bench. Hold one end of a Tension Band in your fist (hold it tightly, so that it won't slip). Anchor the other end on a hook. Then alternate with supinating and pronating rotations. This way, tension will be on the muscles of the forearm throughout the range of motion, and you will benefit much more than if you tried to hold two heavy dumbbells while spinning them.

At first, however, use no weight at all. Do the movements from one end of the range of motion to the other until you've warmed up the muscles and tendons involved. Then put the tension to them. What we've described may sound easy, but many a pro ball player has found his forearms burning after a few minutes with the Tension Band.

If you have access to a line of Hydra-Fitness machines, you'll find that the curling and pressing movements can be done with a resistance range from practically zero to as much resistance as you can handle. You will recall that Hydra-Fitness machines do not use weights or cables, but instead use hydraulic cylinders for resistance. The machines are omnikinetic: the faster you try to do the movement, the more resistance you will encounter. The more slowly you make the movement, the less the resistance. Thus by varying the speed at which you make the movements, you can benefit from the machine's ability to accommodate to whatever resistance demands you make of it. Further, the Series III machines feature six-position adjustable cylinders for progressive resistance. Hydra-Fitness machines are rapidly becoming popular with physical and corrective therapists as well as sports trainers for precisely this reason. If you have pain in the joint, work at a speed just below where you would feel the pain. Try to work a little bit faster each day.

Hydra-Fitness also makes a forearm rotation machine that operates on the same omnikinetic principle. If you have trouble with your elbows when you do rotational movements, try to find yourself a Hydra-Fitness Forearm Conditioner machine. They're easy to use, and very effective.

THE SHOULDER JOINT

The shoulder joint has been called a "cup and saucer." The cup is the head of the humerus or upper arm bone, and the saucer is the glenoid cavity of the scapula or shoulder blade. A variety of ligaments hold the shoulder joint together: the articular capsule, the anterior sternoclavicular, posterior sternoclavicular, interclavicular, and costoclavicular ligaments, and the articular disc. Other ligaments are related to the joint, and bond the clavicle (collarbone) to the shoulder blade.

The shoulder joint has six basic movements, plus combinations of these movements. The movements and their respective ranges of motion are as follows:

Extension: The arm is held straight down to the side.

Hyperextension: The arm is kept parallel to the vertical line of the body, but is brought to the back.

Flexion: The arm is raised to the front.

Abduction: The arm is brought up in an arc to the side.

Adduction: The arm is in the same position as for extension.

Medial rotation: The left arm is rotated clockwise (the reverse for the right arm).

Lateral rotation: The left arm is rotated counterclockwise (the reverse for the right arm).

You can also move the entire shoulder girdle in four directions:

Elevation: The shoulder girdle is lifted vertically in a shrugging movement.

Depression: The shoulder girdle is moved downward vertically in a "drooping" movement.

Protraction: The shoulder girdle is pushed forward.

Retraction: The shoulder girdle is pulled backward. Refer to the photograph of shoulder hyperextension on page 86 for an illustration of this movement. The trainee has retracted his shoulder girdle in addition to hyperextending his arm at the shoulder.

Flexion

Stand with your arm straight down to the side, with the hand against

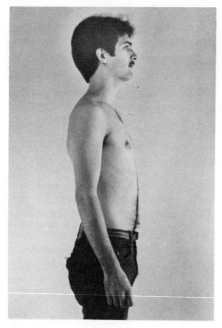 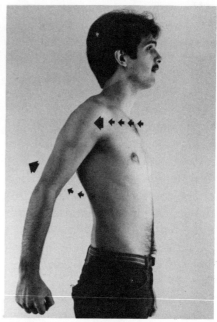

Extension of the arm at the shoulder.   **Hyperextension of the arm at the shoulder, retraction of the shoulder girdle.**

Forward flexion of the arm at the shoulder.

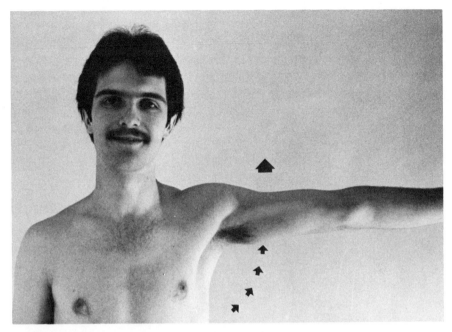

Abduction of the arm at the shoulder.

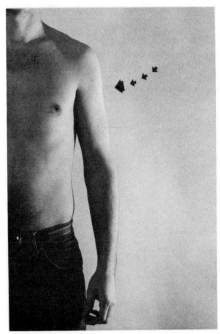

Adduction of the arm at the shoulder.

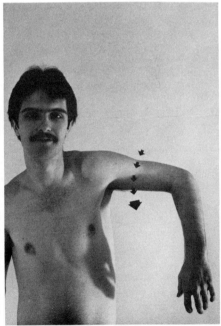

Medial rotation of the arm at the shoulder.

Lateral rotation of the arm at the shoulder.

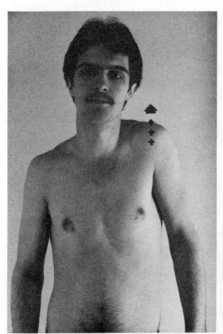

Elevation of the shoulder girdle.

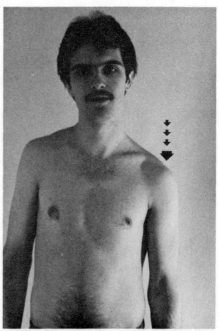

Depression of the shoulder girdle.

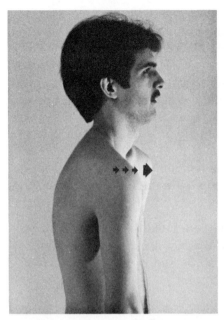

Protraction of the shoulder girdle.

the side of the leg. Raise the arm in front of you. When your arm is parallel to the floor, it will be at 90° flexion at the shoulder.

Hyperextension
Stand in the same starting position as above. Move the arm from its position perpendicular to the floor toward the back. It should hyperextend about 45°.

Abduction
Stand in the same starting position as above. Raise the arm out to the side until it is parallel to the floor. Then see if you can continue the movement until your arm is straight overhead.

Medial Rotation
Stand with your right arm abducted 90 degrees at the shoulder, and flexed 90 degrees at the elbow. Immobilize the elbow and the forearm: don't let the radius and ulna rotate! Then rotate the right upper arm bone in the shoulder counterclockwise. Do the reverse for the left shoulder.

Lateral Rotation
Same as the above, except make the rotation clockwise for the right arm and counterclockwise for the left arm.

You may hear popping noises or grating sounds when you do these movements. These can indicate anything from fibrous material between the upper arm bone and the shoulder blade, thickened ligaments as a result of injury, small fractures, or torn cartilage from previous injuries. If pain accompanies these sounds or any of these movements, you should see an orthopedist for a complete diagnosis. Often injuries sustained when you were younger will show up in your forties, especially if you've had a long inactive period and are only now beginning to get back into shape.

Some of the exercises for the shoulder joint and the muscles that move the upper arm within it have popular names:

Forward Raise (Flexion)

This is done with dumbbells or a barbell. Hold the dumbbells or barbell in the hands palm down, keep the elbow locked, and slowly raise the weight toward the front. There is no need to go higher than 45° above the horizontal plane.

Lateral Raise (Abduction)

This is done with dumbbells. Hold the dumbbells at your side. Bend the elbows slightly as you raise them out to the side. Rotate your entire shoulder girdle to the front, and you'll see that you will not be able to raise your arms past the horizontal plane. If you want to go on overhead, rotate the shoulder girdle backward and continue the movement. There is no reason to go past 45° above the horizontal plane.

Posterior Raise

This is a combination of abduction and hyperextension and is also done with dumbbells. Bend over to the front at the waist (if you have lower back problems, rest your upper body on a narrow bench), and let the arms hang down toward the floor. Without swinging them, bring the arms up in an arc until they are parallel to the floor.

Rotational Movements

There are many ways to do the rotation movements, each working the muscles and the joint from a slightly different angle. These exercises do not have popular names because few people around the local gym realize their value in strengthening the shoulders. These exercises are best done with cables or with a length of surgical tubing, so that the tension can be kept on the muscles throughout the range of motion.

Medial Rotation—Arms at the Sides

Lie on your back, with your elbows bent at right angles and your upper arms against the side of your torso. Keep the elbow solidly in place. Grasp a dumbbell or a cable handle in each hand and bring the hand up in an arc until the forearm is pointing toward the ceiling. As you can see, if you do this one with dumbbells, the tension ends before you approach the end of the movement; but if you do it with a cross-over cable apparatus, the tension remains through to the end.

Medial Rotation—Arms Abducted

Lie on your back with the upper arms out to the sides at a 90° angle to the body. Bend the elbow 90° so that the hands are in line with the top of your head. Use dumbbells, a barbell (light weight!), or a cable apparatus. Rotate the upper arm in the shoulder joint until the forearms are perpendicular to the floor.

Lateral Rotation—Arms at the Sides

This one can be done when you are either lying face down on a bench, or kneeling with the knees bent 90° and the body parallel to the floor. Hold the elbows firmly at the top of the hips at the side, with the elbow bent 90°. Grasp a dumbbell or a cable handle and rotate the upper arm bone in the shoulder joint until the forearms are parallel to the floor.

Lateral Rotation—Arms Abducted

The best way to do this one is to lie face down on a narrow bench. Use a piece of padded board as a crosspiece to support the upper arms. The crosspiece should be about the number of inches from the inside of your elbows, measured across the chest. This way, the upper arms will be supported and you can concentrate completely on the rotational movement. The elbows should be bent at a 90° angle, and the forearms should be pointed toward the floor. Grasp a dumbbell or a cable handle and rotate the upper arm bone in the shoulder joint until the arms have come up in an arc to a position parallel to the floor.

Each of these movements should be done at first with no resistance, to see how far you can move your upper arm in the various directions described. Stretch at the end point of each movement, to see if you can go a little bit farther. When you've warmed up the joint, you can begin to work with dumbbells or with a cable apparatus.

Use enough weight to tire you at 12 reps. Add a rep each day until you get to 20 reps, then drop back down to 12 reps and either add weight or add a set. Again, the goal here is not to lift a lot of weight, but rather to improve the flexibility of the joint while adding some strength and endurance. This is the same for all the exercises in this section. That's why they're called "pretraining" exercises.

MEANING AND VALUE OF PRETRAINING EXERCISES

Since you are not working with enough weight in these exercises to exhaust the muscles, you can do them every day. Try for a full range of motion in each movement, and work for smoothness. Don't jerk the weights or the Tension Bands around. *Concentrate* as you perform each movement, and try to get the feel of the muscles, bones, ligaments, and tendons that move in the various joints.

There's nothing mysterious in all this. It's simply that few people really get to know themselves physically. Think about the movements that you are making. Develop sequences of movements of your own, and try them in combinations. Try to think of your body and your mind as two aspects of the same thing: *you.*

You'll find that while each of the exercises taken separately sounds easy, taken together they constitute a full-fledged workout. Consider it your warmup routine. If, after you get into the basic training program, you begin to feel a little stiff in the joints, repeat the appropriate sections of the pretraining program. It'll work the kinks out.

Think of the pretraining program as insurance against injuries and as a way to reacquaint yourself with your body and what it can do. By building for both flexibility and strength, you will increase the range of motion that each joint can allow, and you will increase the strength of the muscles that make such movement possible. You can't depend on your sport itself to give you overall conditioning and flexibility. To do so would violate what exercise physiologists call "The Principle of Specificity." You strengthen a specific group of muscles by working that specific group of muscles, not by working others. The pretraining program will enable you to overhaul all of your major joints, and to increase the strength and flexibility of the components of those joints.

Further, the pretraining program will provide you with a solid foundation to proceed with basic training and sports training with more determination and vigor. It's like putting new shock absorbers, tires, tie rods, and bushings on a sports car. The ride is not all that's improved.

The more you feel your way into your body's fundamental movements, the more control you'll have when you get out on the tennis court, on the jogging trail, or at the plate with the company softball team. By actively learning what your body can do, you will be far better able to make it do what you want it to do. The pretraining program is the first step toward getting your body under control. And remember: in sports, control is the whole ball game.

Chapter 3

BASIC TRAINING

This chapter is divided into three parts. In the first section, we'll describe the kind of equipment you need. In the second, we'll outline the basic training exercises. In the third, we'll show you how to use these exercises to develop your own program for strength, power, stamina, and endurance training. At the end, we'll list some sample programs for you.

By the time you finish the basic training program, you'll be ready to start on what we call "movement clusters," a concept which is one of the cornerstones of sportspower training. Basic training is a natural step up from pretraining, and it will give you the foundation that you need to go on to more vigorous types of physical activity.

Equipment for Basic Training

FREE WEIGHTS

Free weights are the basic equipment for any strength program. All the pro ball clubs use them, especially football teams, where there is no substitute for the kind of strength it takes to break through a line or bring a runner down. More importantly, strength training is the foundation for any kind of physical activity. Coupled with a good cardiovascular program, strength training is the key to giving you the kind of muscular size, resiliency, and explosive power you need in sports movements.

Because of the growing popularity of weight training and the inter-

The basic home gym: bench, barbell, curling bar, iron shoes, ankle weights, barbell plates.

national popularity of bodybuilding and weightlifting, barbell sets are no longer rare and esoteric pieces of equipment, but can be found in almost any sports equipment store, from sports departments in department stores to heavy metal shops. The basic free weight set consists of the following:

Steel Bar with Collars and Plates
The bar can be either a small bar made of tubular steel, a concrete-filled tubular bar, a solid steel bar, or a full-sized Olympic Standard bar.

The smaller bars use disc-shaped plates with holes about an inch in diameter. Olympic bars use disc-shaped plates with 2-inch holes. All of the bars have collars that keep the plates from sliding off. Some bars are curved for special applications.

Dumbbell Handles

Dumbbell handles are short metal bars, with collars and sleeves. The collars keep the plates on the bar, and the sleeves keep them apart so that you will have something to grip.

Benches

You will need a sturdy bench on which you can lie supine in order to do exercises such as the bench press, flyes, and seated presses. These benches can be of metal or wood. The metal ones are the sturdier of the two, and can be purchased at sporting equipment shops. The bench should be upholstered with Naugahyde or Mylar, so that it will not disintegrate from perspiration.

Some benches have racks to hold the barbell. Bench press benches have racks that enable you to lift the barbell off at arm's length. Don't use it, however, unless you have a spotter to help you in case you can't make that last rep.

Racks

Bench press and squat racks hold the barbell so that you can concentrate on the exercise itself instead of having to worry about getting the bar off the floor and into position. If you have the cash to spare, a good set of squat racks and a bench press rack are as good an investment as the barbells themselves.

There are as many accessories for free weights as there are manufacturers to sell them. Curved bars for curling exercises, deeply knurled bars for bench pressing, head straps for neck exercises, iron shoes for knee extensions and flexes, and kettlebells (dumbbells with bucket-type handles) for shoulder exercises are only a few of the popular enhancements that you can buy for your barbell set.

Most barbell sets include dumbbell handles and all of the necessary collars and plates. A 110-pound set still costs less than $40 and you can buy a full-sized 350-pound Olympic barbell set for under $300. Look in the advertising pages of *Strength and Health, Muscular Development, Muscle and Fitness, Muscle Training, Muscle Digest, Muscle Mag,* or

Iron Man and you'll find all the equipment you'll ever want, including racks, benches, cables, machines, and old-time strongman equipment.

ISOKINETIC AND PROGRESSIVE RESISTANCE MACHINES

The popularity of the modern health club is based on the utility of exercise machines. For a complete description of these machines, with advice on how to use them for the development of various kinds of programs, take a look at our book, *Bodypower: The Complete Guide to Health Club Exercise Machines and Home Gym Equipment* (St. Martin's Press, 1981). It is estimated that there are presently over 20,000,000 people now enrolled in 54,000 health clubs nationally and exercising with machines two or three times a week.

The major machine manufacturers are Hydra-Fitness, Nautilus, Paramount, Universal, and Mini-Gym. If the machines in your club are painted metal, chances are they're made by Nautilus. If they're chrome, they're either Paramount or Universal. If they're blue metal with no plates, but a black box, they're Mini-Gym, and if they're russet-painted metal with adjustable hydraulic cylinders, they're Hydra-Fitness. Most of these machines are excellent in their various applications.

Mike Singletary, middle linebacker for the Chicago Bears, pours on the power with a Hydra-Fitness Omnikinetic Jump Squat machine. (Extension of the leg at the hip and at the knee.) Photo by Sue McClaren, courtesy of Hydra-Fitness of Texas.

Seated press/pulldown on a Hydra-Fitness total power machine.

The controversy between machine exercise and free weight exercise has been raging ever since machine sales began to cut into free weight sales. Both sides have a case besides the economic one, and both sides do a good job at trying to convince you that if you have *their* kind of equipment, you don't need any other kind.

The controversy is not limited to free weights vs. machines. The different machine manufacturers are competing with one another, and their claims and counterclaims are as exciting as the sales pitches in a growth industry always are. The muscle magazines frequently run articles about the controversy, because they know that the readers are constantly beset by the sales talks given to them by health club owners. All of the claims, counterclaims, and assorted hoopla can be boiled down to the following list:

The Free Weights Position
1. Only free weights give you "natural" movements, against the pull of gravity. Since sports movements are made on a playing field and not on a machine, free weights are superior to machines in training you for sports.
2. Free weight exercises work the collateral stabilizing muscles around the joints, thus giving you more strength in the joints and less likelihood of injury.
3. Free weights move in your own natural "groove" and not in a groove (or motion path) that is built into the machine. Thus you can find your proper groove and build strength in a way that is ideally suited for you.
4. Everybody has a different lever system. A machine's lever system is restricted to what's engineered into it. If your lever system doesn't match that of the machine, you may injure yourself. At the best, you won't get a good workout.
5. You can isolate muscles with free weights just as you can with machines.
6. Free weights are significantly cheaper to buy and use than machines.

The Machine Position
1. Machines enable you to vary the resistance according to the demands of your lever system through a complete range of motion. When you do curls on a machine, the tension stays on the biceps all the way to the end of the lift. With free weights, the tension lessens as you get to the end of the movement: at exactly the place where you need it.

2. Machines enable you to work without a spotter. If you can't make the last rep, just let the machine down and walk away from it.
3. Machines are designed to maximize the workout given to specific muscles or muscle groups. You can't "cheat" on a machine; thus, the workout is of higher quality.
4. Machines are adjustable according to height. Anybody can fit into a well-designed machine.
5. You can do circuit training on machines, hopping from one machine to another, for a good cardiovascular workout without the hassle of changing plates on the barbell. You can go from one machine to another without resting in between, thus improving the quality of your workout.
6. Machines offer isolation and intensity for specific muscles in a way that free weights cannot. If you want to concentrate on biceps development, use the biceps machine. If you want to concentrate on triceps, use a triceps machine.

Not surprisingly, both sides are right. Free weights do indeed allow you to exercise in your own natural groove in a way that machines do not. It is quite true that each machine has its own range of motion and its own lever system, neither of which necessarily matches up with your own. If they don't, you may very well suffer injury as you try to move in ways for which your bone structure wasn't designed.

Further, the very isolation that machines offer individual muscles precludes their ability to work muscles in groups. Nobody ever threw a ball with the wrist flexors alone. You don't need a spotter with the machines, but then again, with the exception of the squat and the bench press, you don't need a spotter with free weights either.

Machines emphatically *do not* (unless they are specifically designed for it) work the collateral stabilizing muscles around the knees, ankles, wrists, elbows, and shoulders. By now, everybody should have heard about people dropping their bench press capability by 40 or 50 pounds after giving the machines a few months of work.

Some machines are frightfully expensive, and pay off economically only in a commercial health club or a school gym setting where large numbers of people use them. Almost all the modern clubs now use machines, and some of them are completely replacing free weights with machines.

So what's the truth? If you want to give yourself the fullest possible workout, use both free weights and machines. Don't expect machines to increase your bench press poundages. The bench press is the bench press, and uses muscles that are not necessarily used on a chest exerciser or an arm machine. The bench press, for example, involves not only the pectorals, anterior deltoids, and triceps, but the rotator muscles of the shoulder, the stabilizing muscles of the forearm, the core muscles of the torso, and even the legs. If you don't believe it, try doing bench presses with your feet in different positions. Or try it with your back arched and then with your back straight. You'll see what we mean.

On the other hand, you *can* isolate muscles on the machines in such a way that you can even out your physique and your strength. Remember that some of the machines started as physical therapy equipment. You can overcome problems and treat injuries with judicious use of machines as well as free weights.

A recent study in Houston, Texas (reported in the July 1981 issue of Joe Weider's *Muscle and Fitness*), on machine usage vs. free weights is revealing. It gives an insight not only into the psychology of people who work out, but of health club sales strategies as well. In the study, Dr. Warren Chaney of the University of Houston worked with three groups: people who chose to work out with free weights alone, those who opted for machines alone, and those who chose to use a combination of machines and free weights.

The people who chose to use free weights alone were more aggressive than members of the other two groups (as scored on a psychological test), and only 14.3 percent of the group dropped out of the program after three months. The people with the lowest aggression index chose to use machines exclusively, and of their number, 96 percent dropped out after three months. The middle group had an aggression index almost as high as the free weight group, and had a much higher I.Q. rating than either of the other groups, but half of them dropped out after three months.

Free weight users stick with it and keep their interest up more than machine users and people who use both machines and free weights. Machine-alone people drop out at the rate of 96 percent after three months.

Health club economics are sometimes based on dropout rates. If you sell a year's membership, paid either all at once or to a finance company acting as a factor for the club, then except for the renewal potentiality, it makes no difference to the club if you drop out after three months. A 96 percent turnover of members means the opportunity for continuous sales efforts, even though space in the gym is limited. It means that you can replace your membership every three months and never have a crowded gym. What if everybody decided to come on the same day? Don't worry. People who join health clubs are notoriously inconsistent in their attendance.

It is interesting that the most intelligent of the three groups used both machines and free weights, probably realizing that the best progress could be made by judicious use of all types of equipment. The primary factor here, however, is motivation. And people who use free weights alone are usually more highly motivated about gaining the kind of training that weights have to offer: strength, power, and increased muscle size. There is a lot of lore concerning free weights, just as there is about everything else in the world of physical training, and many guys wouldn't be caught dead using a machine because they identify with the musclebuilding superstars, none of whom has trained exclusively with machines.

TYPES OF MACHINES

Machines are divided roughly into two categories: isotonic and isokinetic. Isotonic machines use plates or other kinds of iron or steel weights, attached either to pulleys or cams by cables or direct connection. By altering the shape of the cam (as Nautilus and Paramount do), the resistance can be altered during the range of motion of the exercise movement.

Isokinetic machines do not use weights, but offer a resistance that accommodates itself to the amount of force being applied to it, and regulates the speed at which the force is applied. In short, the faster you try to make the movement, the more resistance you meet. The slower you go, the easier it is. The Hydra-Fitness omnikinetic hydraulic cylinder machines allow you to accelerate during the movement (thus enhancing power training) while also offering all the advantages of the less-sophisticated inertia-reel isokinetic machines.

One of the great advantages of the isokinetic equipment is that the two major manufacturers, Hydra-Fitness and Mini-Gym, have designed their machines with sports performance improvement in mind. Mini-Gym has equipment that simulates the movements of everything from overhand tennis serves to scrimmage line blocking. Hydra-Fitness has designed a line of equipment to provide power, endurance, and physiological conditioning to athletes of all sports.

The following is a list of machines manufactured by Hydra-Fitness, Mini-Gym, Nautilus, Paramount, and Universal (the list is far from complete, but it consists of those machines that you are most likely to find in your local club or school gym).

Hydra-Fitness
Unilateral Quad Hamstring (for knee extension and flexion)
Pro-Power (for knee and hip extension—simulates scrimmage line work)
Total Power (for elbow extension and flexion, plus shoulder and back work)
Leg Press (for knee extension and hip extension)
Jump Squat (for knee and hip extension—simulates squat)
Biceps/Triceps (for elbow extension and flexion)
Hip Flexion/Extension (for hip work—simulates running movements)
Ab/Ad Hip (for hip abduction and adduction)
Bench Press and Row

These machines come in three series—from simple, nonadjustable resistance to precision-calibrated, adjustable hydraulic cylinders.

Mini-Gym
Squat Thrust (a scrimmage line trainer)
Forearm and Hand Shivers (for more scrimmage simulation)
Swim Bench (simulates swimming motions)

Extension of the leg at the hip and at the knee on a Mini-Gym leaper.

Andy Dumpis of the National Olympic Style Volleyball team doing a seated press on a Mini-Gym isokinetic machine.

Seated press (extension of the arm at the elbow, elevation of the shoulder girdle) on a Nautilus machine.

Leaper (does just what the name suggests)
Lats and Shoulder Unit (for *latissimus*, triceps, and deltoid work)
Isokinetic Tennis Unit (simulates tennis movements)
Ankle Rotation and Flexion Machine (does what it says)
Hamstring and Quad (for knee flexion and extension)
Passing Station (for throwing movements)

Nautilus
Leg Extension (for knee extensions)
Duo Hip and Back Machine (for hip and back extension)
Leg Curl (for knee flexion)
Torso Pullover (for pectorals, deltoids, biceps, abdominals, and *serratus* muscles)
Behind-the-Neck Machine (for *latissimus dorsi* and biceps)

Double Chest (for pectorals and deltoids)
Double Shoulder (for shoulder abduction)
Omni Biceps Machine (for elbow flexion)
Omni Triceps Machine (for elbow extension)

Dynacam (no longer made but found in many gyms)
Seated Bench Press (for pectorals, anterior deltoids, and triceps work)
Floor-Type Bench Press (for free weight bench press simulations, squats, and leg presses)
Hip, Thigh, Back, and Buttocks (works the areas named)
Leg Curl (for knee flexion)
Seated and Standing Calf-Raise machines (for the calves)
Leg Extension (for knee extension—works the quadriceps)
Multistation machines (for leg press, bench press, pulley pulldowns, low pulleys, seated press, parallel bar dips, chins, calf raises)

Paramount
Pec-Deck (for the pectorals and firming the bustline)
Hack Squat/Calf Raise (for the thighs and calves)
Lower Buttocks and Hamstring Developer (does what it says)
Arm Curling Machine (for elbow flexion/biceps work)
Floor-Type Bench Press (for anterior deltoids, pectorals, and triceps; also for squats and leg raises)
Triceps Machine (for elbow extension)
Multistation Machines (for leg press, leg curl, leg extension, pulley pulldowns, low pulleys, bench press, seated press, chins)

Universal
Multistation Machines (for leg press, leg curl, bench press, seated press, calf raise, pulley pulldowns, low pulleys, abdominal work, chins, parallel bar dips, leg raises)

At any given gym, you may see these pieces of equipment, plus assorted machines and free weights made by smaller companies. Some gyms have a mixture of equipment by various manufacturers. Since no machine is made precisely to fit everybody, the wider the range of equipment your gym has, the better off you will be. If you're getting ready for sportspower training, count yourself lucky if your gym has Hydra-Fitness and Mini-Gym equipment. If it doesn't, we show you how to simulate sports movements on what you do have.

Seated toe raise (plantar flexion) on a Dynacam seated calf machine.

Arm curl (flexion of the arm at the elbow) at a Paramount multistation machine.

In addition to the usual range of equipment, some gyms also stock rotational movement machines such as the Hydra-Fitness Power Forearm Conditioner. This machine will give a thorough workout to all of the forearm muscles, as it takes your arms through the full range of motion in wrist flexion and extension, radial and ulnar deviation, and supination and pronation—in short, all the exercises that we outlined in Chapter 2 when we talked about pretraining exercises for the wrist and elbow.

You may also run across neck exercisers, skiing simulators, balance beams, and a variety of body conditioners. All of them can be used to your advantage. Get to know everything your gym has to offer, and you can't go wrong.

For cardiovascular conditioning, many gyms have running and jogging tracks, and some have the new ergometric stationary bicycles such as Schwinn's new Excelsior Ergometric. These bikes have a variable resistance setting, all done electronically with a flip of a dial. You can literally dial the amount of resistance you want, and pedal your excess weight away. When you use these machines, remember that if you

Triceps extension (extension of the arm at the elbow) at a Universal pulley station, starting position.

Triceps extension, completion of movement.

place the seat high, you will get a lesser range of motion, but will be able to use more resistance. If you place the seat low, you will get a greater range of motion in your knee joint, but the load on your quadriceps muscles (and your knee joint) will be greater. Choose the seat height carefully. If you want to work the legs, put it low (but watch out for knee stresses). If you want to go for 30 minutes or so for a cardiovascular workout, put it high, attain your target pulse rate, and go.

Don't think that you have to use all the machines every day, just because they are there. That's not the way to get your money's worth. Work out a sane, scientific, progressive program utilizing both free weights and machines, and then stick to it consistently. Work out three times a week, or every other day. Don't miss workouts. All the machines in the world can't make up for sloppy training habits. If you don't work out, you won't make gains. It's as simple as that.

In the next section, we'll describe the basic training exercises. They can be done on either free weights or machines. We'll tell you how to do them with free weights, and we'll list the machines that work more or less the same areas.

Basic Training Exercises

Before we describe the exercises themselves, we should establish an exercise terminology, to parallel the terminology for training that we gave in Chapter 2. Few gym members use the technical language of kinesiology, although if they did, there would be far less confusion about how individual exercises are done. In general, here's how the argot of the gym corresponds to the language of professional trainers.

Curls

These are flexing movements. The arm curl flexes the elbow, and works the biceps. Leg curls flex the knee, and work the hamstring muscles. The limb always moves in an arc.

Presses

Presses are basically extension movements. Military presses (the name comes from the erect stance) extend the elbow and work the triceps. Leg presses extend the knee and work the quadriceps. Seated presses extend the elbow and work the triceps and shoulders. French curls are actually elbow extension exercises. They probably got the label "curl" from the fact that the arm moves in an arc when you do them.

Extensions

The terms "extension" and "flexion" properly refer to the joints. However, around the gym, people usually talk about "triceps extensions" (which are French curls), or "leg extensions," which are properly knee extensions. Spinal "extensions" are exercises that involve straightening the spine. Spinal "hyperextensions" involve going past the point where your spine would be straight. Hip "hyperextensions" do the same thing: they take the upper leg bone past the point where the pelvic bone and the femur would be in a line.

Pulldowns and Pushdowns

Pulldowns refer to cable exercises (usually for the *latissimus dorsi* muscles or "lats") in which a bar that is fastened to a weighted cable is pulled down to the chest or behind the neck. Pushdowns refer to triceps or elbow extensions performed with a weighted cable.

Kickbacks

These are triceps or elbow extensions, done with dumbbells.

Shrugs
This is a *trapezius* exercise, in which the shoulder girdle is elevated.

Elevation and Depression
These terms mean just what they say. When you shrug your shoulders, you are elevating the shoulder girdle as in the *trapezius* exercise mentioned immediately above. When you pull your shoulders down toward the floor (or raise your body vertically when you are suspended between your arms on a set of parallel bars), you are doing shoulder depressions.

Retractions and Protractions
To retract the shoulder girdle is to pull the shoulders to the back. To protract the shoulder girdle is to push the shoulders forward. These terms are often confused—we've even seen a retraction bench that was called a protraction bench by its inventor.

Keep in mind the planes of the body and the directions of movements that we outlined in Chapter 2, and you're ready to go to work. We'll use the technically correct "extension" and "flexion" to refer to joint movements. Also, instead of talking about "flexing" the muscles (which leads to confusion with flexion movements of joints), we'll use "contraction" when we talk about muscle tension and "relaxation" when we talk about letting muscle tension release itself.

The basic training exercises are designed not only to make you stronger and give you more endurance, but also to develop your general coordination and timing. While the popular conception of the weight trainer used to be that of a slow, ponderously moving clunker, athletic trainers everywhere now know that weights and other types of resistance exercises can give you speed, agility, and timing as well as strength.

Here are the exercises themselves. After we've described them to you, we'll tell you how to work them into a program that uniquely suits your needs. The exercises are arranged by body parts.

CALVES
The two standbys of calf exercises are the standing calf raise and the seated calf raise. The standing raise concentrates the load on the *gastrocnemius* muscles high on the calf, and the seated raises seem to put the load more on the *soleus*, which is the inner and lower calf muscle. Calf raises can be done with the feet parallel (to work both sides of the back of the calf), with the toes together (to work the inner portion), or with the heels together (to work the outer portion). Calf raises can also

be done on one leg, if you don't have enough weight to give you a real workout.

Standing Calf Raise (Plantar Flexion, Knees Extended)

Hold a barbell on your shoulders, right behind the neck. Keep your back straight and slightly arched so that the *erector spinae* muscles are tensed. Also, keep the other muscles of the core tensed (the abdominals, the obliques, and the *iliopsoas*). This will give you a solid foundation to hold the weight. Raise yourself up on your toes, then slowly let yourself back down to the floor. If you want a better stretch, stand on a piece of board. Avoid standing on a thick book. You'll tear up the book and you might slip off and turn your ankle.

Seated Calf Raise (Plantar Flexion, Knees Flexed)

Sit on a bench with your feet flat on the floor. Hold a barbell or a barbell plate on the tops of your thighs at the knee. Use a pad so that you won't hurt your knees. Raise your heels as far as you can go. Be sure to get a complete range of motion. Don't bob up and down. See the photograph on page 104.

Donkey Calf Raise (Plantar Flexion, Knees Extended)

Stand in front of a bench or a low ballet *barre*—anything that will allow you to bend at the waist so that your torso is parallel to the floor.

**Toe raise (plantar flexion)
on a Dynacam calf machine.**

Get somebody to sit across your back over the hips (not on the small of the back). Do the calf raises the same way as described above.

These exercises can also be done on Nautilus, Dynacam, and Paramount standing and seated calf raise machines. Some multistation machines advise you to do calf raises at the leg press station, but these are awkward and not really advisable.

THIGHS

The thighs are made up of the quadriceps muscles in the front and the hamstrings in the back. The quadriceps consist of the *rectus femoris* along the top, the *vastus intermedius* (under the *rectus femoris*), the *vastus lateralis* along the outside, and the *vastus medialis* along the inside. These muscles extend the knee.

The hamstrings consist of the *biceps femoris*, the *semitendinosus*, and the *semimembranosus*. These muscles flex the knee.

Thigh exercises should be done so that a quadriceps exercise and a hamstrings exercise are done alternately. You shouldn't do two quadriceps exercises in a row, nor should you follow hamstring exercises with more hamstring exercises. Alternate the two.

When you do squats, the knee and hip joints are moving. When you do extensions and flexes (curls) the knee and the hip joints are usually stationary. Exercises in which the affected joint is stationary put more strain on the joint, so be sure that you warm up with a few lightweight reps before going on to the full poundage.

Squats (Knee Extension, Hip Extension)

Hold a barbell on your shoulders, right behind the neck. If your calf muscles are tight, you may have to place a board under your heels. Squats can be done partially or fully. If you want to work the quads, but not the hips, then stop one-quarter or one-half of the way down. If you want to work the hips as well as the quads, do full squats or parallel squats. The knees should be kept over the feet. Don't let the knees come inward or go outward. If you do, you will put undue stress on the knee joint and you will undermine your form in the squat. Keep your back arched, with the lumbar sacral muscles tight. Look straight ahead. Resist the temptation to look at the floor or at the ceiling. Keep the upper back muscles bunched tightly, as you hold the bar to the sides of your shoulders with your hands. To start the squat, allow your knees to bend and slowly let your hips move in a straight line toward the floor. Control the movement all the way. Don't bounce up and down, and don't drop suddenly, or you will overstress the knees and the arches. When

Squatting with an Olympic barbell and a power rack for safety.

Squatting with an Olympic barbell and a power rack for safety.

you've gone down as far as you want to go, slowly straighten the knees and stand erect again.

Some machines, such as the leg press, work the quads and hips, but not in the same way as the squat. In the leg press, the knee joints move during the lift, but the hips remain stationary. There are several new squatting machines on the market that actually simulate the squatting movement, but they do the balancing for you instead of forcing you to develop the collateral stabilizing muscles that are worked in the free weight squat.

Leg Extensions (Extension of the Leg at the Knee)

These exercises can be done with free weights or on a variety of machines designed for extension exercises. If you do them with free weights, use either ankle weights or iron shoes. Sit on a bench with your knees flexed, and your feet hanging off the edge of the bench. Make sure that you have some substantial padding under the knees in order to avoid discomfort or injury. Straighten the legs until the knees are straight. Then lower the legs back down to the starting position. If you want to work the entire quadriceps, do the full range of motion. If you want to concentrate on the *vastus medialis,* work in the last 11° of motion below full extension.

Extension of the leg at the knee at a Paramount leg extension station.

Leg press (extension of the leg at the knee, extension of the leg at the hip) at a Paramount leg press station.

Leg Press (Extension of the Leg at the Knee)

Don't try this one with free weights. Long ago it used to be popular to balance a loaded barbell on the arches of your feet. If it rolls off, the results can be disastrous. Use a leg press machine. Every machine manufacturer has some form of leg press machine, so your gym will undoubtedly have one. Just climb into the seat and straighten your legs.

Leg Curl (Flexion of the Leg at the Knee)

These can be done either with free weights or with a machine. If you do them with free weights, you should use either ankle weights or iron shoes. Many people lie on the floor and bring the legs up in an arc. When you do the exercise this way, you lose tension on the hamstrings once you've passed the 45° angle on the way up. It's better to do the exercise one leg at a time, standing erect. This way, tension is kept on the muscles throughout the range of motion. Stand erect, and flex (bend) the knee, bringing the heel up in an arc toward the buttocks. You can also do this one with a little help from a friend or training partner. Lie on the floor on your stomach and have a friend hold your feet at the

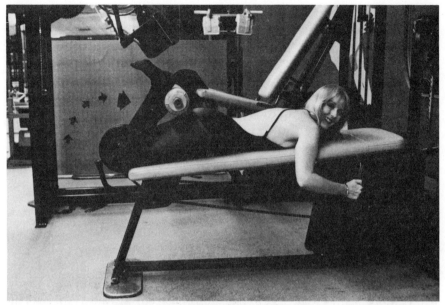

Leg curl (flexion of the leg at the knee) on a Nautilus leg curl machine.

heels, so that he can resist your attempt to bring your legs up. Both of you will be surprised at how little effort it takes to keep you from doing the leg curl.

ABDUCTORS, ADDUCTORS, ROTATORS, AND FLEXORS OF THE THIGH AT THE HIP

The thigh is abducted (brought out to the side) by the *gluteus medius* muscle. It is brought inward toward the body's centerline, or adducted, by the *gracilis, adductor longus, adductor magnus, adductor brevis,* and *pectineus.* The *sartorius* flexes the thigh and rotates it laterally. The *tensor fasciae latae* flexes the thigh and rotates it medially. The upper portion of the *adductor magnus* flexes the thigh and rotates it medially, while the lower portion of the muscle extends the thigh and rotates it laterally. In addition to adduction, the *adductor longus* flexes and rotates the thigh medially, as does the *adductor brevis.* The adductor muscles make up the inner side of the thigh, and the abductor muscles make up the outer side. The *gracilis* runs directly along the inner edge, and the outer edge at the top is the location of the *gluteus medius.* In a sense, the *gluteus medius* is the "deltoid" of the thigh.

Partly because of the popularity of leg extension and curl machines, full squats are no longer performed by many athletes. This omission is regrettable, since neither the extension nor the curl works the hips enough to make a difference. Leg press machines immobolize the hips, so that the work they do get is not the kind that translates easily into sports movements. Further, many people, in an effort to use heavier poundages, don't bring the legs all the way back when they do leg presses, so that the hips miss what workout they could have gotten.

Few machines offer rotational movements for the thighs, and with the notable exception of the Hydra-Fitness Ab/Ad Hip machine, none of the current abduction/adduction machines really give the abductors and adductors the kind of workout overload that is necessary for significant gains in strength and endurance. Here are a few exercises for the hips, together with the thigh flexors, extenders, and rotators.

Lateral Leg Raise (Abduction of the Thigh at the Hip)

Attach ankle weights or an iron shoe to the ankle or foot of one leg. Either lie on your side or stand erect. Lift the weighted leg out to the side as high as you can lift it without tilting the pelvis. This movement can be done with great effectiveness on the Hydra-Fitness Ab/Ad Hip machine. If your gym doesn't have one, protest until they get one! You can also do lateral raises on a low pulley machine. Attach the cable end to your ankle (with an ordinary leather dog collar if there is no attachment on the machine) and lift the leg away from the machine.

Medial Leg Raise (Adduction of the Thigh at the Hip)

This is an awkward one to do with free weights. Lie on your side, and lift the leg on the side on which you are lying toward the centerline of your body. In short, if you're lying on your right side, lift your right leg toward and past the other leg. See the photographs on pages 66–67. You can do this more easily with a low pulley machine. Attach the collar as described for the Lateral Raise and move the leg in the other direction. The best way to do it is with the Hydra-Fitness Ab/Ad Hip machine, which gives you omnikinetic resistance in both the abduction and the adduction movements.

Medial and Lateral Rotations of the Thigh at the Hip

There are no popular names for these exercises, which means they are generally neglected in exercise sessions. Here's a way to do them that will get you some curious stares down at the local health club. See the photographs on page 67.

For lateral rotations lie on your back in front of a low pulley station or a pulley crossover station. You should be lying perpendicular to the direction in which you will be pulling the cable. Start with your right side to the machine in order to perform lateral rotations with your right leg. Attach the collar (as described in the Lateral Raise) to your right ankle, and flex your right thigh (bend it at the hip) so that it is vertical. Flex the right knee so that it is bent at a 90° angle. Support your thigh by placing both hands solidly around the leg above the knee. Then, rotate the thigh in the hip joint so that the lower leg swings in toward the other leg. This exercise will place some stress on the knee joint, so be careful. Reverse your position for the left leg.

For medial rotations lie in the same position on the floor by the low pulley station. Loop the collar around your right foot. You should be lying with your left side next to the machine. Again, flex the hip and knee so that the thigh and lower leg are bent at 90° angles. Start with your right foot near the machine, and again support your thigh with your arms. Rotate the thigh in the hip joint and swing your lower leg around away from the machine and away from the body's centerline. Reverse your body position for the left leg.

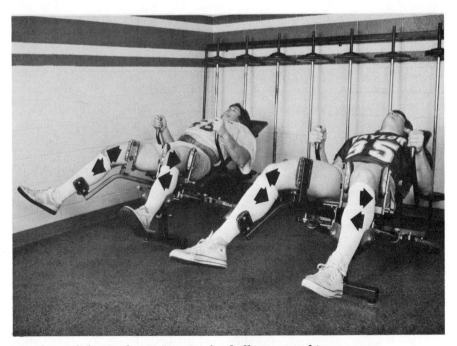

Members of the Baylor University football team working out on Hydra-Fitness AB/AD hip machines (abduction and adduction of the legs at the hips). Photo by Ron Dorsey, courtesy of Hydra-Fitness of Texas.

Leg raise (flexion of the leg at the hip).

Leg Raises (Flexion of the Leg at the Hip)

This exercise is usually done to work the lower abdominals. It is actually a flexion of the hip joint, and involves not only the abdominals, but all of the hip flexors as well. If you do alternating leg raises, it doesn't work the abdominals at all, but works the *iliopsoas* muscles instead. The best way to do this one is to hang between parallel bars (or inside a vertical leg raise bench, such as those made by Dynacam and Paramount). You can support yourself on your hands, with your arms straight, or you can bend your arms at the elbow and support yourself by resting on your armpits. Lift the legs by flexing (bending) the knee and flexing or bending the hips. Your knees should remain bent (so as to take pressure off the lower back), and you should continue to raise your knees as high as you can. Do the motion slowly and don't swing the legs up. If the exercise is too easy for you, attach weights to your ankles or feet.

Hip Extension (Extension of the Leg at the Hip)

There's no popular name for this one either, which means that it too is often omitted in workouts. Lie on the floor on your back. Bend your knees and bring your heels as close to your buttocks as you can. Raise the pelvis vertically while you are resting on your shoulders and feet.

Your back will arch, giving your *erector spinae* a workout. Your *gluteus maximus,* or hip muscles, will contract and extend the hip. If the exercise is too easy, lay a 25-pound plate on your stomach when you do the movement. Don't let it slide down and hit you on the chin.

Squats are still the best exercise for the *gluteus maximus.* If you really want to give the glutes a workout, do full squats or deep knee bends, going all the way down until the backs of your heels touch your buttocks. The first several inches of upward movement is all glutes.

Hip thrust (extension of the leg at the hip).

Flexion and extension of the leg at the hip on a Hydra-Fitness machine.

You can also work the hip flexors and extensors with such machines as the Hydra-Fitness Hip Flexion/Extension and the Nautilus, Paramount, and Dynacam hip and back machines. Low pulley stations will work out the hip extensors. Stand facing the machine, attach the collar to your ankle, and lift the leg to the back away from the machine. For hip flexion, lie on the floor with your head away from the machine. Attach the collar to your ankle, and flex the hip and knee at the same time as you pull the cable toward your head with your thigh flexor muscles.

Let's move on now to the muscles of the "core." You will recall our discussion of them in the chapter on pretraining.

THE CORE MUSCLES

These are the *rectus abdominis,* external and internal obliques, the *erector spinae,* and the *iliopsoas* muscles. The abs run up the front, and flex the spine forward. The *erector spinae* run up the back and extend and hyperextend the spine. The obliques give you lateral spinal flexion, and the *iliopsoas* muscles flex the thigh at the hip and the hip at the thigh. To neglect these muscles is to neglect the muscles from which all torso movements generate.

In sports such as karate, in which twisting movements are made by the torso as a "kickoff" for fist and foot techniques, the core muscles are the originators of the movement. For example, when performing the right-hand lunge punch in karate, the initial muscles to contract are the left side external obliques as you start to lift the right foot from the floor. During the step as the hands and arms are held in position to fire off a punch, the core muscles stabilize the torso. When the punch is thrown, at the point of impact the instantaneous contraction of all the muscles begins in the core and radiates out to all the limbs.

We have seen bodybuilders and powerlifters who neglect the core muscles. They usually have weak lower backs, a lack of stability in the bench press and squat, and do not have well-defined obliques.

We've already talked about exercises for these muscles in the chapter on pretraining. Now, let's add some resistance and build some strength.

ABDOMINALS

The purpose of the abdominals is to shorten the distance between the *symphysis pubis* and the *sternum.* Situps, therefore, are only marginally effective for abdominal work, since the abs finish their contraction during the first few inches of the movement. The following exercises will isolate the abs and give them the workout they need.

Upper Abdominal Crunch (Spinal Flexion)

Lie on the floor with your feet on a bench. Your knees should be bent at a 90° angle. Place your hands at your temples. Don't put them behind your head. If you do, you'll tend to help yourself up with your arms. Concentrate on the abs themselves, and don't think about contracting any other muscles. Curl your body up and bring the shoulders off the floor. Continue the body curl until you feel a full contraction in the abs. Hold for a count of 3, then slowly lower your body back to the floor. This will concentrate the work load on the upper abdominals. When you can do 20 reps, drop back down to 10 reps and hold a 10-pound plate on your chest just under your chin.

Lower Abdominal Crunch (Spinal Flexion)

Assume the same position on the floor as you did for the upper abdominal crunch. This time, instead of lifting your shoulders off the floor, keep the shoulders on the floor and lift the hips. Do not use the legs to lever the hips upward. Let your toes or heels rest lightly on the bench, and bring the hips off the floor with the abs alone. It will take a little practice, but the results are worth it. When you can do 20 reps with no trouble, drop back to 10 reps and hold a 10-pound plate flat against your legs with the edge of the plate resting on your *symphysis pubis* bone. It might be a good idea to use a towel for padding.

Double Crunch (Spinal Flexion)

This exercise combines the two described immediately above. It should be divided into four distinct movements:

Upper abdominal crunch (spinal flexion).

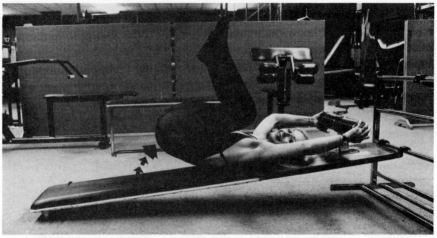

Lower abdominal crunch (spinal flexion).

1. Lift the shoulders off the floor
2. Lift the hips off the floor
3. Lower the shoulders back down to the floor
4. Lower the hips back to the floor

If you can do 20 of these, you need to add weight. Pull a barbell plate off the rack (from 10 to 45 pounds, depending on how strong you are), lie on the floor in the position described above, and hold the barbell plate with your outstretched arms so that it is parallel to the floor with the edge touching the tops of your knees. Hold the plate by the edges. Keep your elbows straight, but not locked. Then do the double crunch as you would with no weight. See the photograph on page 72.

Leg Raises (Hip Flexion)
See page 116 for a description of how to do the leg raise. If you want to work the abs, raise both legs at the same time. If you want to work your *iliopsoas* muscles, raise the legs one at a time, alternating from one to the other. Your legs should pass each other when they are at about a 45° angle from the floor. See the photograph on page 121.

There is a great deal of controversy about how to work the abs. Some bodybuilders recommend an hour of situps a day, while others work their abs the same way they work their other muscles. One thing is certain: if you want your abs to be strong, you have to add weight when you do situps. Being able to do situps or crunches for an hour at a time will not give your abs the kind of explosive strength that you need, for example, when doing the karate lunge punch. Further, you'll need gen-

Alternating leg raise (flexion of the leg at the hip).

uine strength, not endurance, when you use the abs to help stabilize the body while doing squats, bench presses, and deadlifts. It goes without saying that if you are training for sports movements, the abs need to be strong as well as conditioned for endurance.

Current orthodoxy has it that you can't get definition in the abs by doing lots of ab work; "cuts," as they are called, are the result of diet. Yet hardly a month passes by without at least one of the muscle magazines running an article about how you can "chisel out" your abdominals by doing certain exercises.

Some people achieve abdominal definition in a hurry. Others take longer. Try high reps and low reps and decide for yourself when you assess the results. But remember: if you want your abs to be strong, you're going to have to use some resistance. Nautilus has a new abdominal machine that is fun to use and effective once you get the hang of using your abs to do the work instead of your arms. If your gym has one of the new machines, give it a try. Grasp the handles above your head with both hands, and put your shins behind the footpads. Use a light weight at first until you learn to isolate the abs. The machine is pin-loaded so that changing resistance is simple. When you do the movement, try to keep your shoulder joints rigid—don't let your upper arm bones move within the joint. This will help you to isolate the abs.

EXTERNAL OBLIQUES

Many people do endless twists with a bar, a barbell, or a broomstick in an effort to grind away the fat that lies on top of the external obliques. Twisting motions with a weight on your back should be done while seated on a bench or the floor, in order to immobilize the hips. Otherwise, you'll simply twist the hips instead of twisting the torso.

The resistance that you encounter when doing twists is at the end of each twisting movement, when you have to overcome the momentum of the movement and start back in the opposite direction. At the start of a twist in either direction, you have to overcome the inertia of the bar or broomstick. A broomstick doesn't have much mass, so it's not very hard to start a twisting motion when that's all you're using. On the other hand, a barbell, because it has more mass, gathers more momentum. The result is that if you use enough weight to give you some inertial resistance, the resistance will peak abruptly at the extremes of the range of motion. Unless your obliques are already well developed, you run the risk of injuring your spine, since it is largely the vertebrae themselves that are stopping the twisting motion at the end of the range.

Twists with a broomstick are, therefore, largely a waste of time except for the massaging action that they perform. Twists with a heavier bar can be dangerous. The danger that you risk with a bar also exists for twisting machines if you are not careful. It's better to have a resistance to move against that is constant through the range of motion instead of just at each end. *The resistance should also be applied on the line that the motion traverses.* If you are sitting on the floor holding a bar across your back, the bar will be parallel to the floor. To work the obliques *the resistance should also be parallel to the floor.* With a loaded barbell, the weight is trying to move toward the floor, not parallel to it. You'll meet some resistance when you try to twist, simply because of the mass of the bar, but the resistance is neither consistent nor easily calculated.

There are several ways to get around this problem, and give the obliques a workout.

Pelvic Rolls (Spinal Rotation)

Lie on the floor on your back. Bend your legs at the knees and flex your thighs at the hips so that your thighs are in a line perpendicular to the floor. Stretch your arms out to the sides until they are at a 90° angle to the body, with the elbows straight. Roll your pelvis to the right until the side of your leg touches the floor. Then roll in the other direction until the side of the other leg touches the floor. This movement will

Pelvic roll (spinal rotation).

work the obliques for the first 45° of motion from the floor upwards. If this is not enough of a workout for your obliques, try it with the knees straight so that the entire leg is perpendicular to the floor. This will give you less leverage, with the result that the movement will be considerably harder to do. If you still aren't getting enough workout, put on ankle weights or iron shoes. If you get into really heavy weights, you will have to get some friends to sit on your arms to keep the rest of your body from rotating when you do the movement. Be careful with this exercise. Few people have well-developed obliques, and it is easy to pull muscles if you're not in shape.

Torso Rolls (Spinal Rotation)

This one is the converse of pelvic rolls. Lie on the floor on your back next to the low pulley station of a multistation machine (such as the ones made by Paramount, Universal, etc.), with your right side toward the machine. Your body should be in a line perpendicular to the direction in which the cable moves. Reach across your body with your left hand and grasp the cable handle. Place your right hand across the top of your left hand and grasp your left forearm. You should be positioned so that your elbows are bent at 90° angles, and your forearms are held tightly against your body just under the rib cage. Immobilize the hips with a strap, a weight, or a friend, so that your pelvis will not move when you rotate the upper body. Then rotate your body to the left, pulling against the cable. Don't pull with your arm, but instead think of your arm and hand as a hook to hold the cable handle. Do the pulling with the left oblique. Do 10 reps and change positions for the other side.

Torso roll (spinal rotation).

Twistaway Tension Band Twists

When Bob Gajda, former Mr. America, Mr. U.S.A., and Mr. Universe, was at the Sports Fitness Institute in Chicago, he found an ingenious solution to the problem of adding resistance to the twist. He placed the gym's Dynacam Twistaway machine close to a wall, mounted an eyebolt to the wall and an eyescrew to the machine's rotating disc (on which the user places his or her feet), and looped one of Ira Hurley's Unique Tension Bands through the bolts. The result was a Twistaway that provided progressive resistance throughout the range of twisting motion. The people who were serious about working their obliques loved it, because they realized that Gajda's solution worked. The ones who thought they were grinding the fat away always took the Tension Band off the machine, so that they could get a more dramatic twisting action. If your club has one of these machines, try to convince the owners that the addition of a Tension Band or some surgical tubing will make the machine doubly effective. We doubt that they'll listen, but if they do, you will have gained an effective piece of equipment.

Side Leans (Lateral Spinal Flexion)

This is an old favorite for those who want to build strength in the obliques. If you're fat and want to use side leans to tone up the muscles, you may find that your obliques develop in size very rapidly, with the result that the fat does not come off but is merely pushed out more. If

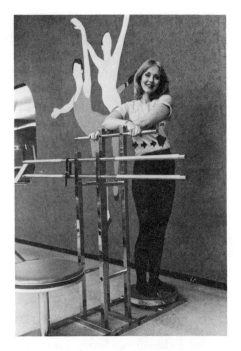

Standing twist (spinal rotation) on a Dynacam Twistaway machine.

Seated twist (spinal rotation) on a Dynacam Twistaway.

you are more concerned about strength than the way you look, then by all means do side leans. Use a dumbbell to do the exercise. Stand with your feet about shoulder-width apart, with a dumbbell in one hand. Don't use two dumbbells at the same time, or one will cancel out the weight of the other. Bend the torso to the side at the waist as far as you can go and still stay in a vertical plane to the side. It's a negative or eccentric movement on the way down, and a positive or concentric movement on the way up. It will build strength as well as size in the obliques. If you want to shift the load to the back side of the obliques, do the same movement, but do it so that the body moves forward as well as to the side. Do 10 to one side, then do 10 reps to the other. See the photograph on page 73.

ERECTOR SPINAE

We discussed spinal hyperextensions in the pretraining chapter. If you've been doing hyperextensions on the Roman chair, you're ready to add some resistance and build up that lower back. There are several other exercises for the erectors, so let's cover them all.

Spinal Extension, Hyperextension

When the spine is straight, it is extended. When it is curved to the front, it is flexed, and when it is arched to the back, it is hyperextended. You can do hyperextensions while lying on your stomach on the floor or on a bench, or while lying face down on a Roman chair bench. Many people prefer the Roman chair bench, because they can bend at the waist and hang down so that their upper body is perpendicular to the floor while their legs are parallel to the floor. They then swing upwards until their spine is first extended and then hyperextended. It should be noted that unless you relax the spinal muscles when the body is perpendicular to the floor, the spine will remain hyperextended throughout the movement. Actually, spinal hyperextensions on a Roman chair are isometric: the spinal muscles contract and hold the contraction throughout the movement upward, keeping the spine in the same position throughout the movement. Thus, once the spinal muscles have hyperextended the spine, the rest of the movement is made by the hip and hamstring muscles. Try it and you'll see what we mean. If you want to isolate the spinal muscles and give them a workout while moving the spine through a range of motion, try relaxing the back muscles while contracting the abdominals before you start the upward swing into hyperextension. This can be done on the floor or on a bench, with someone holding your legs down. If you do this exercise on a Roman chair,

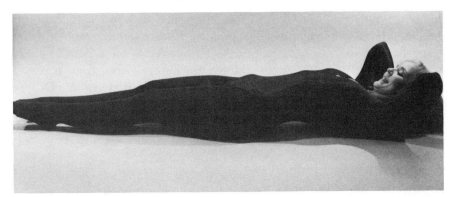

Spinal extension.

Extension (RLC) and hyperextension (VBC) of the spine.

be sure to keep your arms pulled back behind your back, elbows straight and locked, hands together. Bunch up your upper back muscles. This will keep your spine straight while you do the movement and will prevent injuries that might result from side-to-side movements. If you want to add weight, don't put a barbell plate behind your head. This puts too much of a load on the lower back. Instead, grasp a dumbbell (a light one at first) with both hands and lift it off the floor as you pull up into an extended or hyperextended position. You can drop the dumbbell any time you feel too much strain, and you can shift the dumbbell back toward your pelvis in order to take the leverage off your lower back. Spinal extensions and hyperextensions on a Roman chair bench are controversial. Some trainers absolutely forbid their trainees to do extensions and limit them to isometric hyperextensions. Others are equally vehement that hyperextensions damage the spine and that extensions are the only way to work the spinal erector muscles. Try both ways, be cautious at the slightest suggestion of pain, and see which way works best for you.

Stiff-Legged Dead Weight Lift
(Spinal Extension, Hyperextension)

This is another controversial one. Stand erect, holding a barbell in front of you, elbows straight, hands pronated. Bend forward at the waist while keeping the knees locked. Go down until the barbell almost touches the floor, then come back up. It's obvious why this one is controversial: such a movement puts tremendous pressure on the lower back, in the spine as well as in the muscles. Many trainers advise their trainees not to do the lift. We agree wholeheartedly. While some people have the lever system to do the lift with huge poundages without risk of injury, others will injure and reinjure themselves until they have chronic back pain. Don't take the chance. There are other, better ways to work the lower back. We recommend that you omit the stiff-legged dead weight lift and do regular dead lifts or spinal hyperextensions.

Regular Deadlift (Spinal Extension, Hyperextension)

There are great differences between the regular deadlift and the stiff-legged dead weight lift described above. In the regular dead weight lift, one hand is supinated and the other is pronated. This enables you to maintain a far better grip than you would with both hands pronated. When the lift is done, the legs are bent at the knees, so that the initial upward thrust is provided by the legs, not by the lower back alone. The back comes into the lift, but as part of a coordinated effort of legs and back. The feet can be placed about shoulder width apart, so that the arms come down on the outside of the legs (regular style) or the feet can be placed wide apart, so that the arms come down between the legs (Sumo style). The former works the quadriceps primarily, and the thigh adductors secondarily. The latter style seems to distribute the load more evenly between the adductors and the quads. Both styles of lifting also involve the hamstrings and the glutes heavily. If you want to get a hyperextension movement from the regular deadlift, simply arch your back at the top of the lift.

Regular dead weight lift, sumo style (spinal extension, extension of the leg at the knee and at the hip), starting position.

Regular dead weight lift, completion of movement.

Good Morning Exercise (Spinal Extension)

This movement is similar to the stiff-legged dead weight lift, but with important differences. In this one, the barbell is held across the shoulders instead of in front of you at arm's length. The forward movement is the same, but since the weight is on the shoulders, you have more freedom to make compensatory backward movements with the pelvis to relieve the strain on the lower back. It can still hurt your lower back, so do the lift with extreme caution, especially if you add weight.

Dumbbell Swings (Spinal Extension)

Hold a dumbbell with both hands (your hands will overlap), bend at the waist, and swing the dumbbell from between your legs in an arc until it is over your head.

ILIOPSOAS MUSCLES

The *iliopsoas* muscles are actually a combination of the *iliac* and *psoas* muscles. They lie alongside each other, and share functions. Hence they are usually referred to as a muscle group by the term *iliopsoas*. These muscles flex the thigh against the pelvis by bringing the legs up as they do on the vertical leg raise bench. They also flex the pelvis

Good morning exercise (flexion and extension of the spine).

against the thigh, as they do when you do straight-legged situps. Consequently, you can work the *iliopsoas* with several exercises.

Straight-Legged Situp (Hip Flexion)

Sit on a slantboard or on the floor with your knees extended, legs straight. Anchor your feet under something (or somebody) so that your legs won't fly up when you do the movement. Put your hands either in front of you at chest level, or behind your neck. Sit up until you are almost perpendicular to the floor, then lower yourself back down. If you need some resistance, hold a barbell plate across your chest. This exercise will put a tremendous load on the lower back, so be careful. If after a few workout sessions you develop pain in your lower back or pain that radiates across the tops of the pelvic bone (along the "crest of Ilium"), abandon the exercise.

Alternating Leg Raise (Hip Flexion)

We discussed this movement on page 120. If you want to relieve some of the pressure on the lower back, bend the knees slightly. See the photograph on page 121. These leg raises can be done either on the floor, on a bench, or on a vertical leg raise bench. The latter is the most effective.

Leg Raises (Hip Flexion)

Some exercise physiologists maintain that the *iliopsoas* bring the legs up when you do alternating leg raises, but that the abdominals bring them up when you do both legs at the same time. While it is true that it

Straight-legged situp (spinal flexion).

is possible to do alternating leg raises without contracting the abs (you have to concentrate on it, because the abs have a natural tendency to contract in a hip flexing movement), it is equally true that the *iliopsoas* can contract when you do leg raises with both legs at the same time. See the photograph on page 116. The function of the *iliopsoas* group is to flex the thigh against the hip and to flex the hip against the thigh. That means that it is activated when you raise the legs while the torso is stationary, and when you raise the torso while the legs are stationary. If you want to work the *iliopsoas* and the abdominals at the same time, do both legs at the same time. If you want to concentrate on the *iliopsoas*, concentrate on *not* using your abs and do alternating leg raises.

Now, let's proceed up the back to the *trapezius*, the *rhomboids*, and the other muscles and muscle groups that make up the upper back.

THE UPPER BACK AND CHEST

Most athletes neglect the development of the upper back. It's not as visible (to them) as big pectorals and big arms, and it tends to get lost in the shuffle from the bench press to the curling machine.

Upper back development, however, is essential for any person who plans to participate in a sport. All movements that involve pulling an object toward the body involve the upper back to some degree. Further, without upper back development, the upper portion of the spine is left without the double column of muscles that it needs for support.

The movements of the upper back involve the *trapezius,* the *rhomboideus,* the *levator scapulae, teres major, infraspinatus, supraspinatus,* and *latissimus* (although the *latissimus* constitutes the bulk of the middle back, its origins range from thoracic, lumbar, and sacral vertebrae and it inserts all the way up into the upper arm bone, or *humerus*).

The chest consists of the *pectoralis major* and *minor.* Movements that involve pushing to the front or pushing up (as on parallel bars) work these muscles. The lower pecs respond to parallel bar dips and bench presses with the back arched. The upper pecs respond well to incline bench presses. There are a variety of dumbbell exercises for the chest also, which we will cover below.

The muscles listed above move the shoulders to the front, upwards, downwards, and to the back. The forward movements are protractions, the backward ones are retractions, the upward movements are elevations, and the downward ones are depressions.

We discussed these movements in detail in the pretraining chapter. Now let's add some exercises as well as some weight or resistance.

Shoulder Shrugs (Shoulder Elevation and Retraction)

Grasp a barbell with both hands, palms pronated, elbows straight.

Shoulder shrug (elevation of the shoulder girdle).

Use your arms only as "rods" with hooks (the hands) to hold the barbell. Don't do any of the lifting with the arms themselves. This caveat means that you should not bend the elbows as you bring the weight up. Shrug your shoulders and try to touch your earlobes with your lateral deltoids. You won't be able to do it, but this is the direction that the movement should take. Some people rotate the shoulder girdle when they do the lift. Others strongly advise against it, because of the danger of injury to the shoulder joint. Many people can rotate the shoulder girdle during this lift with no ill effects. Others should stay away from the movement.

If you're one of the lucky ones, here's how it's done: When you reach the top of the lift and your shoulders are as close to your earlobes as they will go, retract the shoulders (pull them to the back) and let the weight down with the shoulders back and the chest thrown out. As you repeat the movement, you will be moving the shoulders in a vertical circle. If you can't do the circular motion without problems, you should still pull the weight up and back in a straight line, in order to get a full contraction of the *trapezius* muscles (traps). If you can't handle as much weight as you want in this lift, try holding the bar with a deadlift grip (one hand supinated and one hand pronated) for several reps, then reverse the grip in order to give the traps a balanced workout.

Shoulder Shrugs with Dumbbells
(Shoulder Elevation and Retraction)

Do the same movements as described immediately above, but this time do them with a pair of dumbbells held down by the sides.

Retractions

Lie face down on a bench that is high enough to allow you to reach down to a barbell at arm's length. Don't bend your elbows. Bring the barbell off the floor by using the upper back muscles alone. You will work up to respectable poundages in a hurry with this one, so a word of caution is in order. If you have ever had a chest injury, such as a broken or cracked rib, you should remember that you are putting considerable pressure against the rib cage when you do this lift. Be sure to place enough padding between your chest and the bench to distribute the load over a large area.

Protractions

Lie on your back on a bench or on the floor, with a barbell held at arm's length above you. Your arms should be perpendicular to the floor, as if you were going to do bench presses. Instead of letting the barbell down to the chest, contract the pectorals and push the barbell toward the ceiling. Keep the elbows locked (or at least solidly stabilized by simultaneous contractions of the biceps and triceps). Try to lift your shoulders off the floor or bench when you do this lift. The range of motion is only a few inches, so don't expect anything dramatic in the way of movement.

Shoulder Depressions

Grasp the handle of an overhead pulley cable as if you were going to do pulldowns behind the neck. Instead of bending the elbows as you would in the pulldown, keep your arms straight and pull the shoulder girdle down. Again, there will be only a few inches of motion here, so don't expect a lot of movement. Concentrate on doing all the pulling with your *latissimus dorsi,* the lower part of the *rhomboideus,* and the *pectoralis major.*

Partial Parallel Bar Dip (Shoulder Depressions)

Hang between parallel bars, resting either on your hands or on your elbows and forearms. If you have access to a vertical leg raise bench, you can rest comfortably on your elbows with your forearms on the padded boards. Allow your body to sag downward while keeping your

Parallel bar dip (depression of the shoulder girdle, extension of the arm at the elbow).

arms stationary. Then raise your body, using the muscles of the shoulder girdle alone.

Parallel Bar Dip (Elbow Extension, Shoulder Depression)

Parallel bar dips will develop the triceps as well as the lower pectorals. Hang between parallel bars, resting on your hands. Bend your elbows and lower yourself down between the bars until your elbows are almost fully flexed. Then raise yourself back up to the starting position.

Bench Press (Pectoral and Anterior Deltoid Contraction, Shoulder Flexion and Protraction)

The bench press is probably the most popular exercise in any gym. You will work up to respectable weights pretty quickly, and it is a good "social" exercise: you should never do it without a spotter to help you if you can't make that last rep back to the rack. Lie on your back on a bench press bench or rack. The barbell will be on the rack. Extend your arms upwards, grasp the barbell, and lift it off the rack. Your back should be slightly arched when you begin the lift. Lower the barbell until it touches your chest. You will have to find your own natural "groove" (the path of motion in which you can exert the greatest amount of power). When the bar touches your chest, lift it back upward until your elbows are extended again. Use a light weight at first. It's easy to injure your elbows in this one if you're not used to handling heavy weights. As you develop strength in the lift, don't go overboard

Bench press (extension of the arms at the elbow, forward flexion of the arm at the shoulder, protraction of the shoulder girdle).

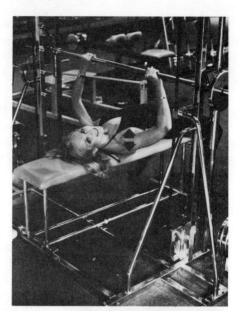

**Bench press on a Paramount
floor-type bench press machine.
Courtesy, Al Phillips,
Chicago Health Club.**

Bench press/row on a Hydra-Fitness total power machine.

and try to lift more than your joints can handle. Ralph injured both his
right shoulder and his right elbow doing partial movements with about
50 pounds over poundages with which he could do full movements. The

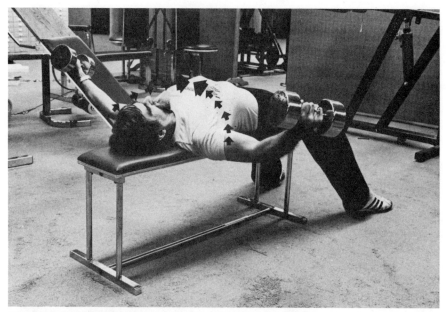

Flyes (forward adduction of the arms at the shoulders, protraction of the arms at the shoulders).

injury entailed four months of rehabilitation before he could get back up to the poundages he was using with no trouble before the injury.

Flyes (Pectoral Contraction, Shoulder Flexion and Protraction)

This exercise is named after the motion that it mimics: flapping the wings. Lie on a horizontal bench (or an incline bench if you want to concentrate on the upper pectorals). Swing two dumbbells up toward the ceiling, then let them down to the sides until they are below the line of the body. Then take them back up again, without making a pressing movement with the triceps. Do all of the work with the pectorals and the anterior deltoids. You may do it with the palms facing at the beginning, or with the hands pronated. Keep the elbows slightly bent in order to take the pressure off the elbow joint. Variations of this lift include straight-arm flyes (with the elbows fully extended) and bent-arm flyes, with the elbows bent at about a 45° angle.

Incline Bench Press (Pectoral and Anterior Deltoid Contraction, Shoulder Girdle Protraction)

This exercise is done the same way that the regular bench press is done, except that you use an incline bench instead of a horizontal

 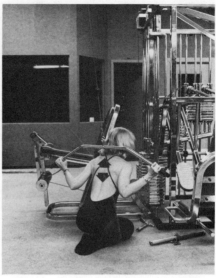

Incline bench press (forward adduction of the arms at the shoulders, extension of the arms at the elbows).

Pulldown behind the neck (vertical adduction of the arms at the shoulders, flexion of the arms at the elbows) at a Paramount pulley station.

bench. Be careful: you won't be able to handle nearly as much weight in this one as you do in the regular bench press.

Pulldowns behind the Neck (Scapular Rotation, *Latissimus Dorsi* Contraction)

Position yourself below an overhead pulley station on a multistation machine. Reach up and grasp the cable handle with a wide grip. Pull the handle down until it touches the back of your neck at the top of the *trapezius* muscles.

Pulldowns to the Chest (Scapular Rotation, *Latissimus Dorsi* Contraction)

Position yourself as you did for the behind-the-neck pulldowns. Grasp the bar or handle with your hands supinated instead of pronated. Pull the handle down to the top of your chest.

Low Pulley Work (*Latissimus Dorsi* Contraction)

Sit in front of a low pulley station on a multistation machine. You'll need a pulley handle that allows you to grasp it with your palms facing

Pulldown to the chest (extension of
the arms at the shoulders, flexion
of the arms at the elbows) on a
Nautilus pullover machine.

Low pulley rowing (extension of the arms at the shoulders, flexion
of the arms at the elbows) at a Paramount low-pulley station.

each other. Keep your back slightly arched for strength in the lower
back, and pull the handle to a position directly in front of your stomach.
The elbows will bend as you bring the handle back. Keep the elbows
close to the sides. When you let the handle go back to the starting position, allow your shoulders to protract so that you will get a full range of

motion when you pull back again. Don't allow your back to bow. Keep the spinal erectors contracted.

Many machine companies manufacture various pieces of equipment for back and chest work. Almost all the multistation machines such as Dynacam, Paramount, and Universal feature bench press stations, low pulley stations, and overhead pulley stations. Nautilus has an upper torso machine for shoulder girdle elevations and *latissimus dorsi* contractions, as well as another machine for pulley pulldowns behind the neck and to the chest. Some companies also make seated bench press simulators, such as the Nautilus Double Chest machine and Dynacam's Chest and Bust Bench Press machine. Remember, these machines offer excellent isolation work for the chest and anterior deltoids, but do not give you a workout of the collateral stabilizing muscles the way that regular free weight bench pressing would.

Pullover (*Pectoral* and *Latissimus* Contraction)

Lie on a bench on your back. Hold a dumbbell at arm's length with both hands over your chest. Bend the elbows slightly and rotate your upper arms medially at the shoulder joint. This position will bring the lats into play with more force. Lower the dumbbell in an arc toward your head until it almost touches the top of your head. As you become more flexible, you will be able to lower it past the horizontal line of the bench on which you are lying. Don't overdo it at first, however, or you

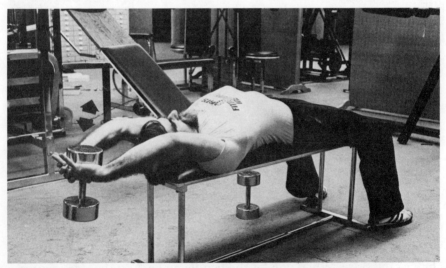

Pullover with a dumbbell (extension of the arms at the shoulders).

may injure your shoulders. Bring the dumbbell back up in an arc until your arms are about 45° from the floor. Repeat the lowering action. As you lower the dumbbell, take a deep breath. Let it out only after you have started back up. Don't use too much weight, or you won't be able to do the exercise in good form. You'll find that the more you bend your arms at the elbows, the more weight you will be able to handle. Nautilus, Dynacam, and Paramount all manufacture pullover machines that more or less allow you to duplicate this exercise. Remember, however, that your lever system may not match the machine's, so be cautious.

DELTOIDS

Let's turn now to the deltoids. In the pretraining chapter, you learned that there are several possible movements involving the shoulder joint. These movements have popular names. Abduction of the arms is called a lateral raise. It works the lateral deltoids. Flexion to the front is called a forward raise, and involves the anterior deltoid. Hyperextension (a movement to the back while standing erect) is not done as an exercise, but bentover raises do involve a hyperextension movement. The arms are held not at the side but perpendicular to the line of the torso.

Medial and lateral rotation are rarely done as exercises, which is a shame because the movements are vital to the development of the collateral stabilizing muscles in the shoulder. See pages 85–89 for a complete description of these movements. All you have to do to make the pretraining exercises part of your basic training program is to add weight in the form of heavier dumbbells or pulleys.

Do the movements in strict form, and don't worry about heavy poundages. These are isolation exercises for the deltoids and the muscles around the rotator cuff of the upper arm bone, so your poundages will not be great. Try Nautilus' and Dynacam's shoulder machines for a variation on the dumbbell or cable work.

Below are two additional exercises for the deltoids. They are compound exercises, and involve the triceps and the anterior and the lateral head of the deltoids.

Military Press (Elbow Extension, Shoulder Abduction)

Stand erect, holding a barbell or dumbbells in your hands at shoulder level, and at the top of your chest. Extend your arms overhead until the elbows almost lock out. The barbell will move in a line that is slightly diagonal to the floor, and will reach a point overhead at the end of the lift that is in line with the back of the head. It is in the first part of the

Military press (elevation of the shoulder girdle, extension of the arms at the elbow, abduction of the arms at the shoulders).

Seated press (elevation of the shoulder girdle, extension and abduction of the arms at the shoulders) at a Paramount Press station.

lift that the anterior deltoids are worked. The lateral deltoids are brought into full contraction at the end of the lift. This exercise also works the *serratus magnus* muscles under the arms.

Seated Press behind the Neck
(Elbow Extension, Shoulder Abduction)

Do this one while you are seated on a bench. If you are handling heavy poundages, slide a bench under a squat rack, straddle the bench, and take the barbell off the rack. Sit down on the bench, get a wide grip on the bar, and do the lift. The press behind the neck concentrates on the deltoids. You may want to get a training partner to sit on the bench with his or her back braced against yours in order to stabilize the torso during the lift. When you sit down on the bench, do it carefully and slowly. A sudden jolt with a heavy weight on your shoulder could result in lower back injuries.

In both the standing press and the seated press, keep the lower back muscles firmly contracted, so that you will have a solid foundation of muscle on both sides of the spine. This position will help you do the lift symmetrically, and it will protect the spine from injury.

Both of these lifts can be done on Paramount's and Dynacam's Floor-type Bench Press machine. These machines feature a bar with hooks that catch on pegs along the vertical shafts on either side of the machine. Rotate the bar, release the hooks, and do the exercise. When you're finished, rotate the bar back and snag the hooks on the pegs. You don't need a spotter with either machine, and you will be able to change poundages easily. You will not, however, work the muscles that stabilize the shoulder as much as you would if you used free weights alone.

Lateral Raise (Abduction of the Arm at the Shoulder)
Holding a dumbbell in each hand, stand erect with arms by the sides. Raise the arms in an arc out to the side and slightly backward while bending very slightly forward at the waist. The arms will find a natural stopping point if you do this one right.

Upright Rowing (Abduction of the Arm at the Shoulder, Elevation of the Shoulder Girdle)
Sit at a low pulley station, grasp the pulley handle with both hands, palms down, and close together on the bar. Bring the arms up and back so that the elbows are high and the pulley handle is close to your chin. Keep your back slightly arched (hyperextended) when you do this one. This exercise can also be done with a barbell. Stand erect, holding a barbell in front of you with the arms extended downward. Raise the barbell upwards, keeping the elbows high, so that the barbell ends its motion under your chin. You can involve the *trapezius* muscles by raising the barbell above the level of the chin.

TRICEPS AND BICEPS (ELBOW EXTENSION AND FLEXION)
As we move on down the arm, the next muscles to be developed are the triceps and the biceps. These muscles oppose each other on the front and back of the arm. The triceps are used in pushing movements, and the biceps are used in pulling movements. The triceps constitute about two-thirds of the mass of the upper arm, while the biceps and the *brachialis* (to the side and under the biceps) make up the other one-third. Here are exercises for these muscles; first the triceps, and then the biceps.

Military Press (Elbow Extension and Shoulder Abduction)
See the description and photo on pages 141–142.

Lateral raise (abduction of the arm at the shoulder).

Upright rowing with a barbell (abduction of the arm at the shoulder).

Upright rowing (flexion of the arms at the elbows, elevation of the shoulder girdle, abduction of the arms at the shoulders) at a Paramount low-pulley station.

Seated Press behind the Neck (Elbow Extension, Shoulder Abduction)

See pages 142–143 for a description and photo.

Bench Press (Elbow Extension, Shoulder Flexion, Pectoral Contraction)

See pages 135–137 for description and photos.

Pulley Pushdowns (Elbow Extension)

Stand in front of an overhead pulley station on a multistation exercise machine. Grasp the cable handle with both hands pronated. Keep the elbows close by the sides, and straighten the arm as you push the handle down toward the floor. See the photographs on page 105.

Kickbacks (Elbow Extension, Isometric Contraction of the Posterior Deltoid)

Stand erect, with a dumbbell in one hand. Bend at the waist until the torso is parallel to the floor. You may want to rest your forehead against a padded bench for support if you have lower back problems. Keep the upper arm by the side, parallel to the torso. Keep the elbow in one place, and don't let it move when you do the lift. Extend the arm backward until the elbow is straight. Don't swing the dumbbell back, but do the movement slowly and steadily.

French Curl (Elbow Extension)

The French curl is actually an extension movement, not a curl, but the popular misnomer has stuck for years. The movement can also be done while you are standing erect. Raise the upper arm until it is perpendicular to the floor and against the side of the head. Keep the upper arm stationary (you can brace it with the other arm by reaching across the top of your head) and raise and lower a dumbbell in an arc. These lifts are not as effective as kickbacks, since the tension is off the triceps about three-fourths of the way through the lift.

All the major machine companies manufacture some kind of triceps or elbow extension machine. Nautilus has an especially good one, which is pin-loaded for easy weight changes.

Standing Curls with a Barbell or Dumbbell (Elbow Flexion)

Stand erect, holding a barbell or dumbbell at arm's length so that the barbell crosses in front of you. If you use dumbbells, they will be to the

Kickback—extension of the arm at the elbow.

Seated triceps extension (extension of the arm at the elbow).

front and slightly to the sides. Keep the elbows stationary and the upper arms close to the sides. Raise the weight in an arc until it is about 6 inches from the top of your chest. Don't let the weight "fall" toward the chest, or the tension will be released.

Concentrated Curls (Elbow Flexion)

Sit on a bench with the feet wide apart. Grasp a dumbbell with one hand. Keep the elbow braced against the inside of the leg. Bring the weight up in an arc until it is as high as you can get it. Don't let the bracing leg move, and keep the elbow stationary.

Incline Bench Curls (Elbow Flexion)

Lie back on an incline bench, with a dumbbell in each hand. Bring the weights up in an arc as high as you can get them. This exercise prevents help from other muscles, and also prevents you from swinging the dumbbells up.

Supinating or Zottman Curls (Elbow Flexion—Involves Both the Biceps and the *Brachialis*)

This exercise can be performed on an incline bench or while standing erect. Instead of starting the upward movement with the hands supi-

Military curl (flexion of the arm at the elbow).

Concentrated curl (flexion of the arm at the elbow) with a dumbbell.

nated, start it with the hands pronated and rotate the forearms as you bring the weight up in an arc. See the photographs on page 82.

The last set of arm exercises is for the wrists. See pages 79–80 for a complete description of the movements.

SPECIAL EQUIPMENT

In addition to the resistance exercises described in this chapter, there are a few other exercises that enhance performance in recreational sports. Here are a few of them:

Kineaesthetic Primer Board

The kineaesthetic primer board is a small teeter-totter board, about a foot and a half square, with either a single plank or a square post on the bottom. To use the board, you have to learn to keep the core muscles flexed, and the body perfectly straight. You can tilt to the front and back, or you can tilt to the sides, depending on how you place your feet on the board.

Practice standing on the board until you can stand completely still,

Incline bench curl (flexion of the arm at the elbow).

Squatting on a kinaesthetic primer board as a coordination exercise.

with no bobbles or false moves. You'll find that you will greatly improve your balance. Some people practice the squat with light weight while standing on the kineaesthetic primer board.

Mini-Trampolines

These are small trampolines, about 2 feet in diameter. They stand about a foot off the floor, and can be carried with you on trips. They are great for strengthening the ankles and feet, and stabilizing the knees and hips. Try changing the position of your feet while you're bouncing. The mini-tramp will also help you with your balance.

Jump Boxes

These are usually adjustable for heights ranging from a foot all the way up to 4 or 5 feet. They have two functions: to provide practice in developing explosive jumping power useful in sports such as volleyball, tennis, and basketball; and to provide practice in landing from a jump.

It's the latter function that is usually neglected in training. Rick Butler and Kay Rogness, former trainers at the Sports Fitness Institute in Chicago, and trainers for the National Champion Olympic-Style Women's Volleyball Team, include jump box training as an integral part of their intensive program. They especially stress the importance

Bob Gajda coaches Valerie on the balance beam.

of landing from a jump so that there is no sudden jarring or loss of balance. When you jump down off the box, bend your knees at the instant of impact. Practice so that you land "lightly" instead of with a thud. This training will improve not only your leg strength, resilience, and agility, but your timing as well.

Balance Beams

We mentioned the oscillating balance beam in the chapter on pretraining. It is also useful as a base for any sports movement. Learn to stand on the balance beam while you do side-to-side shifts, jumps, and pitches and catches. You'll be amazed at the improvement in balance, timing, and power.

Strength, Power, Stamina, and Endurance Training

First, let's define our terms, so we'll all be talking about the same things:

● *Strength* is defined in sports training as the ability of a muscle or muscle group to exert force against a resistance through a range of motion, without regard to time. The resistance can be anything: weights and the force of gravity, hydraulic cylinders, inertial reels, Tension Bands, surgical tubing, or another person. The resistance is overcome by the force generated by the muscles, and the limb that does the pushing or pulling moves through a range of motion. The muscles contract, the limb moves, the object offering the resistance moves, without regard to the amount of time it takes for all this to happen. The more force you can exert, the more *strength* you have.

• *Power* is defined as the ability of a muscle or muscle group to exert force against a resistance through a range of motion, within a specified length of time. The greater the weight and the faster the time, the more *power* you have. Again, the resistance can be anything that resists being moved.

• *Stamina* is defined as the ability to sustain the exertion of force against a resistance through a range of motion while performing successive and rapid repetitions of the motion. The length of time involved is usually not more than 30 or 40 seconds, and is related to the amount of time it takes for your muscles' anaerobic energy supply to be depleted. If you are not very athletic, you will not store a great deal of glycogen in your muscles themselves. If you've trained, on the other hand, your muscles will learn to store greater and greater amounts of glycogen, until you reach your natural limit. "Stamina," then, is a measure not only of the amount of force that you are capable of exerting, but also a measure of the ability of your muscles to store and use glycogen. The longer you can sustain rapid movements against greater and greater resistances, the more *stamina* you have.

• *Endurance* is defined as the ability of a muscle or muscle group to exert force against a resistance through a range of motion for an extended period of time. The rapidity of the movements is not a factor in estimated endurance (which is one of the differences between measurements of stamina and measurements of endurance). Trainers usually set 2 to 3 minutes as the minimum for endurance measurements. The longer you can do the movements against the resistance, the more *endurance* you have.

As you can see from the definitions, each of these kinds of physical activity makes slightly different demands on the muscles, in terms of stored energy and what is called "fiber recruitment." Fiber recruitment refers to your nervous system's ability to make the muscle fibers "fire" or contract. Here's how the different kinds of activity make different demands:

> *Strength* is a matter of the number of muscle fibers you have and the number of those fibers that can be recruited to exert force against a resistance.

Power is a matter of the number of muscle fibers you have and the number of those fibers that can be recruited in the shortest amount of time.

Stamina is a matter of the number of muscle fibers you have and your ability to recruit them repeatedly in maximum numbers over a period of 30 to 40 seconds.

Endurance is a matter of the number of muscle fibers you have, the number of those fibers that you can recruit, and your ability to recruit them repeatedly for extended periods of time, at least for a period of time greater then 2 or 3 minutes.

As you can see from these definitions and their implications, strength, power, and stamina make demands directly on the anaerobic energy supply in the muscles themselves, and endurance makes demands on the aerobic energy supply. Consequently, strength, power, and stamina training work the muscles, but do not train the cardiovascular system. Endurance training, on the other hand, works the cardiovascular system as well as the muscles themselves.

We've said earlier that the muscles are composed of two types of cells: white, fast-twitch fibers and red, slow-twitch fibers. The white fibers are the fibers that give us strength, power, and stamina. The red cells are the fibers that give us endurance. The white fibers are *anaerobic*, meaning that they do not use oxygen in the contractile phase. Red fibers are *aerobic*, meaning that they do use oxygen in their contractile phase. They both use oxygen in their recovery phase.

The only way you can train the cardiovascular system is to make demands on that system's capacity. Consequently, the only way that you can train the cardiovascular system is aerobically: by using the muscle fibers that demand oxygen to do their sustained work. This fact has caused many trainers to conclude erroneously that you can't train the cardiovascular system with weight training. A little reflection will show how wrong this conclusion is.

There is nothing magical about running or jogging. These activities require sustained effort over an extended period of time. Depending on which trainers you believe, cardiovascular training occurs when you are working at 60 (or 80) percent of your capacity for a period in excess of 20 (or 45) minutes.

Running is a high-repetition exercise movement, involving a small amount of resistance. If you run 5 miles, and you cover 3 feet every time you take a stride, you cover 6 feet every time you complete a cycle of putting first one leg and then the other in front. Simple arithmetic will show you that running 5 miles involves doing one set of 880 reps.

If you run 10 miles, you are doing one set of 1,760 reps. If you run 20 miles, you are doing one set of 3,520 reps, and so on. The leg muscles are the largest muscles in the body. Consequently, in addition to the white fibers, they have the largest number of red fibers in any single muscle group. Running or jogging is an efficient way of training the cardiovascular system because it recruits the greatest number of red fibers available in a single exercise movement. There are red fibers in the arms, too, but it would take you a lot longer to get the same amount of cardiovascular training if you worked the arms instead of the legs.

Cycling, skating, skiing, and a number of other sustained effort activities will give you cardiovascular training. Some are more efficient than others. That's why Dr. Kenneth Cooper, in his book *Aerobics*, offers a rating list in which a number of physical activities are graded according to the amount of cardiovascular training "points" they offer. The activities with the highest ratings are those that involve sustained movements of the legs. It makes sense.

What does not make sense is to conclude that resistance training is *never* aerobic. Resistance training becomes aerobic when you achieve your target pulse rate and sustain it for the period of time necessary (given your age and other factors) to condition the cardiovascular system.

You don't train aerobically when you do strength, power, or stamina work. You do train aerobically when you do endurance work, given the stipulations of capacity and pulse rate mentioned in the preceding paragraph. But you can train the entire muscular system (not just the legs) by using light weights and moving from one exercise to another, or one machine to another. In fact, circuit training was developed as a way to combine muscle toning and aerobic training.

There is no doubt that running, jogging, or cycling are the more efficient aerobic trainers, at least in the sense that you get the greatest amount of conditioning in the shortest amount of time. However, exercises that stress leg movements to the exclusion of other body movements (except for the balancing and coordination movements done by the arms and torso during running) are not necessarily the best kind of exercise for the body as a whole. While it is certainly true that many powerlifters are woefully short on endurance, it is equally true that many runners are woefully short on strength, power, and stamina.

Two cases in point will illustrate the problem. In a 1980 speech in Chicago, Dr. Cooper cited a former Mr. Texas who tried the treadmill at his testing center. The champion bodybuilder did not last 15 minutes. Dr. Cooper's interpretation was that bodybuilding did not give you cardiovascular conditioning. No mention was made about whether or not the former Mr. Texas was in competitive shape, still trained regularly, or had recently lost or gained bodyfat. Since training is specific, and bodybuilding is not necessarily aerobic, however, it makes sense that even if he had been in contest shape, he would not have done as well as would someone who ran or jogged regularly.

We work out three times a week at the Chicago Health Club. A friend of ours, who also works out at the club, can turn in mile after mile on the running track. Yet after only three machines, working with relatively light weights, he is always completely exhausted. He has neither strength, power, nor stamina.

This is the point that we would like to make. Training is indeed specific. If you want to be strong, you have to lift heavy weights or work against a strong resistance. If you want to become progressively stronger, you have to use progressively heavier and heavier poundages. If you want to train for power, you have to exert force against a resistance and do it in a hurry. If you want stamina, do rapid movements with as much weight as you can handle for 20 to 40 seconds. If you want endurance, go at it for an extended period of time.

Sports training involves conditioning your body so that you can perform well in the sport of your choice. If your sport is powerlifting, then all the running in the world won't help you in the bench press. If your sport is running, all the bench presses in the world won't help you make that last mile. If your sport is baseball, and if you play shortstop on the company team, you need strength, power, stamina, and endurance. Sports movements demand a total-body approach.

Some sports, however, have different demands. Baseball players are often notoriously out of shape, even at the height of the season. Football and soccer players, on the other hand, will drop like flies if they don't stay in shape. To stay in shape here means being in the kind of condition that it takes to play the game. Football players, for example, expend tremendous amounts of energy over short periods of time, with rests in between bouts. Basketball players are in constant motion. Baseball players sit in the dugout, take their turn at bat, then run around (or stand on) the bases. The demands on the cardiovascular system of a game like soccer is much greater than the demands of a game like baseball.

You must also remember that the pro ball players have a different set of goals from yours. Their game is their source of livelihood. Their performance is their ticket to staying in the profession. Everybody would rather be healthy than unhealthy, but when you are a professional *somadynamic*, when you play to win, and will and must do what you have to do to keep on winning, you are in a radically different ball game than if you are playing a game for the fun of it and to keep in shape.

The cardinal rule of any amateur, recreational player, or weekend athlete, should be: *don't do anything that would destroy your health for the sake of something that is supposed to be a recreational activity.*

Some trainers will tell you that strength training and endurance training are mutually exclusive. Don't believe them. If you are training for a title or for a new record poundage, you may find that endurance training on top of strength or power training may deplete your energy reserves to the point where your performance will suffer. But if you want simply to be above average in strength *and* endurance, there is no reason why you can't have both. We've been doing it for years. Valerie runs 3 to 5 miles three or four times a week, and on Monday, Wednesday, and Friday she weight trains with maximum and near-maximum poundages: heavy weights, low reps, training for power because she's become interested in it.

Certainly, as part of any general conditioning routine, we would recommend that you do not train in one direction to the exclusion of the others. You'll be healthier, happier, and more capable of doing all the kinds of physical activity that you like to do if you make your program as comprehensive as possible. This program will provide you with a solid foundation for whatever specialization you want to pursue.

The exercises in the pretraining chapter and in this basic training chapter will give you that foundation. You should add to the resistance exercises a consistent program of aerobic training, either on machines, with free weights, or on the running or jogging track. If you have problems with your feet, ankles, or knees, try a stationary bike. If you have biking trails handy that are not gauntlets between cabs and buses, ride your bike. But remember, if you want aerobic training, don't coast. Keep pedaling.

We've said that training is specific. Therefore, your goals should be specific, too. Here are a few pointers on various types of training.

STRENGTH TRAINING

Here the task is multiple. You must:

1. Build muscle tissue.
2. Train your muscles to contract properly on demand.
3. Recruit greater and greater numbers of muscle fibers each time you lift a weight or exert force against a resistance.
4. Develop the proper form in the exercises so that you will be able to make the maximum amount of progress in the least amount of time.

5. Develop a proper diet and mineral supplement program that will enable your muscles to build in strength and (if you're male) in size.

To accomplish these tasks, you need to do the following:

1. Begin a systematic program of resistance exercises, incorporating not more than 10 exercises per workout.
2. Work out at least three times a week (when you read in *Muscle Builder* magazine that Boyer Coe works out six days a week, twice a day, remember, he's getting ready for a bodybuilding contest, not training for strength).
3. Start your exercise program with 8 to 12 reps in movements that involve the arms and 12 to 14 reps in movements by the rest of the body.
4. Add 1 rep to the arm work and 2 reps to the other work every other workout. When you reach 16 to 18 reps for the arms and 18 to 20 reps for the rest of the body, drop back down and add weight. Do the movements *slowly* and in perfect form. Think of your body as a strength machine: no jerks and jumps. Keep it smooth and sure.
5. Continue to go through this cycle of adding reps, dropping reps, and adding weight for the first three months of training.
6. After three months of "background" muscle building, drop down to 3 reps on the lifts in which you want to specialize, and work up to 8 reps.
7. Start your program by doing one set only. After one month, add a set. After three months, do three sets.
8. Confine your early training to compound exercises such as squats, presses, bench presses, shoulder shrugs, etc., and leave the isolation stuff for later.
9. Maintain a good balanced diet, with the protein, carbohydrate, and fat levels outlined in the diet section.
10. Get at least 8 hours of sleep a night.
11. Cut out the alcohol and the tobacco.

Do these things and unless there is something structurally wrong with you, you'll become stronger. It's worked for thousands and thousands of people over the last century. You may not have the genes to become another Alexiev, but you will be significantly stronger in three months. Your lean muscle weight percentage will be up and your body-fat percentage will be down. You'll feel better and you'll look better, whether you're a man or a woman.

POWER TRAINING

Power training presupposes that you have done some strength training. Here the task is to be able to recruit the maximum number of muscle fibers in the shortest amount of time. Unless you've done the kind of basic background training that you do in strength training, you won't have the muscle size or the joint strength to do power training without injuring yourself.

If you're already doing weight training, and you are becoming interested in going into powerlifting or Olympic lifting, be sure that you already have a solid foundation of weight-trained muscle before you begin. When you make the transition from strength training to power training, remember that you are making a different kind of demand on your body. You'll be training the nervous system as much as you are training the muscles themselves.

Further, remember that power training is what gives you that explosive ability to move against a resistance that can be valuable in sports. When you come off the line of scrimmage, you want to come off like a 747 plane that's just lost its brakes, not like a Chicago Transit Authority bus lumbering through a snowbank. Power training is not the exclusive property of powerlifters. Power training is beneficial to anyone who wants to develop the ability to move with explosive speed as well as great strength. Sprinters are power athletes, as are most swimmers.

Let's assume that you've done the strength training and the general muscle building as outlined under Strength Training above. Here's what you should do now to develop your power:

1. Each exercise movement has two phases: the concentric or positive phase and the eccentric or negative phase. Let's take the bench press as our example. When you lift the barbell off the rack above your body and start downward toward your chest, you are in the eccentric, negative phase of the lift. When you lift the barbell back up, you are in the concentric, positive phase of the lift. When you are training for strength, you should bring the barbell down slowly and push it back up slowly. In power training, however, you move slowly in the eccentric phase and move as fast as you can in the concentric phase. In other words, when you power train in the bench press, let the barbell down to the chest slowly, and explode off the chest on the way back up. Slowly down, fast back up.

2. This fundamental principle is true for all the muscles. The bench press power trains the pectorals, the anterior deltoids, and the triceps. It gives these muscles the ability to resist a weight during the eccentric phase of the lift, but also to push the weight during the

concentric phase with explosive force. The same holds true for the legs if you apply power training to squats. Go slowly on the way down, and then explode out of the squatting position. You will find also that negative movements seem to work the red cells as well as the whites.

3. If you are training for power in a particular sports movement, you must perform either the movement of that sport or a movement that involves the muscles that are used in the sports movement, and you must do the movement slowly in the eccentric phase and fast in the concentric phase. If you want to come off the line in a hurry, do power training in the squat. If you want to develop explosive power in throwing a ball, make sure that you move explosively during the concentric phase of working the muscles that you use when you throw a ball. If it's an overhead throw, the main muscles are the anterior and lateral deltoid, the pectoral, the forearm (especially the flexors for the wrist), and the obliques. Work against a resistance in the line that the force must be exerted, and do it explosively.

4. The other suggestions about diet, rest, and abstinence from debilitating beverages, drugs, and tobacco hold true for power training as well as for strength training.

5. Pay special attention to your warmup. Since you will be making movements with explosive speed, the risk of tendon, muscle, and ligament pulls is significantly greater than it is in strength training.

6. Do no more than 3 reps per set for each exercise. If your progress slows down, try doing 1-rep sets after you've warmed up sufficiently.

7. Instead of adding reps, then dropping down to the original number of reps and adding weight as you do in strength training, add sets. If you start out with three 3-rep sets on the bench press, on the third workout day, do four sets. When you get up to six sets, drop back to three and add weight.

8. Once you've warmed up, make the jump right up to about 70 percent of your maximum. Either once a week (if you work out three times a week) or every fourth workout (if you work out every other day), go ahead and "max out": try for a new maximum poundage.

9. Regardless of the specific muscle group that you are working, remember that there are stabilizing muscles that help them do their work. If you are power training on the bench press, you should pay attention to the muscles of the shoulder girdle in addition to the pecs, delts, and triceps. Work the traps, the *rhomboids,* and the *infraspinatus,* in addition to the abdominals and the muscles of the

lower back. Remember the advice that champion powerlifter Andy Jackson gave us: "When I want to get in powerlifting contest shape, I work my abs as much as my arms and chest."

10. Don't try to power train more than one major muscle group each workout. You'll exhaust your recuperative energy stores. Don't, for example, do bench presses *and* squats the same day and expect to make gains. You should especially not try to max out in two major muscle group lifts on the same day. It's okay to max on calves and bench presses, but don't try full squats and heavy bench presses.

STAMINA TRAINING

In this type of training, you will be making rapid movements for 20 to 40 seconds. Obviously, you won't be able to handle the kind of weight that you would if you were doing strength or power training. Use a lighter weight, and make the eccentric and concentric movements both at a rapid pace.

Here are a few tips that will help you with your stamina training:

1. At first, use less weight than you can handle. The reason for this is simply that the stresses on the tendons and muscles can be severe in stamina training, since any kind of weighted object gathers momentum as it moves. When you stop motion in one direction and begin to move in the opposite direction, the muscles and tendons must bear the stress of the direction change. The greater the speed and weight, the greater the momentum and subsequent resistance to stopping. The effective weight of a 10-pound dumbbell at the end of repeated rapid movements is considerably greater than 10 pounds. Try bending your arm at the elbow as fast as you can for 10 reps. Now put a 10-pound dumbbell in your hand and try to do the same movement. See what we mean? Did you pull anything loose?

2. Given the problem with weights and momentum, stamina training can best be achieved through means other than barbells, dumbbells, or weighted machines. The obvious choice is some kind of isokinetic device, provided it can be set to allow for rapid movements. Hydra-Fitness's new omnikinetic machines have adjustable cylinders that make just such movements possible. As you remember, isokinetic machines operate on the principle of regulated speed and accommodating resistance. With omnikinetic resistance, the resistance is self-accommodating according to the speed of the movement. There is no problem with momentum, since you are not pushing against weights. Another method of attaining the same resistance would be to use a Tension Band or surgical tubing.

3. Try to do as many reps as you can within the allotted time span of 20 to 40 seconds.
4. If you are working on a Hydra-Fitness machine, set the cylinder so that you can barely finish 20 seconds of rapid movements. Count the number of reps that you do within these 20 seconds. To gain in stamina, do either of two things: (a) set the cylinder for more resistance, so that you can do fewer reps within the same 20 seconds, and then work up to the original number of reps, or (b) set the cylinder so that you can barely finish "x" number of reps in 40 seconds, and work at doing the same number of reps in fewer seconds. The first method will help you to gain strength as you gain stamina, and the second method will help you gain power as you gain stamina.

ENDURANCE TRAINING

When we talk about endurance, we are talking about two things. First, endurance has to do with the ability of a muscle to sustain a series of movements over an extended period of time. Second, endurance has to do with the condition of the organism as a whole in terms of cardiovascular conditioning, levels of muscle and liver glycogen, and both general and specific muscle tone.

It is possible to flex your index finger for an extended length of time without increasing its strength, power, stamina, or endurance. There is no resistance except for the thickness of the skin, the veins, etc. When you add weight and do the same movement, you will gain in strength, and, depending on the way you train, you will gain in power and stamina too. You will also increase the endurance of the muscles in your index finger, but you will not get any cardiovascular conditioning.

If you alternately flex and extend your hips and knees (that is, if you run), you will work muscle groups that are considerably larger than those in your finger and forearm, and you will be doing it under the load of your body's weight. If you reach the right pulse level and sustain the movements for the required length of time, you will receive cardiovascular conditioning.

If you worked with light weights, sat down on a leg extension machine, and did extensions for a long time, you could work either slowly or fast. If you worked slowly, you would condition the muscles for endurance. If you worked faster with the same weight so that your pulse rate rose into aerobic territory, you would condition the muscles for endurance, and you would also condition your cardiovascular system.

So we are talking about two kinds of conditioning, both of which can be done at the same time. One is the conditioning of muscles themselves—increasing strength, power, and stamina—and the other involves conditioning an organic system other than muscles, namely, the cardiovascular system.

If you are going to do sports movements, you need both kinds of conditioning. You need muscular endurance—the ability to perform movements over an extended period of time. And you need cardiovascular endurance—the ability of your oxygen supply system to sustain the activities that you are doing.

Muscular endurance conditioning begins when you perform a movement with moderate resistance over 2 to 3 minutes duration. Cardiovascular conditioning begins when you've sustained a correct target pulse rate for a specified length of time. There is no simple, infallible method for determining a correct target pulse rate. Many factors intervene, such as age, body weight, general physical condition, sex, and medical history. If you want to learn exactly what your target pulse rate should be, you should consult your doctor.

Any of the exercises in this book can be used for endurance training, which is simply a matter of working the red fibers instead of the whites. The red fibers are worked when you perform movements for over 2 minutes. A simple muscular endurance routine would be as follows:

1. Perform the exercise movement at moderate speed for 2 minutes.
2. When you do endurance training, forget about reps and set a timer for the amount of time you will be performing a specific movement.
3. To gain in endurance, add 30 seconds to the movement each successive workout. Work out every other day.
4. When you reach 5 minutes, drop back to 2 minutes and add weight. Work up to 5 minutes again.
5. If you want to continue to gain in endurance, keep working until you reach 10 or even 15 minutes. Then drop back down to 5 minutes and add weight.
6. Don't be in a hurry with the movements themselves. Just continue doing them at a moderate speed until you hear the timer bell.
7. Be especially careful that you do not injure your joints when doing endurance movements. If you have an arthritic condition, endurance training may aggravate it by the constant flexing and extending of the joints. If you have had joint injuries, listen for grating or popping noises. If pain develops, stop the program. If you have any injuries or any other kind of joint problem, be sure to see your physician or an experienced orthopedist before going on an endurance program. He or she may recommend the same exercises that you'll find in the pretraining section of this book.

8. If you decide to add cardiovascular conditioning to your muscular endurance routine, be sure that you have consulted your physician before you tax the system. Remember that running and jogging are especially hard on the feet, ankles, knees, and hips, especially if you have been inactive for a long time. Do the foot, ankle, knee, and hip exercises in the pretraining chapter if you want to protect your joints. See your physician if you want to protect your heart.

PLANNING A PROGRAM

When you develop your own basic training program, you should remember the following things:

1. Continue your pretraining exercises for areas that are still lagging behind, or are injured.
2. Avoid basic training exercises for those body parts that are still injured.
3. Build your basic training routines around compound exercises such as the squat and the bench press.
4. Don't get in a hurry with your training. You've got the rest of your life.
5. Don't expect startling results unless you're willing to put out the effort.
6. Be consistent. Don't miss workouts. All other things being equal, consistency is the one thing that will ensure progress.
7. Include around 10 exercises for each workout.
8. In the beginning, do one set for each body part each workout. As you advance, you can add sets, weight, and other exercises.
9. Train for strength and size will follow. This is not original with us. Bob Hoffman, the Olympic weightlifting coach, Olympic official, and President of the York Barbell Company, has been saying it for years.
10. Work out either three times a week or every other day. If you're under thirty-five years of age, you should have no trouble with the every-other-day system. If you're over thirty-five, cut down on the number of days per week that you work out. You're trying to build, not tear down. Ralph is fifty at this writing, and he does three heavy workouts a week, alternating between legs, lower back, the core muscles, and the *latissimus* one day and arms, chest, shoulders, upper back, and the core muscles the next day.
11. Give yourself enough time to recover and rebuild. Don't get off into six-day-a-week routines. Save them for the time when you're a thoroughly conditioned athlete.

12. Don't forget a balanced diet, with mineral supplements, vitamins, and the proper amounts of protein, carbohydrates, and fats.
13. Cut down on the alcohol and the tobacco.
14. Cut out drugs altogether, unless your doctor prescribes them. If you're under medication, see your physician before you start any training routine.
15. Whether you work out at home or in a gym, keep your eyes open for new training techniques. If you have a question about how to do something, look around and ask the guys and girls whose bodies themselves are proof that they know what they're talking about.
16. Even the experts are sometimes wrong when it comes to your body. We once saw a pudgy corrective therapist trying to tell the then-current Mr. Illinois that he didn't know how to do abdominal work. Mr. Illinois had abs that looked as if they'd been chiseled out of marble. You be the judge.

Here's a sample basic training routine that will give you general muscular conditioning. Follow the sequence as given.

Beginning Sequence
1. Squat
2. Bench press
3. Calf raise
4. Arm curl
5. Double crunch
6. Shoulder shrug
7. Spinal hyperextension
8. Pulldown behind neck
9. Side leans
10. Neck exercise

Follow the strength training procedures with the beginning sequence. Do all the exercises in the sequence in which they are given for each workout.

Intermediate Sequence
1. Squat
2. Bench press
3. Calf raise
4. Arm curl
5. Seated press
6. Double crunch

7. Shoulder shrug
8. Spinal hyperextension
9. Pulldown behind neck
10. Side leans or twists
11. Wrist flexion
12. Wrist extension

Advanced Sequence A
1. Squat
2. Pulldown behind neck
3. Leg extension
4. Leg curl
5. Double crunch
6. Pulldown to chest
7. Spinal hyperextension
8. Calf raise
9. Side leans or twists
10. Shoulder shrug

Advanced Sequence B
1. Bench press
2. Arm curl
3. Double crunch
4. Seated press
5. Spinal hyperextension
6. Triceps extension (kickbacks or French curls)
7. Side leans or twists
8. Concentrated curl
9. Incline bench press
10. Lateral raise
11. Flyes or pec deck

If you belong to a health club or gym, or if you have access to pin-loaded machines, there are a variety of ways that you can do the exercises given in this chapter in terms of combinations of sets, reps, and poundages. The process is called "pyramiding," and it has proved to be effective not only as a way to jar the muscles out of a rut, but also as a general conditioning method. Here are several kinds of pyramiding.

Regular Pyramid
Start your set with 4 or 5 reps at a weight that is only about 50 percent of your maximum. Then, with no rest between sets, move the pin

to a setting that is 75 percent of max. Do 6 reps at this setting, then move the pin down another plate. Do 6 more reps, then move the pin down another plate. Continue this process until you have reached your maximum poundage and can do only 1 rep.

Regular Pyramid with Stamina Pump

Do the regular pyramid, and then drop the poundage back down to about 70 percent of maximum. Do 10 to 20 reps as fast as you can.

Reverse Pyramid

Do 4 or 5 reps as a warmup, then move the pin to about 80 percent of max. Do 1 rep. Move the pin down a plate and do another rep. Move the pin to 90 percent of maximum and do 2 reps. Then move the pin one position lighter and do 4 reps. With no rest between sets (get a training partner to move the pin so you can't rest), move to the next lighter pin position and do 6 reps. Go to the next lighter pin position and do 8 reps. By this time, your muscles should be burning.

The advantage of the reverse pyramid is that it gets the fibers that do not ordinarily contract. When you do the regular pyramid, chances are that you will not feel a real "burn" by the time you do your max. When you do the regular pyramid with a pump, you have a tendency to go light throughout the lift in order to have enough energy to finish the pumping set. The reverse pyramid method takes you to within 90 percent of your maximum poundage very quickly, then continues to stress the muscles all the way down the range. You'll go to muscle failure (i.e., the point beyond which you simply can do no more reps) if you do it right, but you will be less likely to tear the muscles or tendons at the failure point, since you will be handling a lighter weight. It's a way to work to failure while minimizing the risks involved in that kind of training. Reverse pyramids should be alternated with regular pyramids or with regular multiple set exercises so that you will go to your maximum heavy poundage once a week for each muscle or muscle group. When Nautilus' new tricep extension machine appeared at the Marine City Chicago Health Club, Ralph could max out with only half the stack of 14 plates. Within a month using the reverse pyramid method, he was using the entire stack of plates at the 90 percent 2-rep max at the third stage of the exercise. He also added 20 pounds to his bench press weight during the same period. It works. Try it.

Now you know how to pretrain yourself, and how to work out a basic training program that is tailored to your individual needs. The next step is training for the sports movements themselves.

Chapter 4

SPORTSPOWER TRAINING

What Sports Performance Training Is

Sports training is a controversial field, characterized by outrageous claims, arcane knowledge, conflicting theories, medically sound and unsound advice, esoteric training methods, farfetched dietary and nutritional schemes, and mixed results. Sports trainers range from licensed physical and corrective therapists, sportsmedicine and orthopedic physicians, to grizzled old coaches whose knowledge of human physiology is limited to what they read in the muscle magazines.

Every gym has its guru, and every guru has his or her following. Trainers persist in loading their players with salt tablets, in spite of physiological evidence that it's a dangerous, useless practice. Corrective therapists and people with bachelor's degrees in health education disseminate information based on elementary undergraduate course work in anatomy and physiology, sometimes accurately and sometimes with disastrous results.

For every person with a solid background in sports training, there are a thousand who have done no reading in the literature of the field at all, much less actually trained real athletes to win real games. The field is in a state of flux, and professionals in the field are the first to admit that there is a horizon before them beyond which they know little or nothing.

The following are a few cases in point.

165

Two years ago, when we were creating a women's program for the Sports Fitness Institute, we got into an argument with a person about the proper height for a stationary bicycle seat. Sounds silly, but the implications are serious. This person, who held a degree in athletic training, advised club members to ride the stationary bikes with the seat in the highest position, on the grounds that (a) they would injure their knees otherwise, and (b) if they set the seat in the highest position, they would get a greater range of motion with the leg movements.

We questioned the person about both points, since it was obvious that a lower seat position would work the quads more and would also give the user a greater range of motion. The response was predictable. When we pointed out that there wasn't enough pressure on the knees to do injury, and that Sergio Oliva, the former Mr. Olympia, rode a bicycle regularly with the seat in the low position in order to increase the definition in his thighs, the point was conceded (reluctantly). On the other point, we had to take the person out to the bike and force him to look at the angle of the knee at different seat settings to convince him that the knees get a greater range of motion with the seat lower than with the seat higher.

What happened? The "expert" had never actually looked at a person riding a bike before.

Another one: Years ago, when Ralph lost his left eye in a hunting accident, he was told that he had also lost his stereoscopic depth perception. This, of course, was quite true, since as far as neurophysiologists can tell, two eyes are a necessity for depth perception. Ralph was also told that there was nothing that could be done about the clumsiness that such a loss entailed. It was a distressing message for an active sixteen-year-old boy.

It occurred to Ralph that it might be possible to relearn the visual cues that he had worked with before he lost the eye. He knew, for instance, that aviators land airplanes not on the basis of stereoscopic depth perception, but through changes in the perspective field. In fact, the last thing that a student pilot needs to do is to try to look down at the runway as he zips along trying to get rid of enough air speed to touch down.

He worked out a series of graded neuromotor exercises. First, he got his stepfather to toss a basketball to him. At first, he caught it with his face instead of his hands. Then he began to get the hang of it, and moved to a smaller ball. At the end of three months, he was catching a golf ball 9 out of 10 tries at a distance of 75 feet. It was at this time that he paid a visit to his physician, and tossed a tennis ball to him. The good doctor missed the ball, but Ralph didn't. They discussed the therapy, and the doctor thereafter suggested it to his patients who had lost an eye.

Years later, Ralph was talking to a corrective therapist about new therapy programs, and suggested one based on what he had done. The therapist indignantly informed him that (a) without professional credentials, he had no business suggesting therapy methods, and (b) such a method wouldn't work anyway. All the while, Ralph was touching his index fingers together in front of himself to illustrate his point. The therapist didn't notice.

Valerie has little kinaesthetic sense. She has difficulty visualizing the position and the movements of her body in a three-dimensional field. She has always had this trouble, and consequently never learned to ride a bicycle or participate in other physical activities in school.

When she was working with Ralph in the development and implementation of the Bodysculpture program (which later became the basis for a very successful book on weight training for women), she discovered that if an action was described in words, she could do it. She was verbally oriented, not spatially oriented. Ralph worked out carefully worded descriptions of all the exercises, and she learned from the descriptions how to do them. When she started on the program, she weighed 185 pounds, and could not support a 35-pound weight on her shoulders. Now, she weighs 110 pounds, and does half squats with 235 pounds, runs up to 7 miles three times a week, and does all the weight room exercises with skill and perfect form.

The problem is that she was told by her phys. ed. counselor in high school that she was hopelessly uncoordinated, and would never be able to do any of the sports activities that the other girls enjoyed. That was the day that she was kicked out of ballet class.

There are several points to be made here. First, if you have a disability, don't believe the "experts" when they tell you that you can't do what you want to do. We know one-armed motorcyclists, one-eyed aviators, one-legged skiers, and weight trainers with heart conditions. If you really want to do it, there is probably a way. You may not be a champion, but you will be able to do the work, have the fun, and get the benefit from the recreational sport of your choice.

Another point: having credentials in a field does not necessarily mean that a person knows what he or she is talking about. We aren't denigrating credentials. But we are saying that physical training is a field that is new to most physicians, and is only now beginning to gain respectability in medical circles. Many doctors still don't know what it is that physical therapists do, although these fine people have been helping injured athletes back onto the playing field for decades.

Further, the field of sportsmedicine is really in its infancy. Not until the national boom in sports activities did the field even become institutionalized to the point where budget money was allocated for it by medical school budget committees. If you don't believe it, call your local medical school and ask for the sportsmedicine department. You'll get the message.

Let us hasten to say that medical doctors are swarming into the field now, and you can look for a revolution in sportsmedicine over the next few years as it attracts more and more talented researchers. It's part of the evolution of the field of medicine, and we can all be thankful that more physicians are being attracted to the problems of sports and athletic training, exercise physiology, and biomechanics.

At the other end of the credentials scale are the people who know, quite simply, what works for *them*. Obviously, if Arnold Schwarzenegger, Franco Columbu, Boyer Coe, Sergio Oliva, or any of the other physique stars had any really *secret* knowledge that, if applied to a workout method, would produce bodies like theirs, everybody at the gym would look like Arnold, Franco, or Boyer. Yet people buy bodybuilding courses from these people like mad, expecting to find the magic road to big muscles. The stars themselves admit that what works for them may not necessarily work for you, because such things as size, strength, agility, and endurance are as much a product of your genes as they are a product of your training, nutrition, and general behavior habits.

The proof is in the pudding. Sports training is a field in which pragmatism reigns supreme. If a training method works, then it is a good training method. If it doesn't, it's not.

Why, then, is there so much confusion about which training method to follow? Simple. Every person is different. While many people have similar bodies in terms of muscle mass, distribution of white and red muscle fibers, lever system, fat distribution, and the ability of the central nervous system to give and carry out orders, many other people are dissimilar physically. Remember our discussion of body types in Chapter 1. Even if you are trying to become better at the same thing that your neighbor is already doing well, you may not have the kind of body that you need. If your neighbor has short upper arms and yours span farther than your height, forget about beating him at the bench press unless he has meager muscle mass or a broken arm.

The differences that we discussed in the opening chapter between various human body types are relevant to the development of any sports training program. They also give a clue as to why some methods work for some people and not for others. These bodily differences are the reason there is no single correct method for building strength and power, stamina or endurance, ability, coordination, speed, or form in sports. If anybody tells you that he or she has the end-all royal road to sports performance, keep a tight hand on your pocketbook, because the pitch is about to begin.

Right now, all the theories about sports performance training can be boiled down to three basic positions:

The Historical View

There is only one way to get better at playing X. Get out there and play X. No machine or barbell set is going to give you the kind of timing and the complex variations of movements that you meet in the actual game. You want to get better at X? Play more and concentrate more on what you're doing.

The Utopian View

In order to improve sports performance, you have to train with movements that simulate or duplicate the movements of the game itself. This training can be accomplished on a variety of machines, each of which isolates muscles or muscle groups and moves them in the same directions that the movements of the game move them.

The Conservative Physiological/Biomechanical View

It is impossible to simulate or duplicate specific sports movements or combinations of sports movements. If you duplicated them exactly, you would simply be playing the game. Further, if you simulate sports movements against a resistance, you'll throw your timing off. Besides, there is no undisputed evidence that such simulations really improve performance. Consequently, the best thing to do is to work the muscles and joints through their various ranges of motion, and then practice the sport itself in order to retain and develop proper timing and so forth.

Each of these three views has its merits, because hordes of athletes have trained under each of them to the exclusion of the others and have won games, collected trophies, and become stars. We can draw some conclusions here, from which you can develop a training methodology that will meet your own particular needs. As you think about specific sports training, keep the following considerations in mind:

• It is impossible to simulate or duplicate exactly, by artificial means, sports movements as they are performed in actual games. This is not to say that it is impossible to build a machine that will simulate swinging a bat at a ball against a resistance. But it would be difficult indeed to build a machine that would simulate swinging a bat at a ball, followed by the tremendous acceleration of a run to first, second, and third base, followed by a long slide into home plate, with the kinds of auditory and visual stimuli that made you take the chance for the slide instead of staying safe on third.

Performing sports movements in an actual game involves not just timing, but long sequences of timing points, where you have to do the right thing at the right time in the right place for the right reasons. We don't foresee a machine this complex in the near future—not until we can create a force field that would enable us to do all of the movements against resistance. Someday someone will invent a magnetic suit that will provide resistance in every direction.

• We have come further than weighted bats in our approach to adding resistance to sports movements. Mini-Gym has a machine with a bat hooked up to it, so that you can meet the resistance in precisely the direction that you would be swinging. The problem with the old weighted bats, of course, is that they don't give you resistance or "weight" in the direction that you're swinging. They give it to you in a vertical line, as gravity tries to pull the bat down to the ground. While a swing with the Mini-Gym machine builds up the muscles that are used in swinging (the posterior deltoids, triceps, biceps, *latissimus dorsi*, obliques, and *rhomboids*), the weighted bat works chiefly the lateral deltoids and the biceps. Further, the little benefit that you do get is nullified at the end of the weighted-bat swing. You have to overcome the inertia of the bat as you start the swing, so you do get a little resistance to the swing itself. However, you also have to stop the bat at the end of the swing, and this calls for an opposite reaction to the initial impulse. Better to use the Mini-Gym machine.

Nautilus, Paramount, Mini-Gym, and Hydra-Fitness, to name but a few of the major machine manufacturers, have designed and marketed machines that allow you to track the path that you would be tracking in actual sports movements, *at least separate movements.* The very isolation of muscles and muscle groups by these machines makes it possible to pinpoint underdeveloped muscles and bring them up to par. While these machines do not re-create the playing field, they do give you the chance to work on the areas of your body that are lagging behind. If you are lacking strength in your quads, give the Paramount Extension machine a try. If you want to build stamina as well as endurance, hop on the Hydra-Fitness Hip Flexion/Extension machine and grind away as fast as you can.

• The crucial question in sports training is raised in the conservative physiological/biomechanical view. If it is indeed true that sports simulation movements do not improve sports performance, then the claims of the machine manufacturers are, if not false, at least misguided. Further, if it is true that a general conditioning routine and increased frequency in playing the actual game is the only way to improve performance, then our task is relatively simple. All we have to do is get in shape and get out there and play. This is simply a restatement of the historical view, with physiological and biomechanical trimmings.

• If all people were equally developed, we could go along with the conservative physiological/biomechanical view without serious disagreement. People, however, are not equally developed, and merely putting someone on a general conditioning routine and sending him or her back into the game does not accomplish much. At least, underdeveloped body areas should be worked on with some specialization, so that they can be brought into line with the rest of the body's development. If you have a problem, then work on it until you overcome it. Work on it in addition to the general conditioning routine. Ralph discovered the value of a general conditioning routine when he went into karate. However, if he had not specialized in eye-hand coordination after he lost his left eye, he would not have been able to pull his punches in practice sessions at the last instant before striking his training partner. General conditioning routines are a must for any sport, but specialization exercises and routines *do* help. Ask anybody who's been injured and who has worked himself back onto the playing field.

• While there may be no undisputed evidence that simulated sports movements on exercise equipment improve performance in the game itself, there is ample evidence that being generally stronger, faster, and more agile, and having more endurance enhances a person's performance in any kind of physical activity, whether it's sports movements or merely taking a stroll. The conservatives are right about general conditioning to this extent. It has an overall value that transcends whatever it may lack in preparing you for specialized movements. The pretraining program in Chapter 2 is especially important in this respect, as it both prevents injuries and provides a solid foundation for the basic training and sportspower training programs that follow.

• If simulations of exercise equipment have not proved to be the panacea of sports performance training, development of the muscles and of the coordination that specific sports movements require at least gives you the foundation that you need to play the actual game itself. If you use your lateral deltoids in boxing, the development of the lateral deltoids should be an integral part of your training program. If you need stronger quadriceps muscles in order to last all the way down the hill when you're skiing, then the development of strength and endurance in the quads is a logical addition to your training goals.

● Human beings adapt pretty quickly to the stresses and loads of particular physical activities. Baseball, football, racquetball, tennis, golf, bowling, swimming all require a certain level of performance. Once you reach that level by playing the game itself, you will not develop further in strength, stamina, power, or endurance. That's one of the chief reasons you need a sports training program. That's why the pro football players spend the off season in the weight room pumping iron. If you are not making progress in playing a particular sport *and your lack of progress is due to a lack of strength, stamina, power, or endurance*, simply continuing to play the game will probably not contribute significantly to further improvement. What you need to do is to push your muscles beyond the exertions of the game. In short, to "overload" them so they will gain in strength.

● The concept of overloading is one of the keys to any physical training program. It is used by exercise physiologists to describe what happens when you push your neuromuscular systems beyond the stresses to which they are already adapted. In simple terms, the body adapts to the stress of increasing loads by becoming stronger, faster, more agile, or by having more endurance, depending on the type of exercise you use to overload your neuromuscular systems. Overloading is the process by which you increase the amount of work you do over what you are already doing. As your body adapts to the new level of activity, your performance improves.

For example, if you've never run before and you begin a running program with a quarter-mile run, you will be huffing and puffing from having overloaded your leg muscles and your cardiovascular system beyond your normal activities. If there is nothing physiologically wrong with you, the next quarter-mile run should be a little easier. The next will be even easier, and so on until it is no strain at all to run a quarter of a mile.

If you increase your running distance to a half mile, you will feel the effects of overloading again. However, as you continue to progress to longer and longer runs, your body will adapt to the ever-increasing loads until you have reached your full potential.

Overloading may be more or less intense. *Intensity* is a term used by exercise physiologists to describe the extent to which neuromuscular systems are overloaded during specific exercise bouts. There are three basic ways that you can increase the intensity of an exercise. Let's hypothesize an exercise bout in which you do 10 bench presses with 50 pounds during one minute's duration. This would be a 10-rep set with 50 pounds. Here's how you can increase the intensity of the exercise bout:

1. Increase the poundage lifted while keeping the number of reps and the duration of the set the same.
2. Increase the number of reps while keeping the poundage lifted and the duration of the set the same.
3. Decrease the duration of the set while keeping the poundage and the number of reps the same.

In each instance, you've increased the work load on your neuromuscular systems by changing one of the variables. In method 1 you've handled more weight during the same amount of time. In method 2 you've handled the same weight in the same amount of time, but you've increased the speed with which you've handled it. In method 3 you've kept the weight and the number of reps the same, but you've had to lift the weight faster because of the decrease in the duration of the set.

Each way of increasing intensity affects the body in different ways, as you might expect from the principle of specificity of training. Method 1 will increase your strength, will not necessarily increase your power, stamina, or endurance, and will not appreciably tax your cardiovascular system. Method 2 will increase your power, speed, and stamina, will tax your cardiovascular system (if you do enough of it), but will not appreciably increase your strength. Method 3 will increase your power, speed, and stamina, and will tax your cardiovascular system (if you do it long enough), but may yield only small increases in strength.

There are combinations of these methods. If you really want to overload your system, raise the intensity of the exercise bout by increasing the poundage, increasing the number of reps, and decreasing the duration of the set. If you're free from illness or from structural or physiological problems, your body will respond by adapting to the increased loads. People who do long, leisurely workouts do not improve as fast as those who do fast, intense workouts. People who reach a plateau and never push themselves to greater levels of intensity and overloading will remain on that plateau.

There is another variable in computing the intensity of overloading in addition to duration and resistance. Each limb is moved by the muscles that insert into the limb's bones. Muscles originate at points on bones that remain relatively immobile and insert into points on bones that move with muscular contraction. Each joint allows a certain range of motion, as we discussed in Chapter 2. Depending on the joint angle of the limb, the muscles will have greater or lesser leverage in moving the limb. For example, the leg, as it extends and flexes at the knee, has a total range of motion of about 135° between being fully extended and being fully flexed against the thigh. The quadriceps muscles that extend the leg have their greatest leverage at about 128°. This means that the quads can handle more resistance at 128° than they can at full extension or at an angle greater than 128°. If you are doing leg extensions with a weight acting as the resistance, this means that the weight that you are able to extend fully will be less than you could handle at 128°. All of which means that unless you find a way to add weight *during* the leg's motion and subtract it as the leverage decreases, you will *not* experience a full intensity overload throughout the range of motion of the limb.

This may sound complicated, but it is really very simple. And it is precisely the reason that Nautilus and Paramount use some form of cam in their machines: to change the resistance effectively as the limb moves through its range of motion.

The most ingenious method of providing maximum intensity overload throughout a range of motion has been developed by Hydra-Fitness, whose hydraulic cylinders have six settings with which the resistance can be lowered or increased. Moreover, they provide self-accommodating variable resistance throughout the range of·motion, regardless of the relative strength of the individual using the machine. This means that the user receives a maximal intensity overload at every joint angle, thus combining the best qualities of both isometric and isokinetic training, while avoiding the limitations of weighted system training.

On the cellular level, overloading involves training muscle fibers to manufacture and store greater quantities of ATP (adenosine triphosphate), the high-energy phosphate which, as it is hydrolized into ADP (adenosine diphosphate), provides the energy for muscular contraction. ATP is a product of what is called the "citric acid" or "Krebs" cycle that is one of the last processes in the conversion of carbohydrates, fats, and proteins into fuel for body functions.

Not only does overloading train the cells to store and produce more ATP, it also trains and expands the capacity of the energy systems that are directly responsible for muscle action: the aerobic and anaerobic energy systems. The aerobic energy system supplies energy for sustained-effort activities, such as jogging, running, and cross-country skiing. The anaerobic energy system supplies energy for explosive, short-range muscle contraction, such as those associated with strength, power, and stamina activities. Both of these energy systems can be overloaded and thus trained to be more efficient in their energy output and faster in their recovery from depletion.

In the same way that muscular systems respond to overloading, so do neuromotor systems. The nervous system can be trained to operate more efficiently and with greater effectiveness through overloading. It is a mistake to think only of muscular systems when talking about training. The nervous system must give the signals that make the muscles contract. Any training of the muscles, then, is also training of the nervous system.

Neuromotor signals to muscle fibers initiate a chain of electrochemical events that ultimately cause microscopically small filaments in the fibers' "myofibrils" to slide by each other. It is the "cross bridges" between these two types of filaments that are the immediate causes of individual fiber contraction, as the actin and myosin of the filaments react. It is the collective force of these millions of contracting fibers that makes the biceps or the quadriceps themselves "contract," thus causing a limb to move.

• Given the principle of specificity of training, which demands that specific movements call for specific training (for example, if you want to develop the power to leap vertically in basketball, you must train to leap vertically), the ideal form of training would be one in which maximal intensity overloading occurred during the performance of the sports performance movements themselves. The *key* to the sportspower training system is that the neuromuscular systems are pre-exhausted during exercise to the overload level, then pushed into maximal intensity overload during the performance of the sports movements themselves. This is why each exercise bout is followed immediately by the sports movements. By structuring the workout in this sequence, intense overloading occurs while the trainee is moving within the space-time matrix demanded by the sport itself. Timing and control are thus enhanced instead of being interrupted as they are by ordinary training methods.

Let's try to synthesize the three basic sports training positions into a single methodology that can be applied to any sport. Let's proceed on the following assumptions:

1. If poor performance is due to a lack of strength, stamina, power, or endurance, then training in these areas will enhance the probability of improvement.
2. If poor performance is due to underdeveloped muscles or muscle groups, or to injuries that have not received proper rehabilitative

attention, then specialized routines designed to develop these specific areas and solve these specific problems will enhance the probability of improvement.

3. If poor performance is due to a lack of coordination in the movements of the game being played, increased frequency in practicing these movements will enhance the probability of improvement. You don't learn to hit a ball by bench pressing. You learn to hit by practicing hitting.

4. Whether you train with sports movement simulations or by general conditioning programs, you must try to balance your training efforts with your efforts in the actual playing of the game. This may mean 10 hours a week in the gym and 1 hour on the field, or it may mean 1 hour in the gym and 10 hours on the field. This sort of thing depends on the individual's needs, and there is no simple checklist that will enable you to find your own balance.

Before you begin your sportspower program, you should keep the following things in mind:

1. Before you begin any vigorous, rigorous physical training program, get a complete or at least a partial physical examination by a competent physician. Don't make the mistake of thinking that exercise or sports will get you into shape. If there's something wrong inside, you may aggravate the condition and wind up with the opposite of what you were after.

2. If you have any old injuries, any underdeveloped body parts, abnormalities of the limbs, joints, or muscles, see your doctor or an orthopedist before you start training. The pretraining exercises in Chapter 2 are designed to help you follow whatever therapy program your doctor puts you on. More than likely, the prescribed exercises are in Chapter 2. They will increase strength and endurance and they will bring individual body parts up to the level of the rest of the body.

3. The basic training chapter is designed to give you the information necessary to work out a general conditioning program suited to your own personal needs. From the various exercises described, choose those that will give you a total body workout. At the beginning, follow the programs that are outlined at the end of the chapter. They will assure balanced development and coordination of muscle groups.

By the time you get to the end of your 90-day basic training program, you will already have begun specialization on specific body parts. Go through all the exercises for individual muscles and muscle groups so that you will understand how to do them. The pretraining program will get you ready for basic training. The basic training program will get you ready for movement clusters and the training sequences of the sports performance program.

4. By the time you finish with your pretraining program, you should assess your physical condition in terms of the need for strength, stamina, power, or endurance training. If you're lacking in strength, then stress strength-building procedures in your basic training program. If you're lacking in endurance, then stress endurance-building procedures. The same goes for power and stamina. Strength training will make you strong. Power training will give you explosive strength. Stamina training will give you short-term speed and strength, and will train your muscles to store more glycogen. Endurance training will enable you to make it through the long haul of continuous physical activity. Whichever aspect of physical conditioning you lack, the training procedures outlined at the end of Chapter 3 will help you to overcome your deficiencies.

When you've achieved the goals set forth thus far, you're ready to start with movement clusters and specialization programs. Here's what they are and how they work.

Sportspower Movement Cluster Training

All physical movements are combinations of movements. It's impossible to move only your hand or your forearm or your upper arm. When you move any part of your body, you move the body parts that lie around the area being moved. Try an experiment and you'll see what we mean. Take this book in your right hand, and flex and extend the wrist. You can see the flexors and extensors of the forearm as they alternately move the hand. You will also notice that the upper arm is moving slightly, to compensate for the shift of the book's mass up and down. The shoulders are probably also moving slightly, as the muscles of the shoulder and back support the movement of the hand. Even when you are sitting in an exercise machine trying to perform (for example) elbow extensions, you are probably pushing against the floor with your feet. No movement is done in a vacuum. No muscle is an island.

When you perform the coordinated movements that are required for walking around the room, you are bringing all, or almost all, of the body's muscles, bones, and joints into play. You never think about the action of the lower back muscles in walking until you injure the lower back. Then you find out with a vengeance that each step requires alternate flexing of the muscles along the sides of the spine.

Watch a karateka as he breaks a board with the side of his foot in a side-thrust kick. He begins with a fluid sidestep and brings his arms up toward the direction in which he will kick. If he is kicking with his right leg, he will plant his left foot solidly on the floor and raise his right foot in a straight line toward the target. The arms will be bent at the elbow, and the fists will be clenched. His head will be turned so that he is looking directly at the target. As he brings his right foot up, his leg will extend and his foot will supinate as his toes draw back to make the side of the foot into a hard ridge. An instant before he kicks the target, he will rotate his pelvis to the front and fully abduct and extend his right leg. At the point of impact, he will flex every muscle in his body, beginning with a wave of muscular contractions in the abdominals that radiates throughout the body and ends in the right foot. Crack! The board breaks.

All of this happens in less than a second's time, and it involves the coordinated activity of every muscle in the body. That's why the real pros—the legitimate black belts—are so formidable in a bout. They have perfect control over the entire neuromuscular system, with the requisite strength, speed, and power that a perfectly executed karate technique requires. Watch the beginners and then watch the black belts. You'll see the difference. The difference is coordinated precision and controlled force.

In any movement of this kind, there are combinations or clusters of movements that occur in particular sequences. If you are off in your timing in any of these movement clusters, you probably won't break the board. You'll just bruise your foot.

The same holds true for any sports movement, whether you are throwing a ball, lifting a barbell, swinging a racquet, or running a mile. Clusters of movements are coordinated into rhythmic and fluid steps, jumps, swings, and strikes. In fine-tuning an athlete, the coordination of these movement clusters makes the difference between exceptional and mediocre performance.

The sportspower concept, therefore, is this:

1. Lay the foundation with pretraining therapeutic programs.
2. Build on that foundation with basic training exercises that increase strength, stamina, power, and endurance.

3. Specialize in strength, stamina, power, and endurance training for the muscles and joints used repeatedly in your particular sport.
4. Do your specialization training so that the muscles and joints that are exercised are worked in the same sequence in which they are worked when you are playing the game itself.

Translated into action, this means that you must:

1. Exercise all of the collateral stabilizing muscles around the joints, and work for full ranges of motion.
2. Exercise all of the major muscle groups.
3. Bring underdeveloped body parts up to par with extra exercises for those specific body parts.
4. Train to equalize your abilities in terms of strength, stamina, power, and endurance.
5. In addition to pretraining and basic training exercises, work the muscles and joints of the limbs that are used in specific sports movements, so that you enhance strength, stamina, power, and endurance in these movements.
6. Think of specific sports movements in terms of *movement clusters:* combinations of muscular contractions in certain sequences, and within certain time frames.

For example, if you want to enhance your performance in throwing a ball, you will want to develop explosive power in the *anterior deltoid,* the *pectoralis major,* the *triceps brachii,* plus the rotators of the forearm and the flexors of the wrist. These are the arm, chest, and shoulder muscles that are used in throwing a ball.

Other muscles are used as well: when you throw a ball, you twist your trunk, change the loading on your feet, and balance the movement with your head and your hips. Throwing a ball is a biomechanically complex movement.

For the throwing arm, you must work not only for power and explosive speed, but for endurance as well. Nobody wants to lose his pitching arm halfway through the game. This means that you will have to alternate exercises that build muscle mass (for strength and speed) with exercises that build endurance (high repetition, sustained contractions). Build the muscle mass first, then work for endurance.

Try to do the arm exercises so that the muscles are worked in the order that they are used when you throw a ball. The same goes for the muscles of the legs and trunk. Try to analyze the sequence in which you make the movements of a pitch, and then work your body parts in that sequence. Following is a possible sequence for pitching:

1. Bench presses, flyes, or pec deck work for the chest
2. Triceps extensions for the upper arm
3. Supinations of the hand for the forearms
4. Wrist flexes for the wrist

This constitutes a single movement cluster: a cluster of movements that are performed in sequence, which constitute one component of the complex act of throwing a ball.

You will need other movement clusters to take care of the torso and the legs. Here's a sample movement cluster for the legs that will give a pitcher the power, flexibility, and stability he needs.

1. Side leans, seated twists for the external obliques
2. Double crunches for the abdominals
3. Alternating leg raises for the *iliopsoas* group
4. Spinal hyperextensions for the lower back
5. Low pulley rowing for the middle and upper back
6. Leg extensions for the quads
7. Leg curls for the hamstrings
8. Knee rotations (both medial and lateral) for the knees
9. Complete ankle routine

As you can see, there will be some duplications between sportspower exercises and pretraining and basic training. The sportspower exercises should be done *in addition* to your regular background training routine. If there are duplications, fine. That's what you need: extra work on specific areas.

Further, you can see that it is not always possible to do the exercises in the sequence of movements that you would be making if you were actually playing the game. You can make a rough approximation, however. If you're working on your throwing, try doing the torso or core muscle sequence first, then the legs, then the throwing arm.

If you're working for speed in the throw, the arm exercises should be done with as much weight as you can handle for 3 to 4 reps (at the most), moving with as much speed as you can muster in the contraction phase of the movement, and with no rest between the different exercises in the sequence. Go fast in the concentric and slowly in the eccentric phase.

Now for the real test. When you finish one series of exercises, then do

10 practice movements of the sports movement itself. Throw a ball. Swing a bat. And do it until you overload your muscles. Do it until you feel them burn. Do the entire movement in pantomime. This not only overloads the muscles, but also helps to translate the exercises into the neuromotor coordination required by the sport itself. When you've done 10 reps of practice movements, do another tour through the exercises. Do three fast series with only a one-minute rest between series.

Get the picture? You're not trying to simulate the specific sports movements with machines or free weights. Instead, you're building a solid foundation of strength, power, stamina, and endurance with pre-training and basic training exercises, followed by a program of exercises that focuses on the muscles that are used in the specific sports movements. Then you coordinate these specific exercises with the actual movements of the sport.

In many ways, this type of cluster training is similar to the practice in karate of performing formalized fight sequences, or *katas*, after the arms and legs have been fatigued by practice punches and kicks. As such, movement cluster training concentrates not only on the development of the muscles used in sports movements, but on the development of neuromotor responses that are peculiar to the specific sport. By doing the sports movements in pantomime, you are accomplishing several things:

• Teaching your body to make the transition from exercise to specific sports movements
• Maintaining the timing of the actual sports movements
• Maintaining and reinforcing the sequence of movements involved in the actual sports movements

There is an old saying in the Japan Karate Association that the best time to take a rank promotion test is when you are so tired from practicing techniques you can hardly stand. There are two reasons for this. First, the rank promotion test is supposed to test your ability to perform all basic techniques properly, both in pantomime, in formalized sequences, and in actual combat. Second, you can't predict your condition when and if you ever get into a real fight for your life, in which you are depending on your karate skills for your very survival.

Technique tends to go out the window when you're fatigued. But if you continue to practice the techniques long after you're fatigued from exercise, you will condition your body to perform better under stress, and you will also literally "beat" your nervous system into the "grooves" that the techniques demand. This is the key to neuromuscular overloading. The same holds true for any movements, whether in karate, judo, baseball, skating, or any other sport.

By repeatedly performing sports movements at the end of a movement cluster, you are increasing intensity overloading for the entire neuromuscular system.

In the pretraining and basic training chapters, there are ample exercises to work every joint, muscle, or muscle group used in sports activities. Series of exercises can be compiled that work the various muscles in more or less the sequence that they are used in actual practice. If you are deficient in development, you'll find out where and to what extent when you begin the movement clusters. Never neglect your pretraining and basic training programs. At the beginning, you should do your pretraining routines every day or every other day. Basic training routines should be done every other day or three times a week. When you've completed your 90-day basic training program, begin the movement cluster training sequences.

Movement cluster training should be done at first as one third of your total training. Spend a third on pretraining exercises and a third on basic training exercises. As you feel the need for more training in movement clusters, shorten the length of time you spend on pretraining activities (by this time, you should have cleared up the problems that pretraining was designed to solve), and make basic training and movement cluster training equal halves of your program.

You will always need to keep up a general conditioning program, composed of the exercises from the basic training chapter. They provide the continuing foundation for the movement clusters and for the sports movements themselves. Vary the amount of time you spend on movement cluster training according to how successful you are in making improvements in your neuromuscular coordination as it applies to the performance of specific sports movements. For some, the general conditioning program will take up most of the time. For others—especially those who are already in generally good condition—most of the time will be spent with movement clusters.

And don't forget: there's still no substitute for playing the game! None of this will work unless you spend time on the field, in the water, on the ice, or on the court. A training program is never a substitute for a game. It's a backup system, to help you get ready and keep you ready to play and enjoy your favorite recreational sport.

And now, one final concept to put a capstone on the program. Biomechanics experts talk about sports movements in terms of whether they are "open" or "closed." This distinction is vital to any sportspower training program. Here's what it means.

A movement cluster is closed when it is always done in the same manner, deliberately, and is controlled by the person doing it. Performing the bench press is a good example. The key to success is in *not* varying the movement from one competition to another. Lie on the bench. Arch your back slightly. Decide on how you are going to place your feet and don't move them during the lift, or you'll be disqualified. Lift the bar off the rack. Lower it to your chest. Pause, and wait for the judge's go signal. Push the bar toward the ceiling, with both arms moving in coordination. Wait for the signal. Put it back on the rack. A closed system.

Racquetball provides the perfect example of an open movement cluster. You're standing in the court, racquet in hand, waiting for the ball. There are a number of things that you do not know—for example:

1. The angle at which the ball will move toward you
2. The speed at which the ball will move toward you
3. The amount of spin the ball will exhibit

Consequently, you also do not know precisely what action will be required of you when the ball comes toward you until it comes toward you. In terms of discrete movement clusters, your options are almost infinite.

You must not merely react. You must anticipate the vast number of possibilities and be ready to react instantly, no matter what happens. No number of elbow extensions or wrist flexions will prepare you for the moment-to-moment unpredictability of racquetball. A perfect open system.

Again, there is an analogy in karate. The Japan Karate Association's Heditaka Nishiyama, the head of the All America Karate Federation, in his book *Karate: The Art of "Empty Hand" Fighting* (Rutland, Vermont; Tokyo: Charles E. Tuttle, 1960), describes the concept of *mizu no kokuro:* a mind like water. You should make your mind like an undisturbed pond of water. Only in this way can your mind truly reflect what your opponent with his actions demands that you do to defend yourself. If the pond is disturbed by fear or tension, the surface will not reflect your opponent, and he will get through your defenses. What is called for here is not total passivity, but a kind of Whiteheadian "pure anticipation," with no prior commitment made to any specific action, but with an almost infinite store of potential actions, from which can be chosen those that will maximize your effectiveness in doing what you have to do.

This is precisely what is called for in any open movement cluster.

You must train yourself to react instantly, automatically, in whatever mode will help you win, but with no preconceived notions about what you are going to do. Consequently, when you perform the specific sports movements during your exercise series, work in as many possible reaction movements as you can. Do them fast, and do them with as much skill as your aching muscles will allow.

This way—*and this is the real secret of sportspower training*—the muscles will be pushed into maximum overload while doing the sports movements themselves, not merely while you're doing a set of exercises. You don't have to simulate the sport movements with exercise equipment in order to overload the muscles and the nervous system. As you perform the movements themselves you're pushing your neuromuscular system into overload.

It's the difference between merely throwing 50 karate punches and throwing 50 karate punches after a sequence of bench press and elbow extension exercises. With 50 punches alone, you will eventually overload only to the extent that the repeated movement itself tires the muscles. With the prior exertion of the exercise sequence, you will pre-exhaust the muscles so that they go into intense overload and remain in overload while you are actually doing the sports movements themselves.

And when you overload the muscles during the performance of the sports movement itself, you also condition the neuromotor responses required to perform those movements with skill in a way that would otherwise be impossible.

In the following section, we'll give you exercise programs for each of your favorite recreational sports. In many cases, the same kind of training is required for more than one sport. For example, throwing a ball is similar to an overhead or lateral swing with a racquet. Further, lateral movements of the body are common to almost all sports that involve being on your feet and moving from one side of a court or playing field to the other. Consequently there will be duplications of exercises from sport to sport.

The sportspower movement cluster exercises stress muscle groups instead of isolated muscles. When individual muscles are worked, however, exercises will follow immediately that work the opposite muscles or other muscles that move with them.

Sportspower movement cluster exercises should be performed with the goal in mind of training the muscles to do what is demanded of them in actual playing. For instance, you wouldn't want to train your legs solely for strength if your goal is to run the Boston Marathon. Likewise, you wouldn't want to do endurance training alone if you want to develop the muscle mass and strength it takes to do the high jump.

Emphasize fluid movement and coordinated effort. Try to tie muscle actions to each other in such a way that you find your natural "groove" for each movement. And don't forget the sports movements between series of exercises. That's the key to the whole thing!

Okay, you've got it. Now all you have to do is the work! To make it easier for you to sort everything out, we've added several indexes to the specific programs, the exercises, and the types of training you'll need.

Sportspower Training Programs for Recreational Sports

The training programs in this chapter are divided into the following categories:

1. Racquet Sports: tennis, racquetball, badminton, squash
2. Sustained Leg Movement Sports: running and jogging, cycling, skating (ice and roller), skiing (downhill and cross-country)
3. Ball Hitting, Throwing, or Kicking Sports:
   baseball and softball, football, golf, soccer, handball, volleyball, basketball
4. Martial Arts: karate, judo
5. Water Sports: swimming, scuba diving, board and platform diving, waterskiing
6. Strength and Power Sports: powerlifting, Olympic lifting

To make it easier for you to follow the programs suggested in this chapter, here is an index to the exercises in the pretraining and basic training chapters:

Index to the Exercises

Terminology for the fundamental movements of the human body 51–53

Pretraining exercise methods 54

Training for strength 55

Sample Pretraining and Basic Training Program for General Conditioning and Rehabilitation

PRETRAINING
1. Foot and ankle sequence
2. Knee sequence
3. Hip sequence
4. Spinal column sequence
5. Hand and wrist sequence
6. Elbow sequence
7. Shoulder sequence

Note: This, of course, covers the entire pretraining program. If you have been sedentary and are just now beginning to expand your physical activities, the entire program is advised as a prelude to basic training and to playing any sport. If you are not sedentary, but are already physically active, choose those pretraining exercises that will recondition injured or lagging body parts.

BASIC TRAINING (WORK OUT EVERY OTHER DAY)
1. Squat
2. Bench press
3. Calf raise
4. Military press
5. Shoulder shrug
6. Curl
8. Double crunch

9. Spinal hyperextension
10. Side lean

INTERMEDIATE BASIC TRAINING
(WORK OUT EVERY OTHER DAY)

Alternate Workout A
1. Squat
2. Seated calf raise
3. Low pulley rowing
4. Leg extension
5. Leg curl
6. Pulldown behind the neck
7. Double crunch
8. Spinal hyperextension
9. Side lean
10. Alternating leg raise

Alternate Workout B
1. Bench press
2. Lateral raise
3. Posterior raise
4. Curl or concentrated curl
5. Triceps extension
6. Shoulder shrug
7. Incline press or military press
8. Pec deck or flyes
9. Double crunch
10. Spinal hyperextension
11. Side lean

ADVANCED BASIC TRAINING
(WORK OUT EVERY OTHER DAY)

Alternate Workout A
1. Squat
2. Seated calf raise
3. Leg extension
4. Standing calf raise
5. Leg curl
6. Regular dead weight lift
7. Low pulley rowing
8. Side lean

9. Pulldown to the chest
10. Double crunch
11. Pulldown behind the neck
12. Spinal hyperextension
13. Alternating leg raise

Alternate Workout B
1. Bench press
2. Shoulder shrug
3. Incline press
4. Lateral raise
5. Retraction
6. Protraction or pec deck or flyes
7. Posterior raise
8. Seated press behind the neck
9. Anterior raise
10. Concentrated curl
11. Triceps extension
12. Double crunch
13. Spinal hyperextension
14. Side lean
15. Alternating leg raise

Sportspower Programs
(Work Out Every Other Day)

RACQUET SPORTS

Racquet sports involve every muscle of the body. The body is shifting from side to side, frontward and backward, as the player anticipates or tries to anticipate the direction from which the ball will come. It is an open sport in that movements vary depending upon the action that must be taken to hit the ball.

Strong ankle and knee joints are a necessity in the racquet sports. Side shifting stresses the knees and the ankles, as well as the hips. Further, given the jumping and spinning that are required, you'll want to work for power as well as endurance in the legs.

Arm movements should be trained for power and endurance, with controlled, explosive power as the key both to serves and to returns. In all racquet sports movements, a sequence of action/relaxation/action/relaxation takes place as you hit the ball and wait for the return. Consequently, you must be able to sustain your efforts over a period of time, but do them in short bursts of completely controlled activity.

The sequences listed in the racquet sports program are designed to provide movement clusters for the specific movements performed in racquet sports. These movement clusters will work your muscles in the order that they are used in making actual sports movements. Refer to pages 177 through 185 to refresh your memory about the way that movement cluster training works. Pay special attention to the discussion on overloading on pages 172 through 175 and 184. You should also add some form of aerobic training such as running or jogging to your total training program.

First Sequence
1. Seated twist or side lean
2. Double crunch
3. Spinal hyperextension
4. Perform sports movements: side-to-side shifting
5. Jump box work

Second Sequence
1. Ankle sequence from pretraining (include balance beam)
2. Knee rotations with Tension Band
3. Leg extension
4. Leg curl
5. Hip flexes
6. Hip abduction
7. Hip adduction
8. Jump box work
9. Perform sports movements: side-to-side shifting, forward and backward shifting, jumping. Perform on the floor and also on a balance beam.

Third Sequence
1. Flyes or pec deck work
2. Anterior raise
3. Lateral raise
4. Posterior raise
5. Dumbbell curl
6. Triceps extension
7. Wrist extension
8. Wrist flexion
9. Radio-ulnar deviation
10. Perform sports movements: side-to-side shifting, jump box, forward and backward shifting, jumping, swinging a racquet. Do all the

movements the sport requires. Try them on the floor and on a balance beam for balance and to help strengthen the collateral stabilizing muscles.

At first, perform 1 set of each sequence. After a week, perform 2 sets. After two weeks, perform 3 sets. Modify the program according to individual needs.

SUSTAINED LEG MOVEMENT SPORTS

Sustained leg movement sports have enjoyed a tremendous growth in popularity over the last decade, due in large part to the influence of Dr. Kenneth Cooper's landmark *Aerobics,* and James Fixx's and Dr. Sheehan's books on running. These books spawned a horde of books, magazines, and workshops on the joys and benefits of running and jogging.

Due partially to the increase in television coverage of sports events, there has been a corresponding surge of interest in other forms of sustained leg movement sports: cycling, skiing, skating, and race walking.

The increase in interest in these sports has also brought a corresponding increase of injuries that are peculiar to sustained leg movement sports: shin splints, sprained ankles and feet, separated joints, torn ligaments, and overstretched tendons. People who did not know that they had structural problems in their hips, knees, and ankles soon found that simply strapping on a pair of skis or skates, or lacing up a cheap pair of running shoes, was not sufficient preparation for an all-out attack on the slopes, the rinks, or the trails.

The purpose of the pretraining exercises is to help you prevent such injuries by giving strength and flexibility to your joints by working the muscles that stabilize those joints. Consequently, pretraining exercises are included in the sportspower program. For overall development, you should do all of the pretraining exercises. Although your sports may emphasize sustained leg movements, your entire body is working when you run, ski, skate, or cycle.

Remember that the sportspower program incorporates both pretraining and basic training exercises in the form of sequences that constitute movement clusters that approximate the movements of the sport. At the end of each sequence, you should perform the sports movements themselves. If you are a runner, you should run. If you are a skier, then you should either ski or go through the motions of skiing. If you are a skater, you should either skate or simulate the motions of skating. Every serious skater will remember the television coverage of Olympic gold medal winner Eric Heiden doing skating movements in his stocking feet across a polished surface.

Review the material on pages 177 through 185 concerning the relation between the exercises and the sports movements that are listed in the exercise sequences. Pay special attention to the discussion of overloading on pages 172 through 175 and 184.

First Sequence
1. Foot and ankle work from pretraining
2. Knee rotation from pretraining
3. Seated calf raise
4. Standing calf raise
5. Knee extension
6. Knee flexion
7. Hip flexion
8. Run around track or ride a stationary bicycle. If you are a skater, try side-to-side movements on a polished floor, with a pair of thick wool socks on, to simulate the side-to-side movement of skating. Be sure to move exactly the way that you would move on the ice or on rollers. If you are a cyclist, assume the riding position you would use while riding a real bike. If you are a runner, run as you would when you really run. If you are a skier, practice partial knee-bending movements, sliding movements similar to skating simulations, and jump box work.

Second Sequence
1. Seated twist
2. Double crunch
3. Spinal hyperextension or regular dead weight lift
4. Retraction
5. Lateral, anterior, posterior raise
6. Alternating arm swings with dumbbells (for skiers)
7. Repeat the sports movements, jump box work

Third Sequence
1. Squats (especially for skiers) plus jump box
2. Regular dead weight lift
3. Repeat sports movements

BALL HITTING, THROWING, OR KICKING SPORTS
Ball hitting, throwing, and kicking sports have many movements in common. Baseball players run after they have hit the ball. Other players throw the ball while the batter is running. Football players must throw, run, and kick, sometimes resulting in movements that are com-

mon not only with baseball but with racquet sports as well. All sports obviously have movments in common with almost all other sports. The fine differences between wrist action in throwing a softball and throwing a baseball are sometimes detectable only by strobelight photo analysis.

Emphasis becomes important when we think of the difference between the demands of one sport and another. In baseball, the players are relatively inactive until it comes time to hit the ball or to take places on the field while the opposing team is up to bat. Even during the game, the team on the field has players who may never run, jump, catch, or throw during an inning, depending on where the ball goes when it is hit.

Volleyball and basketball players must sustain vigorous activity to a far greater extent than baseball and softball players. Consequently, they must train for endurance as well as for controlled strength and explosive power. In comparison to basketball, baseball is relatively static. Football combines some aspects of both games.

At the beginning of each program are a few tips that will help you get the most out of your training.

Baseball and Softball

Remember the fundamental movements that baseball and softball involve: throwing, hitting, catching, tagging, sliding, and running. If your team has the field, you must add to these movements shifting from side to side (as in shortstop and base work), and exploding out of a field position to catch a long fly or a line drive.

Timing, explosive power, explosive speed, and absolute accuracy in pitching, throwing, and hitting are the chief ingredients of performance in this sport. The kind of cardiovascular demands made by basketball or long-distance running are not present on the baseball playing field.

This does not mean that you shouldn't train aerobically. If you're going to sustain your timing and accuracy throughout a long game, you'd better train for endurance. This is especially true of a pitcher, who must train for different types of conditioning in the same muscles (endurance in the pitching arm in order to last through a game, and power in the same arm in order to deliver a fast ball).

In addition to the training program outlined, you should supplement your training and playing with aerobic training (such as running, jogging, or cycling) on alternate days. Each sequence of exercises constitutes a movement cluster that approximates the movements of the sport itself. Review the material on pages 177 through 185 on the relation between the exercises and sports movements. Pay special attention to the discussion on overloading on pages 172 through 175 and 184.

First Sequence
1. Ankle sequence from pretraining
2. Double crunch
3. Side lean
4. Spinal hyperextension
5. Squat
6. Sports movements: running, side-to-side shifting, jumping, bending, stooping

Second Sequence
1. Seated twist
2. Anterior, lateral, posterior raises
3. Flyes or pec deck work
4. Elbow flexion
5. Elbow extension
6. Radio-ulnar deviation
7. Wrist flexion and extension
8. Jump box work
9. Simulated sports movements: throwing motions, windup, throw, and follow-through

Third Sequence
1. Hip abduction
2. Hip adduction
3. Spinal hyperextension
4. Double crunch
5. Seated twist
6. Posterior and anterior raise
7. Triceps extension
8. Barbell curl
9. Sports movements: side-to-side shifting, digging-in movement with the feet, hitting movements

Football
In addition to training for strength, power, stamina, and endurance, a football player, even if he is a recreational player, must never forget that football is a contact sport. You can train for power by performing the exercise movements slowly in the eccentric movements and rapidly

in the concentric movements (refer to the section on training for strength, power, stamina, and endurance on pages 149 through 161). You can train for endurance by doing exercises at 20 percent capacity over an extended period of time. But you have to come in contact with another object, be it a fellow player or a padded post, in order to train to take the body blows that come with playing the game.

The exercises listed in the program below will give you the kind of strength, power, stamina, and endurance you need to improve your game. The sports movements listed at the end of the exercises provide you with the overloading necessary for real progress. You should, however, include scrimmage, blocking, and tackling in the sports movements. You can't make progress in a contact sport without the contact.

In addition to the exercises and sports movements listed in this program, you should supplement your training with an aerobic activity such as jogging, running, or cycling on alternate days.

Each sequence of exercises constitutes a movement cluster that approximates the movements of the sport itself. Review the material on pages 177 through 185 on the relation between the exercises and sports movements. Pay special attention to the discussion on overloading on pages 172 through 175 and 184. Remember that different playing positions demand different kinds of performance, so adjust your routine accordingly.

First Sequence
1. Ankle routine from pretraining
2. Knee rotation from pretraining
3. Squat
4. Hip flexion
5. Hip abduction
6. Hip adduction
7. Hip hyperextension
8. Jump box work
9. Sports movements: side-to-side shifting, jumping, turning, spinning, pushing against an opponent

Second Sequence
1. Regular dead weight lift
2. Shoulder shrug
3. Retraction
4. Protraction
5. Side lean
6. Spinal hyperextension

7. Double crunch
8. Sports movements: side-to-side shifting, jumping, twisting, isometric pushing against a wall or pushing against an opponent, running around the track

Third Sequence
1. Bench press
2. Pulldowns behind neck
3. Posterior raise
4. Lateral raise
5. Anterior raise
6. Flyes
7. Sports movements: jumping, pushing against an opponent or isometric pushing against a wall, throwing motions, catching and pulling-in motions, running around the track and practicing evasive maneuvers while running, with spins and leaps, stiff-arm work, jump box work.

Soccer
Same as football, but with more emphasis on leg, hip, and core muscle work. Drop isometric pushing against an opponent, but stress ankle and knee rotation work. For sports movements, stress sudden starts and stops, explosive acceleration from a standing position and from a crouching position. Also, stress balance beam work for bilaterally symmetrical performance with the legs and feet. Jump box work and minitrampoline work.

Handball
Same as racquet sports above.

Golf
It has jokingly been said that golf is a way to ruin a good walk. Golfers have responded that walking is the way that a good golf game is often ruined. For those who play golf for the first time, it is the memory of walking a long distance that sticks in the mind as much as the tension at the tee.

The movements made when hitting a golf ball involve the arms, the upper body, the torso, and to some extent the head and neck. The legs and feet provide the stable foundation for swinging the club with both power and absolute accuracy. Deviation of a quarter of an inch in shoulder or arm movements can be translated into a disastrously wrong angle when the face of the club meets the ball.

Further, it is the speed with which the face of the club meets the ball that translates into distance. This means that power training—training for explosive but tightly controlled motion—is what the golfer needs to bring his driving distance up to the magical 300 yards that every duffer and divot-maker dreams about.

On the other hand, putting (or, for that matter, chipping out of a sand trap with accuracy) takes a combination of stability, coordination, power, and concentration that at least some golfers think is far harder to develop than the ability to hit fabled 300-yard drives.

In addition to the exercises listed, and the golfing movements that follow them, you should also train for the ability to concentrate on your movements in order to achieve perfect control over them. As you perform the golfing movements at the end of the exercises, train your mind to concentrate on each movement as you make it. Go back to the pretraining chapter and reread the section on the fundamental movements of the wrist, elbow, shoulder, spine, and hips. Try to visualize in your mind how each limb moves and carries its movement onto other parts of the body as you make your swing.

Practice your swings on a balance beam, in order to train for stability. If you can make a perfect swing while balancing on a beam, when you get your feet back on solid ground you'll find stability that you never knew you had.

You should also include some form of aerobic training in your program on alternate days. While golf does involve walking, all too often the walk has been replaced by a ride in an electric cart, with the result that the only exercise you get in golf besides swinging is getting in and out of the cart. Try running or jogging three times a week for the kind of cardiovascular fitness you'll need to keep on enjoying golf for decades to come.

Each sequence of exercises constitutes a movement cluster that approximates the movements of the sport itself. Review the material on pages 177 through 185 on the relation between the exercises and sports movements. Pay special attention to the discussion on overloading on pages 172 through 175 and 184.

First Sequence
1. Ankle sequence from pretraining
2. Knee sequence from pretraining
3. Hip sequence from pretraining
4. Spinal hyperextension
5. Double crunch
6. Side lean
7. Sports movements: practice stance and swings on a balance beam

Second Sequence
1. Hip abduction
2. Hip adduction
3. Wrist flexion
4. Wrist extension
5. Seated twists or standing twists on a Twistaway machine
6. Posterior raise (for deltoids)
7. Lateral raise
8. Anterior raise
9. Sports movements: practice stance and swings on a balance beam

Third Sequence
1. Flyes
2. Shoulder shrug
3. Pulldown behind neck
4. Seated twists or standing twists on a Twistaway machine
5. Triceps extension
6. Curl
7. Medial and lateral rotation of shoulder
8. Wrist flexion
9. Wrist extension
10. Sports movements: practice stance, swings, and putting on a balance beam. Work for fluid movement and smooth acceleration in the swing.

Volleyball and Basketball

Volleyball and basketball are two of the most physically demanding recreational sports. The entire body is in almost constant motion, and neuromotor coordination is of prime importance for both games.

The two sports share common movements: jumping, running, shifting from side to side, overhead arm movements, twisting, and coordinating leg and arm movements. The energy demands are great, as you can deduce from watching any group of out-of-shape people playing either sport.

Ankle and knee exercises from the pretraining section are included here because they are fundamental in providing the kind of strength and flexibility you need to avoid injury during a fast-paced game. Extensive leg and hip work is also included, since these are the areas that get the most work during a game. Strength in the upper body is not particularly stressed, but is important especially in blocking techniques. The training emphasis should be on neuromotor coordination of leg, body, and arm movements, combined with power and endurance training. You will need short bursts of speed and power, but you will also need to be able to sustain vigorous leg activity to last through the game to the end.

Jump box and trampoline work has proved to be helpful in giving you the kind of dynamic power you need for jumps and moving across the floor. Balance beam work will give you the kind of stability on your feet that you need in fast-moving scrambles.

Each sequence of exercises constitutes a movement cluster that approximates the movements of the sport itself. Review the material on pages 177 through 185 concerning the relation between the exercises and the sports movements. Pay special attention to the discussion on overloading on pages 172 through 175 and 184.

In addition to the exercises listed here, you should include some form of aerobic training in your program on off days. Jogging, running, or cycling will give you the cardiovascular conditioning needed to supplement your power and muscular endurance training.

First Sequence
1. Ankle sequence from pretraining
2. Knee rotations from pretraining
3. Squat
4. Hip flexion
5. Hip abduction
6. Hip adduction
7. Leg extension
8. Leg curl
9. Jump box work
10. Mini-trampoline work
11. Sports movements: side-to-side shifting, jumping, spinning

Second Sequence
1. Squat (work for explosive contraction phase)
2. Spinal hyperextension
3. Double crunch
4. Hip flexion
5. Hip abduction
6. Hip adduction
7. Side leans or twists
8. Shoulder shrug
9. Protraction
10. Retraction
11. Sports movements: side-to-side shifting on a balance beam, throw-

ing ball from balance beam, catching ball from balance beam, striking ball from balance beam, jump box work

Third Sequence
1. Shoulder rotations
2. Posterior raise
3. Lateral raise
4. Anterior raise
5. Flyes or pec deck work
6. Lunges with two dumbbells
7. Military press
8. Dumbbell curl
9. Wrist flexion
10. Wrist extension
11. Sports movements: same as in Second Sequence

MARTIAL ARTS

Karate

The chief ingredients in successful karate are speed, power, focus, accuracy in timing, and endurance. Power comes from the proper combination of speed and focus. A punch must be thrown from the side to the target in as small an amount of time as is possible. At the point of impact (whether you pull the punch in practice *kumite* or are hitting a *makawara* board) all of the muscles of the body should contract, beginning in the abdominal region and radiating out through the rest of the body. When the punch, kick, strike, or block connects, it should have behind it a completely rigid body. This rigidity occurs only for an instant, however, followed by relaxation.

The exercises listed in this program are designed to help you increase your speed, power, and neuromotor control. The karate movements listed at the end of each sequence will help you overload the muscles that you have exercised. As a variation, advanced students may complete all three sequences of exercises and then perform a kata that utilizes all the movements included in the exercises. In addition to the exercises listed in the program, you should include an aerobic activity in your training. Running, jogging, or cycling will provide you with the cardiovascular conditioning that you need to sustain you through tournaments or heavy practice sessions.

Review the material on pages 177 through 185 concerning the relation between the exercises and sports movements. Each sequence constitutes a movement cluster that approximates the karate movements.

Pay special attention to the discussion on overloading on pages 172 through 175 and 184. As a karateka, you should especially enjoy the sportspower program, since its central concept is based on the relation between exercise and performance that is integral to the relationship between karate conditioning exercises and the performance of katas. Sportspower training is, essentially, the development of "exercise katas" for every sport.

First Sequence
1. Ankle sequence from pretraining
2. Squat and lunges with dumbbells
3. Hip abduction
4. Hip adduction
5. Hip flexion
6. Hip hyperextension
7. Leg extension
8. Leg curl
9. Seated twists or standing twist on a Twistaway machine
10. Sports movements: stepping into left and right forward stances, stepping into side or *kiba-dachi* stance, front snap kick, side snap kick, back thrust kick

Second Sequence
1. Leg extension
2. Leg curl
3. Hip flexion
4. Hip hyperextension
5. Hip abduction
6. Hip adduction
7. Spinal hyperextension
8. Double crunch
9. Twists or side lean
10. Retraction
11. Protraction
12. Sports movements: front thrust kick, side thrust kick, roundhouse kick, stepping with downward block, stepping with rising block

Third Sequence
1. Twists
2. Shoulder shrug
3. Bench press
4. Low pulley rowing

5. Anterior raise
6. Posterior raise
7. Lateral raise
8. Flyes
9. Curl
10. Triceps extension
11. Hand supination and pronation
12. Wrist flexion
13. Wrist extension
14. Lunges with dumbbells
15. Sports movements: stepping and punching (lunge punch and counterpunch), stepping and blocking, back stance stepping and knife-hand blocks, combinations of techniques

Note: Stances, stepping, kicks, strikes, blocks, and punches should be practiced extensively while standing on a balance beam. If you can perfect these techniques while you are balanced on the beam, you will be rock-solid on the floor. This is especially true of the roundhouse kick. Jump box work should also be included.

Judo

Karate is the art of "empty-hand fighting." The karateka tries to avoid getting close to his opponent except to deliver a punch, strike, kick, or block. The judoka, on the other hand, must get close to his opponent, both with his hands and with the rest of his body, in order to grab him and throw him to the mat. In at least this sense, the training goals of the karateka and the judoka are at opposite poles: the karateka must glide in, make his contact, and glide swiftly away; while the judoka must get in close to his opponent and perform a deft maneuver that will render the opponent helpless. The method is completely different. The results are the same: the opponent has been put out of action.

The judoka needs far greater strength in the arms and the upper back than the karateka needs. Upper back, shoulder, and arm work should be stressed, and training for these areas should include both strength and power training. For a review of power and strength training methods, refer to pages 154 through 158.

The judoka must also condition himself to withstand falls without disorientation. The most common complaint of beginning judo students is their difficulty in taking falls and bouncing right back up to meet the opponent again. Ringing ears, headaches, and problems with balance are as common as sore backsides and palms. By practicing falls after a rigorous sequence of exercises, you will condition yourself to take more punishment.

Each exercise sequence constitutes a movement cluster that approximates judo movements. Review the material on pages 177 through 185 concerning the relation between the exercises and sports movements. Pay special attention to the discussion on overloading on pages 172 through 175 and 184.

In addition to the exercises listed in the program, you should include aerobic activities in your training. On off days, you should run, jog, or cycle in order to give yourself the kind of cardiovascular conditioning you need to sustain yourself through a tournament or a rigorous practice session.

First Sequence
1. Ankle sequence from pretraining
2. Knee rotations from pretraining
3. Squat and jump box work
4. Spinal hyperextension
5. Double crunch
6. Side lean
7. Low pulley rowing
8. Shoulder shrug
9. Sports movements: side-to-side shifting, bending, twisting movements on a balance beam, practice falls on a mat

Second Sequence
1. Twists
2. Double crunch
3. Spinal hyperextension
4. Pulldown behind neck
5. Squat and jump box work
6. Hip abduction
7. Hip adduction
8. Leg extension
9. Leg curl
10. Low pulley rowing
11. Sports movements: load-up throws with an opponent, practice falls on a mat, side-to-side shifting, pulling motions with arms

Third Sequence
1. Side lean
2. Double crunch

3. Spinal hyperextension or regular dead weight lift
4. Curl with dumbbell or barbell
5. Bench press plus protractions
6. Wrist flexion
7. Wrist extension
8. Triceps extension
9. Anterior raise
10. Lateral raise
11. Posterior raise
12. Sports movements: practice falls on a mat, load-up and complete throws with an opponent

Fourth Sequence
1. Hand and wrist sequence from pretraining, with resistance
2. Hand supination and pronation
3. Triceps extension
4. Concentrated curl
5. Low pulley rowing
6. Bentover rowing
7. Double crunch
8. Barbell curl
9. Pulldown to chest
10. Sports movements: same as above, but practice loading and body shifting on a balance beam, load and throw opponent on mat

WATER SPORTS

Swimming is an isokinetic power or sprint activity: it involves movements made in a liquid medium such that the velocity of the movements is governed by the viscosity of the liquid. Usually, the movements made in competition events are made as fast as possible. Movements performed by swimmers are also affected by the strength, power, stamina, and endurance of the individual. Powerful swimmers can move their arms through water faster than weak swimmers. Swimmers with endurance can swim greater distances than swimmers who have no endurance.

Machines such as those manufactured by Hydra-Fitness are ideal for supplementary exercises for swimmers. They are omnikinetic, meaning that the velocity of the movement is determined both by the viscosity of the fluid in Hydra's hydraulic cylinders and by the relative strength of the user. Since Hydra's hydraulic cylinders are adjustable (6 settings from light to heavy resistance on the Series III machines), it is possible to develop omnikinetic movement clusters with self-accommodating resistance. The effect in terms of effort is analogous to what you would have if you were able to increase the viscosity of the water in which you are swimming. If you have access to Hydra-Fitness equipment, you will be able to cut the total time spent training significantly.

If you do not have access to Hydra-Fitness equipment, you can do the movement cluster sequences with either free weights or weighted machines. If you use this type of equipment, you should try to finish the sports movements portion of the sequences in water. *Don't go into the water after a heavy workout without supervision!* If the water is cold, cramping may occur. Never try to complete the movement cluster sequences in water without someone present who can pull you out if you become exhausted or have cramps!

Whatever your swimming goals, you should include both short- and long-distance swimming in your program. If you are a recreational swimmer, you can have more fun if you work for both endurance *and* power. If you do not do long-distance swimming, include some form of aerobic activity in your training so that you will receive the cardiovascular conditioning you need.

Review the material on pages 177 through 185 concerning the relation between the movement clusters and sports movements. Pay special attention to the discussion on overloading on pages 172 through 175 and 184.

Swimming and Scuba Diving

First Sequence
1. Squat
2. Double crunch
3. Leg extension
4. Spinal hyperextension
5. Leg curl
6. Twist or side lean
7. Hip abduction
8. Hip adduction
9. Hip flexion
10. Hip hyperextension
11. Sports movements: these movements should be done in the water. If this is impossible, you should approximate swimming leg movements on isokinetic or omnikinetic equipment (such as Hydra-Fitness) so that the feel of the movements and the speed at which they would be made approximates the natural isokinetic environ-

ment of water. If you are training for competition, move as fast as possible in all movements.

Second Sequence
1. Double crunch
2. Spinal hyperextension
3. Twists
4. Low pulley rowing
5. Curls with a dumbbell
6. Shoulder shrug
7. Pulldown behind neck
8. Triceps extension
9. Leg extension
10. Leg curl
11. Sports movements: see above. This time, include arm movements for crawl, butterfly, etc.

Third Sequence
1. Twists
2. Anterior raise
3. Lateral raise
4. Posterior raise
5. Shoulder rotation sequence from pretraining
6. Bentover rowing
7. Wrist flexion
8. Wrist extension
9. Triceps extension
10. Curls with a dumbbell
11. Alternating leg raises
12. Alternating leg extension
13. Alternating leg curl
14. Sports movements: same as above

Board and Platform Diving
Since your medium is at least partially water, you should combine the swimming movement clusters with the board and platform diving clusters. Diving requires polished neuromotor control and ability to assume and recover from a variety of anomalous body positions. As a consequence, you must parallel the kind of training done by karatekas: condition your neuromotor system by overloading it; accomplish the overloading by diving after an exercise sequence when you are tired.

The same *caveat* applies here that applied in the swimming program, for the same reasons: don't try to complete the movement clusters with diving unless you have a partner present who can pull you out of the water! Never dive under any circumstances without a partner who can help you if you get into trouble! If you perform your diving routine immediately after a workout session, beware of exhaustion and muscle cramps. Don't take unnecessary chances. You're supposed to be doing this for fun.

Review the material on pages 177 through 185 concerning the relation between the exercises and sports movements. Each sequence constitutes a movement cluster that approximates the movements of your sport. Pay special attention to the discussion on overloading on pages 172 through 175 and 184.

1. Squat and jump box work
2. Double crunch
3. Spinal hyperextension
4. Side lean
5. Regular dead weight lift
6. Alternating leg raise
7. Hip flexion
8. Hip abduction
9. Hip adduction
10. Military press
11. Sports movements: practice balance on a balance beam; do not do practice dives when your *erector spinae* muscles are tired (you may injure your spine). This is one sequence in which it is almost impossible to intersperse actual sports movements with the exercises. These exercises, however, will strengthen your core muscles, and the balance beam work will enhance your bilaterally symmetrical performance. Also try a mini-trampoline.

Waterskiing
See the section on sustained leg movements above. Add additional work for wrist flexion and low pulley work for the *latissimus* muscles. Practice low stances on a balance beam.

STRENGTH AND POWER SPORTS
Powerlifting and Olympic lifting are sports that, historically, grew out of a form of exercise. Tradition has it that weightlifting began with the Greek Milo, who lifted a calf every day for a year. As the calf grew in size, Milo grew in strength. Fortunately for Milo (or, perhaps, for the perpetuation of the myth) the daily increase in the calf's mass did not

exceed the daily increase in Milo's muscular strength, so that at the end of the year Milo could lift the full-grown cow. It is assumed that he could not lift a cow at the beginning. Thus, according to pundits, began progressive resistance training.

The sports of powerlifting and Olympic lifting developed out of an effort to lift greater and greater poundages in certain common exercise lifts: the bench press, the deadlift, and the squat for powerlifting; the snatch and the clean and jerk for Olympic lifting (the military press was abandoned because of the danger of spinal injuries that accompany bad form in the lift).

It is helpful, then, to make a distinction: powerlifting and Olympic lifting are sports in which greater and greater poundages are attempted (in competition); weight *training* is a form of resistance exercise which can be used to develop strength, power, stamina, and endurance, regardless of the sport you are training for.

In training for either powerlifting or Olympic lifting, it is important not to neglect the muscles that help stabilize the joints and that act synergetically with the large muscles in making lifts. We've all seen people around the gym who get stuck at a certain poundage on the bench press and can never seem to get past it. They work harder than anybody else, but still don't make gains. Often the problem is lack of proper "background" work with lighter weights. You can't do your maximum every training session and expect to make progress. You have to work below maximum for a couple of sessions, then go for the maximum. You should alternate between sessions in which you do 3 or 4 reps with a weight that is anywhere from 60 percent to 80 percent of your maximum, and sessions in which you perform 1-rep sets, starting with a poundage that is well below maximum and finishing with a weight that is a new personal record.

Further, you should pay attention to the muscles that help the big ones make the lift. For example, the bench press is what is called a "compound" lift. It involves more than one major muscle group. The anterior deltoids, the pectorals, and the triceps all play an integral part in the lift. But the rotators of the shoulder, the supinators of the forearm, and the elbow stabilizers such as the *brachialis* and *brachioradialis* play an equally important role both in the prevention of injuries and the stabilization of the joints involved in the lift.

The same is true of the squat. The primary movers in the squat are the quadriceps: the *rectus femoris,* the *vastus medialis, vastus intermedius,* and *vastus lateralis.* But the *gluteus maximus* is the muscle group that starts the movement upward from the bottom of a squat, aided and then taken over by the action of the hamstrings. The *rectus femoris* is linked not only to the kneecap, but to the pelvis as well. It is a hip flexor as well as an extender of the leg at the knee. The adductors in the inside of the thigh are equally important to the squat, which is why many powerlifters swear by such machines as the Hydra-Fitness Adduction/Abduction Hip machine. It works the inner and outer thigh.

The deadlift involves the legs, the upper and lower back, and the arms. Those of you who keep up with the weight training magazines will recall the startling photos of a world class powerlifter in a 1981 meet whose right biceps ripped loose from the tendon in the middle of a lift. Yet many amateur powerlifters do not include biceps work in their powerlifting workout.

Former national champion Andy Jackson stoutly maintains that his lifts improve significantly from heavy abdominal work. Other lifters, such as former world women's champion Karen Gajda practice squatting on a teeter-totter board in order to train their neuromotor system for stability in the lift.

The same is true for Olympic lifting. The snatch involves principally the muscles of the shoulders, upper and lower back, arms, and legs. The clean and jerk involves the same muscles, but in a different way: the movement stops at the top of the chest, then continues overhead.

For each type of lifting, it is as important to work the collateral stabilizing muscles and the synergistic muscles as it is to work the main movers. This is why we've included the pretraining chapter. It is as important for weightlifters as it is for participants in other sports. If you are just starting in power or Olympic lifting, or if you've had a layoff, you would do well to go through the pretraining exercises for all of the joints before you dive back into regular weight training workouts.

The basic training exercises should be thoroughly familiar to anyone who has done any weightlifting. However, you should review the material on strength, power, stamina, and endurance training on pages 149 through 161, as well as the discussion on overloading on pages 172 through 175 and 184.

And don't forget: never do heavy bench presses without a spotter!

Powerlifting

First Sequence
1. Hip abduction
2. Hip adduction
3. Hip flexion
4. Hip hyperextension

5. Double crunch
6. Spinal hyperextension
7. Side lean
8. Power rack work for partial squat movements
9. Sports movements: squat, squat on a kinaesthetic primer board

Second Sequence
1. Squat
2. Spinal hyperextension or good morning exercise
3. Side lean
4. Hip adduction
5. Shoulder shrug
6. Bentover rowing
7. Double crunch
8. Sports movements: regular dead weight lift

Third Sequence
1. Anterior raise
2. Double crunch
3. Shoulder rotations from pretraining
4. Protraction
5. Retraction
6. Side lean
7. Spinal hyperextension
8. Lateral raise
9. Flyes
10. Posterior raise
11. Sports movements: bench press

Olympic Lifting

First Sequence
1. Squat
2. Double crunch
3. Leg extension
4. Spinal hyperextension or good morning exercise
5. Leg curl
6. Lunges
7. Dumbbell swings
8. Military press
9. Barbell curl

Appendix I.

Injuries: How to Avoid Them
and How to Treat Them
If and When You Get Them

If you've been physically active most of your life, you already know the difference between "good" pain and "bad" pain. Good pain is the deep, warm soreness that you feel when you've recently changed your weight training routine to jar your muscles out of their rut. If you're sore, you know you did it right.

Bad pain, on the other hand, is the kind of nagging, sharp, aching, and sometimes disabling pain that comes after injuries and strains, tears, and breaks. This section is devoted to some of the ailments common to serious amateur athletes. There is a list of the kinds of injuries that often accompany specific sports. There are descriptions of various types of treatments popular with physicians and sports trainers.

We can't overstress the importance of seeing a physician if you suffer an injury. Some finger injuries, if left unattended, can lead to irrevocable loss of movement. Other injuries, such as pull-off fractures and hairline bone cracks, can become sources of chronic pain. Don't rely on your own self-diagnosis if pain persists after an injury. Above all, don't think that this appendix can substitute for professional help. Each injury is different. No injury can be diagnosed without individual inspection. The purpose of this appendix is to acquaint you with different types of injuries and the treatments that you can expect when you have them.

And remember: if you want to avoid injuries, no matter what your particular sport, do *all* of the exercises described in the pretraining chapter.

TYPES OF INJURIES
• Pulled or torn muscles. This one is usually the result of not warming up sufficiently, or from making a sudden move under stress that the muscles are not resilient enough to accommodate. It can also result

212

from using too much weight in resistance training, or from using too much speed in working with isokinetic devices (where the greater the speed attempted, the greater the resistance met by the muscles). Sports that require speed often result in torn muscles when the player tries to go beyond his normal velocity (for example, when making a serve in tennis).

• Pulled or torn tendons. These injuries sometimes accompany pulled muscles. Depending on the amount of muscular development in an individual player, it's a toss-up whether the muscle tears first or the tendon. Tendons sometimes tear loose from the bone surface on which they are anchored. Other times they merely tear internally and become inflamed. The infamous "tennis elbow" is simply a chronic inflammation of the extensor and flexor tendons of the forearm (and, more rarely, of the upper arm). Tendons pull or tear when they are overstressed. Athletes with terrifically strong muscles pull tendons when the tendon is no longer able to cope with the stresses that the muscles put upon them. Sometimes speed alone will pull tendons. Karatekas sometimes execute techniques (strikes, blocks, punches, or kicks) so fast that the speed of the technique exceeds the tendon's ability to accommodate to the demands of the movement. The result is called "tendonitis" (or "tendinitis"), which is an inflammation of the tendons involved.

• Joint separations and dislocations. Separations and dislocations occur when a joint is subjected to stresses that exceed its structural strength. The amount of stress that a joint can take is determined by a number of elements: the structure of the joint itself, the condition of the ligaments that hold it together, the condition of the cartilage in and around the joint, and the size and strength of the muscles and the tendons that attach them to the bones near the joint. Some joints are inherently stronger and more stable than others. The hip joint is a ball and socket, the shoulder is a cup and saucer, and the knee is a loosely constructed partial hinge that depends on cartilage and ligaments for its stability instead of a smoothly articulated pair of convex and concave encapsulated bone surfaces. The hip joint is inherently stronger than the knee. The shoulder joint is stronger than the knee, but weaker than the hip. Joint injuries can range from minor separations, in which the ligaments are stretched but not torn, all the way to major dislocations in which the two bones that connect in the joint are pulled completely out of the joint, with attendant tearing of ligaments, cartilage, and adjacent tendons and muscles. At one end of the scale, if you've merely overstretched a muscle or suffered a minor muscle tear, you can probably treat the injury yourself. At the other end of the scale, if you've suffered a major tear or a fracture, you need the attention of an orthopedist, and you'll probably need some postoperative care, such as physical or corrective therapy.

• Bone chip fractures. These fractures occur as a result of collisions between the bones of a joint or from a blow to the bone from the outside. The result is that a small chip of bone is separated from the main bone. Sometimes tendons or ligaments pull off bone chips as a result of overstressing. When the ligament or tendon pulls the chip away from the bone, it is sometimes called a "pull-off" fracture.

• Stress or fatigue fractures. These bone breaks occur when the bone is not able to stand up under the stresses that are being put upon it. "Simple" fractures involve bone breaks in which the skin is not broken, as opposed to "compound" fractures in which skin tearing occurs. These injuries also range from minor (or in the case of a hairline fracture of the toe) to catastrophic (in the case of a compound fracture of the hip joint and thigh bone). Regardless of the severity of the break, if you do indeed have a break, you should see an orthopedist.

• Triggerpoints. Triggerpoints are thought to be small nodules of degenerated muscle tissue that can "trigger" spasms and pain. They were described by Dr. Max Lange in 1931. Treatment for triggerpoints was pioneered by Dr. Hans Kraus and usually consists of injections of either lidocaine or a saline solution to break them up. If you have small, painful nodules embedded in your muscle tissue (feel for them: they're small and round), ask your doctor about them. They may be what Doctors Lange and Kraus call "triggerpoints." On the other hand, they may be tumors. Don't neglect any lump or nodule! Triggerpoint therapy is still controversial among physicians.

• Sprains. A sprain occurs when a ligament is injured. Sprains come in three grades, depending on the severity of the injury. Ligaments are stretched in Grade One sprains, they are partially torn and weakened in Grade Two, and they are completely torn or ruptured in Grade Three. Grade One you can probably take care of yourself. For Grade Two and Grade Three, you need an orthopedist.

• Bruises. Bruises (or "contusions") are usually caused by a blow to the muscle or to the bones. They can also result from repeated actions, such as stamping the feet during karate techniques. They are areas either in muscle tissue or in bone tissue where small blood vessels are damaged, and surrounding tissue is stressed or damaged. Don't ignore bruises. If they are frequent, or if they won't go away, see your doctor. You may have a bleeding problem.

• Stiffness and muscle cramps. These ailments can result from pulled muscles, calcium deficiency in the diet, infection, or the reaction of muscle tissue to overuse or overstress. Cramps can result from salt depletion, sudden changes in temperature, and failure to warm up adequately.

These are the most common ailments that plague amateur and professional athletes alike. If you are a "weekend" athlete, chances are greater that you'll suffer more of these ills than if you played three or four times a week. This is especially true of such things as stiff muscles, cramps, and torn muscles and tendons. If you don't play the game enough to keep the muscles toned and the tendons elastic, you suffer the consequences.

Because of the similarity in movements, many sports have injuries in common. For instance, the same tendon pulls that give the tennis player "tennis elbow" give the ball player "pitcher's arm." Sudden snapping motions of the wrist during the last few degrees of motion in a pitch or in a forehand or backhand swing put a sudden stress load on the tendons that attach the wrist flexors and extensors to the bones at the elbow. The result: tendonitis, and the nagging pain that it entails.

Here are some of the injuries and the sports with which they are associated:

1. Wrist sprains and fractures: tennis, football, baseball, karate, boxing, fencing, pole vaulting, cycling, gymnastics
2. Neck sprains and fractures: wrestling, football, gymnastics, trampoline, diving, weight training
3. Broken or cracked ribs: football, wrestling, cycling, karate, boxing, skiing, hockey, soccer
4. Lower back injuries: weightlifting, diving, wrestling, football, trampoline, jogging
5. Hip injuries (fractures or dislocations): skiing, football, gymnastics, judo, trampoline
6. Knee injuries: football, skiing, racquet sports, wrestling, judo, basketball, baseball, volleyball, soccer
7. Ankle and foot injuries: jogging, running, football, skiing, basketball, skating, baseball, volleyball, soccer

The list, of course, is by no means exhaustive. Ralph once smashed the tip of a finger doing squats (when he set the barbell back on the rack). We have a friend whose wife lost two fingers wrestling with clothes in a dryer. Everybody knows a story about a freak accident in which someone dropped a barbell plate on a toe and broke it, or separated a shoulder not in football but in table tennis. But the sports listed under the injury headings are the sports in which these injuries are most likely to happen.

What do you do when you're injured? Here are a few tips, with some observations on the state of the art of injury rehabilitation.

The old admonition for the treatment of injuries is called RICE: Rest, Ice, Compression, and Elevation ("elevation" meaning to place the injured area higher than the heart). Stop moving the injured limb, get it out of action, let it rest so that you won't compound the injury. Put ice on the injured area so that the natural tendency toward swelling can be stopped. If the injured area swells, healing will be postponed. Ice will slow down circulation of blood to the area, and swelling will at least be attenuated. Compress the area as another way to keep it from swelling. Elevate the area to the level of the heart or higher so that gravity won't cause more swelling.

RICE is the oldest standby of athletic trainers, coaches, and physical therapists. It is not universally accepted, however, as the best way to treat an injury. Some orthopedists, such as Dr. Hans Kraus, a former faculty member of the Columbia College of Physicians and recipient of the Distinguished Service Award of the President's Council on Physical Fitness and Sports, emphatically does not believe in RICE. Instead, he recommends MECE: Movement, application of Ethyl Chloride, Compression, and Elevation.

In *Sports Injuries* (Playboy Press, 1981) Kraus reminds the reader (and indirectly, the medical profession) that he first reported the use of ethyl chloride as a source of coldness in 1935 in a paper delivered to the Academy of Physicians in Vienna. Kraus cites not only the effectiveness of ethyl chloride spray on minor (and sometimes major) injuries, but the convenience as well. All you need is a can of ethyl chloride. You don't need a refrigerator filled with crushed ice.

Kraus also criticizes the common practice of immobilizing injured limbs and joints. "M" in MECE stands for "Movement." If you expect the injured body part to regain its full use, you have to move it.

Kraus is not alone in this regard. Many coaches and trainers as well as physical and corrective therapists start rehabilitation programs as soon as the swelling goes down. Others, however, insist that the injured limb or joint be absolutely immobilized, with a cast if necessary.

Many people simply "work through" an injury. When they do this, however, they are asking for trouble. Some kinds of injuries, especially torn ligaments in the fingers and wrists as well as the elbow and knee, can become chronic and devastating if left unattended. For certain kinds of finger injuries, permanent loss of movement can occur if the injury is not attended to by a qualified professional within a week.

Shoulder injuries, especially if they involve separations, can lead to long and painful convalescences. Ligaments can be abraded and reinjured after the initial injury, and they can thicken as a consequence. Once they thicken, it may be impossible to move the arm in the shoulder joint without pain.

Knee injuries are the worst of the lot in some ways. Many people have simply lost the use of their knee joints either through neglect of injuries or through repeated reinjury.

Although the experts may disagree about the proper course of action immediately following an injury, there are some things upon which they seem generally to agree:

1. An injured muscle, limb, or joint should be lowered in temperature as soon as possible to avoid excessive swelling. Whether you use ethyl chloride or paper cups full of ice, get the area chilled in a hurry.
2. Once you've chilled the area (but not enough to damage the skin), you should immobilize the joint or limb until you know whether or not there is a fracture involved. If you move a fractured bone around, you can cut nerves and blood vessels, with catastrophic results.
3. If the bone is fractured or if the joint is separated or dislocated, go immediately to an orthopedist. He or she will tell you whether or not you need a cast, a splint, or a brace. If you are injured sufficiently to need therapy, you'll have to go to a doctor anyway, since physical therapists must have a referral from a physician to treat you.
4. If the bone is not fractured and if the joint is not dislocated or separated, but merely sprained, then the ethyl chloride or ice packs should be followed by rest until the danger of swelling is past. Once the danger of swelling is past, then therapy can begin.
5. There are as many types of therapies as there are therapists to give them. Some apply heat, others alternate heat and cold. Some give vibratory massages and some swear by ultrasonics. Some use isotonic exercise, and others use isokinetics (isotonic exercise involves lifting weights to strengthen the muscles, while isokinetics uses hydraulic cylinders or friction-clutch devices to govern the speed and the force with which the movement is made). Some therapists have had significant success by providing resistance to muscular con-

traction with small, wide rubber bands or lengths of surgical tubing.

6. Depending on many factors—age, the extent of the injury, the location of the injury, whether or not there is a fracture—therapy can begin as soon as 24 hours after the trauma. Most people use some form of heat or other circulation-increasing means. The main thing is to bring about an increased flow of blood into the affected area (once the danger of swelling is past) and hence an increased flow of oxygen and the nutrients necessary for the healing process.

7. The objectives of physical or corrective therapy are manifold. Among the most important goals are relief from pain; full or increased use of the injured body part; in the case of joint injuries, a return to a full range of motion; strengthening of the muscles, tendons, ligaments, and other tissues and structures in the damaged area; return of the patient to a normal use of the damaged area. In short, getting him or her back into the game!

8. Once therapy begins, the patient should not be allowed to favor the injured area any more than is necessary to ease the pain. Nobody ever regained the full use of an injured joint or limb by sitting around wishing it well.

9. Therapy takes as much effort (much more, as a matter of fact) on the part of the patient as it does on the part of the therapist. Any good therapist can tell you and show you what you should do to get well. Only you can do the work that it takes to get back in the running.

10. The progress you make depends on a number of things: your age and the resultant rate at which you heal; the extent or severity of the injury; whether or not the injury is simple (involving only one injured body part, such as a simple bone fracture) or multiple (such as a broken hip with related back injuries); whether or not an infection develops; whether or not the bones and joints are reset or rebuilt properly; how promptly you received medical attention; the competence of the attending physician; the competence of the therapist; the competence of the people who attended to your injury immediately after it happened; your own determination to get well and get back into the game.

So, when the injury happens, remember RICE or MECE, don't jostle a fracture around, and get medical attention if the injury looks like more than a simple strain, sprain, or pull. Most emergency clinics are prepared to treat injuries. That's their stock in trade. But don't wait until you're injured before you seek help. If you are at all physically active, you should already have looked up the various professionals in your area so that if and when you get hurt, you can have the odds in your favor instead of trusting to pot luck and whoever happens to be the surgical resident on duty the night you pop your clavicle at the company softball game.

You should also make it your business to know the names of the physicians in your community who specialize in athletic injuries or related orthopedic procedures. If there are physical therapists in your town, seek them out. Their advice may save you time, money, and pain in the future. They're in the Yellow Pages.

A few precautionary words: physical therapy is a relatively new field. Corrective therapy is so new that the state organizations are just now beginning to form. Many physicians, especially those who know little about exercise and athletic injuries, still do not understand what it is that the physical therapist does. The physical and corrective therapist must depend on the physicians for referrals. You can't go to a physical therapist and say, "Here, fix my knee." He or she must have a physician's diagnosis beforehand, and a written referral from the MD.

Only recently, through the efforts of people such as Chicago's Richard Hoover, have physical therapists become known not only to the physicians but to the general public as well. These are the people who treat injuries on a day-to-day basis, and who get the patients off their backs and back into the game. The good ones know all the machines, instruments, and procedures that will help you overcome your injury. If you don't know which therapist is the best, call your local pro ball club. Or try the sportsmedicine department (if there is one) at your state university. They'll know the good ones, too. They're probably teaching courses for them.

Most important of all, if you're injured don't think that the world has come to an end. Ralph overcame rheumatic fever and an enlarged heart to become a weight trainer and Valerie overcame an almost total lack of kinaesthetic sense to become one of the most agile people around the gym. And in 1981, a troupe of handicapped people successfully climbed Mount Rainier.

Most of your injuries will be minor. If you have them, do what you have to do and get back into the game as soon as you can.

And be more careful next time!

Appendix II.

Muscular Anatomy Charts with Nomenclature of Major Skeletal Muscles

KEY FOR SKELETAL MUSCLES, FRONT VIEW

1. TRAPEZIUS
2. LATERAL DELTOID
3. ANTERIOR DELTOID
4. PECTORALIS MAJOR
5. LATERAL HEAD OF THE TRICEPS
6. SERRATUS ANTERIOR
7. BICEPS BRACHII
8. MEDIAL HEAD OF THE TRICEPS
9. BRACHIALIS
10. BRACHIORADIALIS
11. RECTUS ABDOMINIS
12. EXTERNAL OBLIQUE
13. FLEXORS FOR THE FINGERS AND WRIST
14. GLUTEUS MEDIUS
15. ILIACUS
16. PSOAS MAJOR
17. PECTINEUS
18. ADDUCTOR LONGUS
19. GRACILIS
20. ADDUCTOR MAGNUS
21. TENSOR FASCIAE LATAE
22. SARTORIUS
23. RECTUS FEMORIS
24. VASTUS LATERALIS
25. VASTUS MEDIALIS
26. PERONEUS LONGUS
27. GASTROCNEMIUS
28. TIBIALIS ANTERIOR (OR ANTICUS)
29. EXTENSOR DIGITORUM LONGUS
30. EXTENSOR HALLUCIS LONGUS
31. SOLEUS

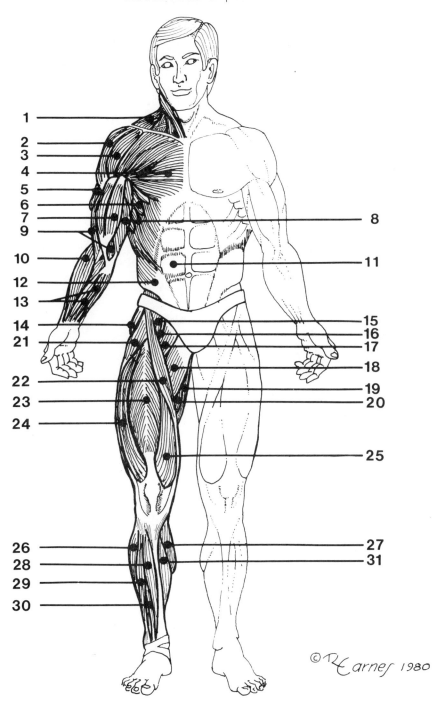

1
2
3
4
5
6
7
9
10
12
13
14
21
22
23
24
26
28
29
30

8
11
15
16
17
18
19
20
25
27
31

©TEarnes 1980

HUMAN MUSCULAR ANATOMY, FRONT VIEW

KEY FOR SKELETAL MUSCLES, BACK VIEW

1. TRAPEZIUS
2. LATERAL DELTOID
3. POSTERIOR DELTOID
4. TERES MAJOR
5. RHOMBOIDEUS MAJOR
6. LATERAL HEAD OF THE TRICEPS
7. LONG HEAD OF THE TRICEPS
8. LATISSIMUS DORSI
9. BRACHIALIS
10. MEDIAL HEAD OF THE TRICEPS
11. BRACHIORADIALIS
12. EXTENSOR CARPI RADIALIS LONGUS
13. FLEXOR CARPI ULNARIS
14. EXTENSOR DIGITORUM COMMUNIS
15. ERECTOR SPINAE
16. EXTENSOR CARPI RADIALIS BREVIS
17. EXTENSOR CARPI ULNARIS
18. GLUTEUS MEDIUS
19. ABDUCTOR POLLICIS LONGUS AND
    EXTENSOR POLLICIS BREVIS
20. TENSOR FASCIAE LATAE
21. GLUTEUS MAXIMUS
22. ILIOTIBIAL BAND
23. GRACILIS
24. ADDUCTOR MAGNUS
25. BICEPS FEMORIS
26. SEMITENDINOSUS
27. SEMIMEMBRANOSUS
28. VASTUS LATERALIS
29. SHORT HEAD OF THE BICEPS FEMORIS
30. GASTROCNEMIUS
31. SOLEUS
32. PERONEUS LONGUS
33. FLEXOR HALLUCIS LONGUS
34. FLEXOR DIGITORUM LONGUS

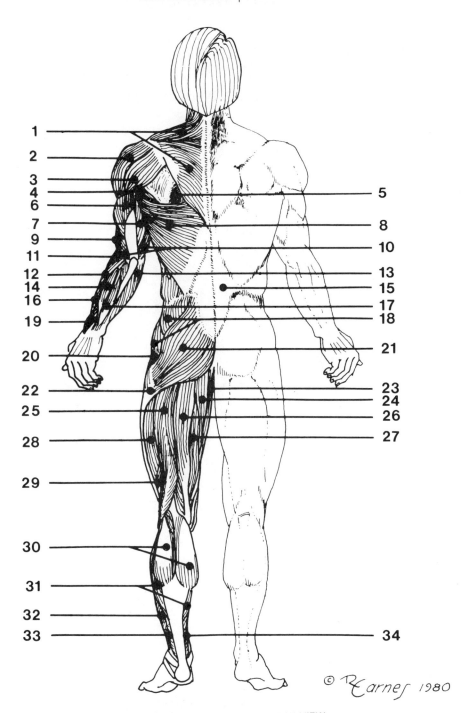

HUMAN MUSCULAR ANATOMY, BACK VIEW

Appendix III.

The Skeletal System:
Approximate Ranges of Motion
of All the Major Joints

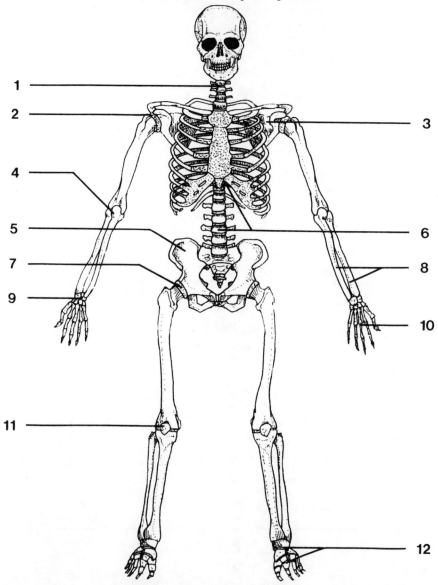

1
2
3
4
5
6
7
8
9
10
11
12

RANGES OF MOTION FOR FUNDAMENTAL MOVEMENTS

Key to the Illustration of the Skeletal System, with Approximate Range of Motion for the Major Limbs and Joints of the Musculo-Skeletal System

Number	Area or Joint	Movement	Approximate Range of Motion
1	Neck or cervical spine	flexion	45°
		extension	0°
		hyperextension	70°
		lateral flexion left or right	45°
		rotation to the left or right	85°
2	Shoulder joint	flexion	90°
		extension (base-line, arm by side)	0°
		hyperextension	45°
		abduction	90°
		adduction (base-line, arm by side)	0°
		lateral rotation	90°
		medial rotation	80°
		horizontal flexion (adduction)	90°
		horizontal abduction	90°
3	Shoulder girdle	elevation	3 inches (approx.)
		depression	2 inches (approx.)
		protraction	3 inches (approx.)
		retraction	3 inches (approx.)
4	Elbow	flexion	150°
		extension (base-line, arm straight)	0°

Number	Area or Joint	Movement	Approximate Range of Motion
		hyperextension (occurs in some individuals)	varies
5	Pelvic girdle	increased inclination	9°
		decreased inclination	6°
		lateral tilt	15°
		rotation to the left or right	10°
6	Thoracic and lumbar spine	flexion	90°
		extension (base-line, back straight)	0°
		hyperextension	45°
		lateral flexion	45°
		rotation to the left or right	60°
7	Hip	flexion	125°
		extension (base-line, standing erect)	0°
		hyperextension	15°
		abduction	45°
		adduction (base-line, standing erect)	0°
		hyperadduction	30°
		lateral rotation	50°
		medial rotation	40°
8	Radial-ulnar movements	pronation of the hand	180°
		supination (base-line, palm to front)	0°
9	Wrist	flexion	85°
		extension (base-line, wrist straight)	0°
		hyperextension	85°
		ulnar flexion	45°
		radial flexion	25°

Number	Area or Joint	Movement	Approximate Range of Motion
10	Hands and fingers	metacarpal-phalan-geal movements (at the knuckles)	
		flexion	90°
		extension (base-line, hand straight)	0°
		hyperextension	10°
		abduction (spreading the fingers)	30°
		adduction (base-line)	0°
		proximal interphalan-geal (at the second joint)	
		flexion (making a fist)	110°
		extension (base-line, fingers straight)	0°
11	Knee	flexion	135°
		extension (base-line, leg straight)	0°
		rotation at 90° flexion	50°
12	Ankle and feet		
	ankle	dorsiflexion	20°
		plantar flexion	60°
		eversion	25°
		inversion	45°
	feet	pronation	20°
		supination	40°

Note: When a movement is given 0° range of motion, it is because the position that the movement indicates is the base-line from which range of motion measurements are made. For example, flexion of the leg at the knee is 135° but extension of the leg at the knee is 0°, since the base-line for measuring the knee joint's range of motion is the fully extended or straightened limb.

Appendix IV.

The Body Planes: Median, Coronal, Sagittal, and Transverse

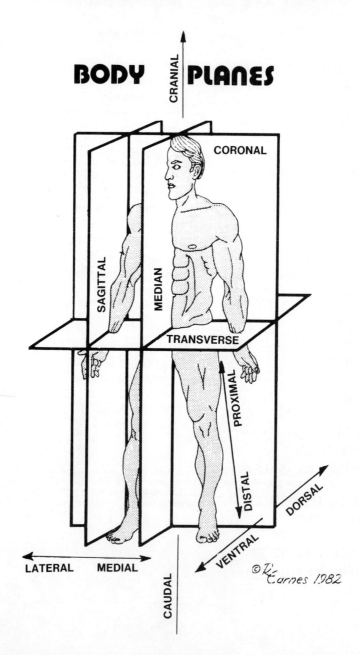

Exercise Equipment Manufacturers

The following list is obviously not exhaustive. As a quick glance at any muscle magazine will show you, there are literally hundreds of small companies all across the country, each grinding out some sort of weight-training equipment. The companies listed below are the major manufacturers, or they are small companies with a unique concept. The equipment that these companies manufacture is what you'll find in health clubs and gyms anywhere in the United States.

BODY CULTURE EQUIPMENT
COMPANY
    P.O. Box 10
    Alliance, NB 69301
    (Iron Man free weights and
    machines)

DIVERSIFIED PRODUCTS
    Opelika, Ala/Compton, CA
    (DP Olympic barbells)

HYDRA-GYM ATHLETICS,
INC.
    2121 Industrial Park
    P.O. Box 599
    Belton, TX 76513

NAUTILUS SPORTS/MEDICAL
INDUSTRIES
    P.O. Box 1783
    Deland, FL 32720
    (Nautilus machines)

PARAMOUNT HEALTH
EQUIPMENT CORPORATION
    3000 South Santa Fe
    Los Angeles, CA 90058
    (Machines, free weights, and
    accessories)

SAF-T-GYM (RICK ADAMS
PRODUCTS)
    815 Alexander Vy Road
    Healdsburg, CA 91364
    (The Saf-T-Gym workout
    bench)

STRENGTH/FITNESS
SYSTEMS
    P.O. Box 266
    Independence, MO 64051
    (Mini-Gym machines)

UNIQUE TRAINING DEVICE
COMPANY
    P.O. Box 1094
    Glendale Heights, IL 60137
    (Tension Bands, benches,
    accessories)

UNIVERSAL GYM
EQUIPMENT
CORPORATION
   17352 Von Karman Avenue
   Irvine, CA 92714
   (Universal multistation
   machines, accessories)

WEIDER INSTITUTE
   21100 Erwin
   Woodland Hills, CA 91364
   (Weider barbells and
   accessories)

YORK BARBELL COMPANY
York, PA 17405
(York barbells and accessories:
the company that started it all)

Index

leg raises
  for abdominals, 120
  for *iliopsoas* muscles, 130–131
  for thighs, 116
locomotor apparatus, testing of, 24
lordosis, 11–12
lower back, exercise equipment for, 49–50
low pulley work, for chests and upper backs,
    138–140

machines, exercise, *see* exercise machines
Mannerberg, Don, 42–43
martial arts, 201–205
Mayo Clinic Diet Manual, 29–30
MECE, 216, 218
medical histories, 17
mesomorphs, 2–4
military press
  for biceps and triceps, 143, 147
  for deltoids, 141–143
minerals, 40–42
  calcium as, 41–42
  in diets, *see* diets
  magnesium as, 41
  potassium as, 41
  sodium as, 40–41
Mini-Gym machines, 49, 96, 100–102
  batting machine in, 170
  specific machines of, 101–102, 170
mini-trampolines, 148
Mirkin, Gabe, 16, 23, 36, 38–39
mitochondria, 29
movement clusters
  examples of, 177–178
  neuromotor system and, 181
  open vs. closed, 182–184
  in sportspower training, 178–185
  for throwing, 180
  in total training, 182
  see also sports movements
Muscle and Fitness, 44, 95, 99
Muscle Builder, 51, 155
Muscle Digest, 95
Muscle Mag, 95
muscles
  aerobic training for, 4, 151
  anaerobic training for, 5, 151
  cramps in, 214–215
  endurance of, 150–151
  injuries to, 212–213
  movement clusters and, *see* movement
    clusters
  overloading of, *see* overloading

power of, 150–151
  pulled or torn, 212–213
  red vs. white cells in, 4–5, 151
  stamina of, *see* stamina
  strength of, *see* strength
  weight and, 25–26
Muscle Training, 95
Muscular Development, 51, 95

National Center of Health Statistics, 26–27
Nautilus machines, 50, 96, 102–103
necks
  exercise equipment for, 50
  injuries and weakness of, 12–13
  pretraining exercises for, 74–76
neuromotor system
  movement clusters and, 181
  overloading of, 175
Nishiyama, Heditaka, 183
nutrition, 28–44
  carbohydrates in, 28–30, 37–38
  diets and, *see* diets
  energy and, 28–30
  fats in, 28–30, 38
  minerals in, 40–42
  "preferred energy fuel" and, 29
  protein in, 28–30, 36–37
  vitamins in, 38–40
  water in, 36

obliques, external, *see* external obliques
Oliva, Sergio, 166, 168
Olympic lifting, sportspower training for,
    208–211
overloading, 172–175
  aerobic and anaerobic systems in, 174–175
  cellular analysis of, 174
  duration in, 173
  Hydra-Fitness machines and, 174
  intensity of, 172–173
  methods of, 173–174
  of neuromotor system, 175
  range of motion and, 173–174
  resistance in, 173
  in sportspower training, 181–182, 184
Owens, Jesse, 4

parallel bar dips, for chests and upper backs,
    134–135
Paramount machines, 96, 103
pelvic rolls, for external obliques, 122–123
physical profiles, 1–44
  muscular problems and, 13–14
  somatotypes in, 2–4